BRIDGES
to PEACE

Ten Years of
Conflict Management
in Bosnia

Edited by

Charles C. Pentland

To David G. Haglund

A special issue of the *Queen's Quarterly*

ISSN 0033–6041

For additional copies, please contact
the Centre for International Relations,
Queen's University,
Kingston, Ontario, K7L 3N6

tel: 613–533–2381

fax: 613–533–6885

Contents

Acknowledgements

THIS VOLUME has its origins in the annual spring conference of Queen's University's Centre for International Relations (QCIR), held June 13–14, 2002 on the premises of our cross-town colleagues at the Royal Military College of Canada in Kingston, Ontario. The Dean of Arts and Science at RMC, and Senior Fellow at the QCIR, Joel J. Sokolsky, ensured that everything ran smoothly. He was ably assisted by Lt (N) Rob Marriott and the other members of RMC's Short Course Unit.

Organizing the conference was the last in an impressive series of projects conceived and conducted by David G. Haglund, my predecessor as Director of the QCIR. After seventeen years at the helm, David went on a year's leave at the beginning of July, 2002, to return as the Sir Edward Peacock Professor in the Department of Political Studies at Queen's. All of us at the QCIR – where David will remain a Senior Fellow – are grateful for his efforts over that long tenure. This volume is dedicated to him.

As always, it is a pleasure to acknowledge the tireless and good-humoured work of Ann Liblik, the QCIR's administrator, in managing the flow of paper, electrons and cash through the office, and in ably conducting so much of the Centre's diplomacy with regard to visitors, government and university officials, and the many people responsible for the infrastructure of such a conference. Her skill and experience are much appreciated.

The QCIR is grateful to the Royal Military College for its financial contribution toward the conference, and to the Security and Defence Forum of the Department of National Defence for its continuing support of the Centre and its work.

In addition to those who presented papers, many others contributed valuable comment, whether as designated discussants or from the floor: John Graham, Dejan Guzina, David Harries, Ron Haycock, Michael Hennessy, Ben Lombardi, Lubomyr Luciuk, Alex Macleod, Kim Richard Nossal, Dan O'Meara, and Johanna Vingerhoeds. We are especially grateful to His Excellency Jacques van Hellenberg Hubar, Ambassador of the Netherlands to Canada, for his thoughtful and deeply personal reflections on what we – the international community – did and did not do, could or should have done, as events in the Balkans ran their course. His remarks are reproduced as the Foreword to this volume.

Finally, my thanks to Boris Castel and Steve Anderson at the *Queen's Quarterly*. Their combination of diligent editing, creative design and fast production is formidable.

Charles C. Pentland

Foreword

Address by His Excellency
Jacques van Hellenberg Hubar,
Ambassador of the Kingdom of The Netherlands
to Canada, at the Royal Military College, Kingston,
13 June 2002.

FROM 1990 until the end of 1993 I served in Israel as Deputy Chief of Mission and point of contact with the Palestinian leadership. Back home, until September 1997, I was dealing with issues like asylum, migration, integration and so on, when I was asked to become deputy Secretary General of the Foreign Ministry, dealing with management and restructuring of the ministry. The Balkans and its regular visitor Mr Sacirbey – the Foreign Minister of Bosnia – simply went a door further. I mean literally one door further, because my room was next to that of the Minister, so I could from time to time partake in the emotionally charged atmosphere hanging around that room and in the staff-meetings.

In September 1997, I became Ambassador to Israel. Subsequently, in March 2000, I was called to Brussels in order to help launch the European Security and Defence Policy (ESDP). Only there, in the Political and Security Committee (PSC) of the EU, did I have to deal with the Balkans.

So I shall tiptoe quickly and superficially through a subject which has developed into an object for lifetime study. Our national report on Srebrenica alone counts several thousands of pages.

I remember the moment when we received at the PSC in Brussels a ministerial delegation from the Balkans. The Presidency at that time, a rather loquacious colleague – for once speechless – gave me the floor to welcome the visitors and explain on behalf of the Committee what the EU expected from them and what they should and should not do. The chair did not beforehand inform me of his move, so this must have been a moment heavy with diplomatic improvisation. Fortunately, our guests were too polite, and too interested in the offerings of the EU, to show anything but good will. There was no sign of astonishment about the unusually direct message about peace, tolerance and co-operation they received.

I am relating this because it is an illustration of what the EU's role mainly is: to serve as a pole of attraction, to use the force generated by that attraction in order to promote politically acceptable behaviour and to project stability by using its soft power.

My next experience however was more impressive. I had been invited to visit Bosnia-Herzegovina and was standing on a hilltop with my more important co-guests, surrounded by frightening soldiers – ours – when my mobile telephone rang: The Hague wanted to give me urgent instructions about elections in the Federal Republic of Yugoslavia (FRY) and was astonished to hear that I was not in Brussels but at the other end of Europe, whilst they had hoped to send me off to the PSC the next morning. Well, it resulted in the longest helicopter flight in my life, and via Frankfurt I arrived in Brussels. I am still afraid to receive the bill for that flight, especially in these days of scrutiny of ethical behaviour. What this illustrates however, is the degree the co-ordination of EU policies has shifted from capitals to Brussels. The process had started to gradually influence the content.

S O I was not around when some fateful decisions with respect to the safe area in Srebrenica were taken, eventually leading to a massive failure of the international community to provide the protection the safe area concept was all about. Because my country happened to be an instrument of the international community, Prime Minister Kok decided, upon the publication of a critical report prepared at the government's request by the Netherlands Institute for War Documentation,[1] to assume responsibility. The government evidently did not assume responsibility on behalf of Gen. Mladic, but on behalf of the faceless international community and it decided to follow the Prime Minister when he tendered his resignation to the Queen on April 16, 2002.

I hasten to add that this decision, in itself laudable, was only grudgingly followed by the Dutch Liberals, partners in the government coalition, who were from the beginning convinced that if there was a reason for resignation at all, it had to come as a consequence of a parliamentary debate and not before. They also doubted the conclusion that there was substantive reason to resign. The Liberals were of the opinion that in earlier debates, years ago, it was already established that no particular minister and *a fortiori* no cabinet needed to resign.

Some could say indeed that this report was published seven years after the event and that the government thus might have taken the decision to resign a couple of years earlier instead of just four weeks before an election, when the coalition had run its course and had completely exhausted its power to govern.

That may be also one of the arguments of a small part of the voters who subsequently booted the government from office. It was only a small part, because the main reason, I believe, that the ruling coalition was thoroughly defeated in the general elections of May 15, 2002 was not the Balkans episode but a subterranean shift in public opinion – a shift which was missed by most of the politicians of the ruling establishment.

Suffice it to say that in view of ongoing societal changes and the profound angst caused by the aftermath of September 11, 2001, people expected government to govern and to protect them, their culture and their nationhood, not to explain why nothing could be done against real and perceived threats. The era of ever retreating government was over. A government which was pragmatically looking after the economy (to the extent governments have much influence over it) but did not address personal security, failures of integration policy or a deteriorating service level in the national health system, that government was out of touch with the sentiments of the public. (The government coalition which resulted from these elections lasted not even a year. New elections produced a revamped Labour party, but coalition talks with the Christian Democrats, the largest party, failed.)

But let me revert to the Balkans. The Netherlands were somehow involved in one of the greatest man-made disasters since the Holocaust. Roughly 7,000 Muslim men and boys are thought to have been killed following the fall of the safe areas of Srebrenica and Tuzla. Dutch forces in Dutchbat III were present in July 1995 when it happened.

This figure of 7,000 victims is impressive in itself, but even more so if you realise that it is the same as the number of Canadians killed in the campaign to liberate my country at the end of World War II. It is also 2.5 times higher than the number of victims of September 11. Therefore, it is understandable that the foreign affairs and security establishments as well as the general public in Holland have been suffering from a serious peacekeeping trauma since the summer of 1995.

I VERY WELL REMEMBER the hand-wringing after the event. A minister literally hid his head under his desk to express the shame he felt for not having been able to protect and defend. He asked me as soon as the tragic facts transpired, to go and talk to some MPs in order to make them change their ill-conceived plan to go and meet with returning peace-keepers. They didn't desist, afraid to give the impression that they or their party would be seen as not supportive of our boys. The minister was right. He was afraid of something else: the political fall-out of images of a happy celebration of their return after what we knew to have been a tragedy. It might at least look incongruous – which indeed it did, at least on TV – when four weeks after the mass murder the peacekeepers and parliamentarians were seen to have a good party. The latter was an exaggeration, but the damage to the image was next to irreparable and still lingers on.

In the public relations area, a number of *faux pas* were made, the grossest probably the statement in an interview that there were no good guys, only bad ones. After the killings, this didn't go down very well at all. There were vain efforts by the military to contain the public relations damage.

More than a few of the servicemen who had been in Srebrenica were suffering from the psychological stress of being accused of complicity in the killings of 7,000 Muslims. They could feel relieved after publication of the NIOD report, which exculpated them. However, families of the victims felt that the world, the West, the UN, had failed to give them the protection which they believed should have been inherent in the concept of safe areas. The NIOD report didn't give them closure.

How could it have come to that, and who was responsible? Questions were raised and the buck was passed on, and on and on. The UN assumed part of the responsibility in its report on the matter.[2]

In Holland some were focussing on the role of bigger EU allies. The suspicion was that there had been a secret deal between the French and Mladic, and that the UN or the French were responsible for withholding the air-support to our boys that might have stopped the advance of Serb forces. This suspicion fed on old antagonisms and recent frustrations acquired since the time of our 1991 EU Presidency. The fact that we were good enough to pay and to supply troops but could never enter into the Balkan Contact Group, was undoubtedly also feeding into the suspicion. Questions were put to the UN. But nothing came of it. Talk about a parliamentary enquiry into the command-responsibilities made the French irritable. Eventually it was decided to give the task to the NIOD to sort out the whole affair. It took them the full second term of the now defeated coalition to do their job. In the meantime, Paris also issued its report, which remained fairly uncontested in Holland.[3]

I cannot possibly give you a resumé of the thousands of pages of the NIOD report. But it is my personal impression that the story of the withholding of air-support to Dutchbat, deserves some closer attention. This will probably also be a subject for the parliamentary inquiry which will take place this year, in order to fill some gaps in the report's conclusions and also to realize politically the closure that the NIOD report did not fully achieve. The issue of the close air support, or rather its refusal, reveals a preoccupation with the safety of UNPROFOR and Dutchbat.

After reading parts of the report, I feel confirmed in my personal view that in spite of all the ethical arguments which convinced the international community to act in Bosnia in the first place, nobody was ultimately prepared to risk the lives of servicemen for the protection of the people who had sought refuge in the safe areas. The most fundamental question which decided the debate before we accepted the commitment so strongly pressed upon us, was not: do safe areas pose a solution or are they going to be part of the problem?

No, the determining question was ultimately whether or not, in accepting this commitment, we were exposing our forces to acceptable risk. The answer given to that question was: acceptable. Therefore we went in, but with a mandate and rules of engagement, and with equipment, that didn't meet the challenges ahead. The inescapable reality is perhaps that no country, no responsible commander, accepts very high risks in the defence of a third party, as long as defeat of this party is not perceived as an unacceptable direct loss for the country concerned. This reality sounds cynical and is understood as such by some relatives of the victims in Srebrenica.

In the eyes of the critics of the international community's operations in the Balkans, including Kosovo – where after all we were objectively trying to defend a Muslim population from ethnic cleansing – the community's reputation is blemished. Although this was more a failure of implementation than of intent, even the credit for our effort is nowadays denied to us.

This leads me to a common issue in foreign policy, the tension between an ethical approach and a more pragmatic approach – the former based on intentions, belief in international vocation and human rights principles and the latter founded on an understanding of the interests of countries and populations and on a cold analysis of the attainable, given the availability of political and military instruments.

The decision-making process which led us into the Srebrenica disaster was fraught with good intentions, ethical considerations, and pressure from the media and the public. At times, ministers were desperate, realising the enormity of the challenge before the international community, the EU and NATO. I vividly remember us looking at maps, with those isolated safe areas, wondering how to cope with the logistics if things were to turn bad. I remember a mood to give up, and to leave the Balkans to the Balkan peoples. This was perhaps because it dawned on us that in reality little could be done. But the ethical considerations took over in the political arena. The minister who, according to the NIOD report, was most forcefully pleading for an activist role and for engaging our military, was the same minister who immediately after the publication of the report called for the resignation of the government because the failure to deliver had been exposed.

All this, and especially the Kosovo operation, led us to reconsider EU security and defence policies. In the fall of 1999, the European Council of Helsinki introduced an effort to improve on the political and military instruments and the architecture of decision making in the EU, required for the execution of the so-called Petersberg tasks. The judgement is still out on that endeavour. In parallel, however, the projection of stability was enhanced by using the civilian dimensions and the financial resources of the EU. These seem to work reasonably well, given the power of the EU as a pole of attraction.

I N CONCLUSION, our concept of a multi-cultural and multi-ethnic society clashed with the concept of homogeneous societies that prevails in the Balkans and in many other parts of the world. We imposed our pluralistic views to a certain extent, because we could not and did not want to deal with the fundamental questions posed to us – and to the way we might deal with the rapid changes in our own societies – by the competing concept of a homogenous society. So the ethical foreign policy we pursued was supported by our dominant assumptions about the unavoidability of the pluralistic society, which considered national homogeneity to be an atavistic concept.

Notes

1 *Srebrenica, a 'Safe' Area: Reconstruction, Background, Consequences and Analysis of the Fall of a Safe Area* (Amsterdam: Netherlands Institute for War Documentation, 2002). Available in English at http://194.134.65.21/Srebrenica/.
2 United Nations. General Assembly. *Report of the Secretary-General Pursuant to General Assembly Resolution 53/35. The Fall of Srebrenica.* A 54/549 (New York: United Nations, 1999).
3 France. Assemblee Nationale. *Evènements de Srebrenica (1995): Rapport d'Information.* Paris: Documents d'Information de l'Assemblée Nationale, Novembre 2001.

Introduction

IN the Balkans, where historical memory is notoriously long and deep, the passage of ten years might seem of little consequence. By any standard, however, the decade that followed the outbreak of war in Bosnia-Herzegovina in the spring of 1992 was momentous, fraught with rapid, wrenching change on a hitherto unimaginable scale. Almost four years of war saw more than 200,000 people killed and over a million driven from their homes, often with a brutality whose malign creativity seemed to know no bounds. In the process, an economy was destroyed, a land despoiled, and a region destabilized. The energy and inventiveness of the protagonists was not, however, initially matched by any notable resourcefulness on the part of the international community, which for more than two years laboured in vain to manage the conflict with traditional tools of mediation and peacekeeping under the auspices of the United Nations and several European organizations. But by the time the fighting ended in late 1995, the international community had, under enormous pressure, not only created and brought to bear the innovative forms of coercive diplomacy that led to the Dayton agreement but also begun to shape a complex model of international management for troubled or failed states. That US-led version of coercive diplomacy has been deployed on several occasions since 1995, including in Bosnia's neighbour, Kosovo. Multilateral protectorates have also proliferated. The results of both, it is fair to say, have been mixed, and the learning curve steep. But it cannot be denied that the ten years up to the spring of 2002 were rich in consequences, most of the immediate ones tragic for Bosnia and its people, but many of the longer-term ones promising, not only for the Balkans as a whole but for the wider world order.

To consider the events of that decade and their meaning for Bosnia, the Balkans and the international community, the Queen's Centre for International Relations convened a conference in June, 2002, focused on attempts at conflict-management both during and after the war. This volume brings together nine papers presented over the two days, plus the personal reflections of the Dutch Ambassador to Canada, especially poignant with reference to the trauma of Srebrenica. The collection cannot, of course, pretend to be comprehensive or definitive. Each paper takes but a facet of the complex, continuing project of conflict-management in Bosnia-Herzegovina, some exploring reactions to the initial crisis and the ensuing war, others the international community's actions since Dayton. Some papers examine the evolution and impact of collective international action in keeping the peace and assisting Bosnia in moving toward its assumed European destiny. Others offer accounts of why various national policies toward the conflict took the form they did, and what difference it made either to Bosnia or to the state in question.

The three papers in the first section of the book are about the interplay of international players and Bosnian domestic politics in keeping and building the peace since Dayton. To achieve law and order in that war-ravaged place it was necessary to establish order before law, working from the "secure environment" provided by IFOR and SFOR, through a far-reaching reform of Bosnia's own dysfunctional security agencies, to the establishment of a domestic legal system compatible with modern European principles.

David Last's chapter offers a view of peacekeeping in Bosnia that draws from the international community's full range of experience from UNPROFOR though SFOR. Unlike many accounts, however, it confronts what might be called the traditional conflict-manager's view of how best to go about things with a revisionist critique based on close – sometimes personal – observation on the ground. Last argues that the early years of the Bosnian war, however frustrating and futile for the those seeking to make and keep peace, proved in retrospect to be an indispensable tutorial in the new arts of domestic conflict-management. Second, he highlights the subliminal labours of "civil society" in humanitarian actions and post-conflict reconstruction – a "bottom-up" process to complement – at least in principle – the "top-down" work of the diplomats. Third, he casts a critical eye on excessive claims about institutional innovation in the international community's response. Fourth, he notes the important strategic shift from regional containment to inclusion in European structures.

Walter Dorn and Jeremy King offer a detailed account – sometimes critical but generally optimistic – of Bosnia's progress toward reform in its key security institutions: the armed forces, the police, the customs and border services, the judiciary, the intelligence services, and the control of small arms. They also document what they see as a dangerous counter-trend in military assistance. Across the board, the problems encountered by the central government and the international community are predictably similar, connected to the need to forge a single, modest-scaled, effective national service out of three bloated, ethnically-based operations tainted by a history of brutality and corruption. The task has been to move each of these services toward European norms and standards. The record, they find, is uneven, and agreements on paper have not always had much resonance or result on the ground.

Fundamental though it is, security is only one of many sectors of Bosnian society in dire need of a modern legal framework. Tufik Burnazovic's chapter looks at the bigger picture – the transformation of the Bosnian constitutional and administrative system from its hybrid post-Tito and shattered post-conflict state, to something approximating a western-style system heavily influenced by Anglo-American legal norms. He traces this slow and painful transformation – dogged by political obstruction but prompted by increasingly sharp and decisive interventions by the OHR – through the adoption of a new laws on central banking, foreign trade policy, foreign investment, customs and border police, as well as provisions for a national court and for the free movement of all Bosnia's peoples throughout its territory. The author's assessment is as cautious as that of Dorn and King, but he conveys the sense that Bosnia is making steady progress toward a coherent, enforceable national legal community.

The second section brings together three papers showing how some elements of the international community have gradually accepted and implemented the "responsibility to protect." John Blaxland's chapter on the Australian-led international action to ensure East Timor's peaceful transition to independence returns us to David Last's theme of learning from experience. By 1999, the international community had accumulated a thick dossier of post-Cold War experience – much of it traumatic – concerning multilateral humanitarian intervention. As Last shows with respect to Bosnia, some of that experience transformed operations in the countries where it had been gained a few years before. Some of it found expression in studies of broader application such as the Brahimi Report and the report of the International Commission on Intervention and State Sovereignty. Blaxland's paper shows how some lessons from Bosnia and elsewhere – the need to establish visible dominance early, for example, or the value of controlling the information environment – informed the enforcement operation in East Timor, and how, in turn, the international community might learn from that case.

My chapter reviews the experience of the European Community (since 1993, European Union) in the Balkans, assessing its performance and prospects as part of the multilateral post-Dayton protectorate for

Bosnia. It explores how, since Dayton, the European Union has gradually emerged from the futility and marginality to which the Bosnian wars had reduced it in the region. It has done so partly by design, partly by default: by design in the sense that it learned from experience that its best assets were still those of soft power – trade, aid, the promise of eventual inclusion – and that it needed to embed its approach to Bosnia in a broader regional strategy; by default in the sense that as American attention began again to stray from the Balkans, it seemed once more the "hour of Europe" with the EU becoming the *de facto* proconsul of the international community in the region. Nevertheless, many of the questions and doubts raised by the EC's first attempt to manage the crisis in the early 1990s remain to be answered.

Jurgen Dobert's paper examines a decade of political-constitutional debate in Germany over the participation of the Bundeswehr in peacekeeping and enforcement operations abroad – a debate precipitated by, though not confined to, events in the Balkans. Not only did Germany have an unhappy recent history of military involvement in the Balkans; one of the first acts of the new "fully sovereign" post-Cold War Germany had been its controversial swift recognition of Slovenia and Croatia's independence. Hence the political debate about projecting German military power abroad was not only driven by Balkan events but haunted by Balkan ghosts. Dobert shows how Germany's geopolitical position in Europe, its economic dominance of the EU, and indeed the very logic of its military doctrine both at the personal level of the individual soldier and at the more abstract level of strategy and morality, led the courts and the Bundestag to find the use of German forces abroad constitutionally permissible.

The third section examines the policies of three countries involved in and affected by the Bosnian crisis in very different ways. Gerald Wright's account of Canadian policy in the period 1991-3 serves to remind us that in Ottawa as in other Western capitals leaders lacked the benefit of our hindsight. They could not have known that reasonable, cautious, traditional approaches to conflict-management would not work in the face of cynical, bloody-minded ideologues bent on rearranging the Balkans according to principles of ethnic exclusivity. Where Wright does find fault is in Canada's inability to convert the political capital gained from its lengthy and costly involvement in UNPROFOR into a significant place and voice in the diplomatic councils of the peace process.

David Hale seeks to explain why the United States delayed engaging fully in the region and why its eventual involvement took the form it did. Despite extensive journalistic and academic attention, these questions continue to trouble those who followed the Bosnian debacle from the outset. The analytical problem here is not any shortage of possible explanations – if anything, the hesitancy of the Bush and Clinton administrations seem over-determined: European assertiveness in taking the initial lead, domestic priorities, the indifference of the American public, lost battles in the bureaucracy, memories of Somalia, Balkan mythology – the list is long. Hale, like a number of others, concludes that the turning point came through the impact of visual images of atrocities, which turned US public opinion and forced the administration's hand.

Louis Delvoie directs our attention to Turkey, often overlooked as a regional actor both during and after the war, but significant as an indicator of the Islamic world's perceived stake in its outcome. How the west's response to the Bosnian war – in particular the plight of Bosnia's Muslims – was read in the Islamic world has assumed a heightened significance since September 11, 2000. Delvoie's chapter reminds us of the historical and demographic ties between Turkey and Bosnia, and of the way in which the evolving crisis played into Turkish domestic politics through, *inter alia*, the Islamic question and the NATO connection. The perception – however accurate – of western governments standing by or, at most, assuming a posture of neutrality as Bosnia's Muslims were displaced and killed, played badly in Ankara and the Turkish street. It is not hard to imagine how it played in other Islamic counties less secular and pro-western in their orientation to begin with.

However fragmentary and preliminary their collective conclusions may seem, these chapters – enhanced by Ambassador Hubar's reflections – provide a broad critical assessment of the international presence in Bosnia-Herzegovina over the past decade. That complex of multilateral agencies is a structure built to bear a troubled society across dangerous times to an imagined future self-sustaining peace. The image of a bridge seems especially appropriate for Bosnia, where it has an almost iconic status: consider the metaphoric power of Ivo Andric's *The Bridge on the Drina* (set in Visegrad, site of some appalling ethnic cleansing in 1992) and of the bridge at Mostar, destroyed in 1993 and now under reconstruction. Bridges may symbolize connection and the overcoming of obstacles to progress, but they are also vulnerable and attractive to attack. Occasionally, a bridge begun is never completed. Lack of funds or lack of will may permit the troubled waters to prevail. Bosnia was not the first multilateral protectorate of the post-Cold War era nor, it is safe to say, will it be the last. Like the rebuilding of the Mostar bridge, it combines local and international resources, human and material. The analyses in this book remind us that while there has been discernible progress over the past ten years, we are still far from the other side of the river.

Charles C. Pentland

I
Order & Law

DAVID LAST

Balkan Operations in the 1990s: Stepping Stones to Improved Peacekeeping

This specific Bosnian hatred should be studied and combated as one would combat a deadly endemic disease. And I believe that foreign scientists would come to Bosnia to study hatred, as they study leprosy, if only hatred were a recognised and classified subject of study like leprosy.

Ivo Andric, "A Letter from 1920" [1]

INTERNATIONAL EFFORTS to prevent the spread of violence and to restore peace and security in the Balkans in the 1990s have stretched the theory and practice of peacekeeping. I believe the experience has led to developments that have the potential to improve the capacity of international third parties to control and prevent violent conflict in the future. This chapter is in three parts. It begins with a brief overview of a decade of international intervention in the Balkans. I draw from that experience four developments that I believe may be stepping-stones to better peacekeeping in the future. Finally, I draw some conclusions about the implications of the Balkan experience for the way peacekeeping may need to be conducted in the future.

Major DAVID LAST is an officer in the Canadian Armed Forces with extensive peacekeeping experience. He has a doctorate from the London School of Economics and teaches in the Department of Politics and Economics at the Royal Military College of Canada.

The Balkan Experience in Perspective

TO PUT the Balkan experience in perspective, we need to consider not just its chronology, but its impact on western thinking about conflict and security. Since 1990 Yugoslavia has moved from state in trouble to state of civil war to states rebuilding. After surviving occupation in the Second World War and breaking with Stalin in 1948, Yugoslavia became a leader of the Non-aligned Movement. With a well-managed economy, it was considered in the 1950s and 1960s the most promising of the socialist states. Its economic decline began with the oil shocks of the 1970s and 1980s. Tito's death in 1980 and a constitutional crisis in 1986 gave an opportunity to ethnic nationalists, many of whom were elected in democratic elections in 1989 and 1990.[2]

Civil war began with the Slovenian and Croatian declarations of independence in June 1991. With a relatively homogeneous population and support from Europe, there was little bloodshed over Slovenia. Croatia was less fortunate, with the Yugoslav National Army (JNA) providing support to Serb enclaves in Eastern Slavonia, Western Slavonia and the Krajina. Serbs there were unwilling to be minorities in a Croatian state. With the European recognition of Slovenia and Croatia in January 1992 and the arrival of UN and European Community observers, the situation began to stabilise in Croatia, but to worsen in Bosnia. Fighting there began in April 1992 after a referendum on sovereignty boycotted by the Bosnian Serbs. Macedonia declared independence, and the UN raced to establish a military presence there to prevent the further spread of the conflict.

Fighting in Bosnia in 1992 was principally between Bosnian Serbs and non-Serbs, but by 1993 aspirations for a greater Croatia and local tensions resulted in increasingly severe fighting between Bosnian Croat and Bosnian Muslim communities. This continued until the Washington Framework Agreement established the Muslim-Croat Federation in February 1994. Creation of the Federation led to the intensification of fighting with the Bosnian Serbs in 1994 and 1995, and to the culmination of Croatian efforts at national consolidation in 1995. By August 1995 the combined efforts of the Federation and NATO air strikes in support of UN resolutions had brought about a redistribution of territory that was conducive to an agreement. The cease-fire came in September 1995 and a General Framework Agreement for Peace was negotiated at Dayton, Ohio in November

1995. The signing of the Dayton agreement in December 1995 was intended to mark a watershed between ineffectual international intervention in an ongoing civil war and robust international support for and enforcement of an agreed peace. International implementation of the peace agreement in Bosnia has been less sure than was hoped, though more successful than the UN mission that preceded it.

Over the life of the United Nations Protection Force (UNPROFOR), more than 70 Security Council Resolutions and Presidential Statements adjusted the mandate and expectations of the UN missions while a series of UN, European, American and other diplomatic initiatives engaged the belligerent parties. NATO became involved in July 1992 when the North Atlantic Council agreed to enforce UN sanctions with a naval force in the Adriatic. It began to monitor Bosnian airspace in October 1992 and to enforce a no-fly zone at UN request in March 1993. Attempts to use air power in February 1994 met with limited success, and resulted in Serbs taking more than 350 UN hostages in May 1995. Not until the deployment of a Rapid Reaction Force to provide security in June 1995, and negotiation of an agreement on use of force between NATO and the UN in July 1995 was NATO ready to use air strikes again.

With the Dayton agreement, a NATO Implementation Force (IFOR) succeeded UNPROFOR. Four principal "pillars" for implementation succeeded the single UN mission with its comparatively unified headquarters. NATO's IFOR, later the Stabilisation Force (SFOR), provided the framework for security. The new UN Mission in Bosnia and Herzegovina (UNMIBH) was responsible for civil administration and policing. The Organisation for Security and Co-operation in Europe (OSCE) provided assistance with democratisation, human rights, and regional confidence building measures. The European Union accepted responsibility for economic reconstruction. Finally, the Office of the High Representative (OHR), reporting to the Peace Implementation Conference (PIC), was to provide unifying direction for these four missions, each with its own organisational responsibilities. The European Union Monitoring Mission (EUMM) maintained a presence in the affected countries and regions outside Bosnia.

While the peace was being implemented in Bosnia, the powder train had reached Kosovo. The civil war between Yugoslav authorities (predominantly Serb) and the predominantly Albanian population was launched with the repeal of Kosovar autonomy in 1989. It accelerated after 1995 with the settlement of Bosnian Serb refugees in Kosovo, and the increasing availability of small arms from Albania, itself in crisis.

Systematic ethnic cleansing probably began in 1998, and with the failure of the Rambouillet negotiations, NATO was at war with Yugoslavia by March of 1999. By June 1999 the first elements of NATO's Kosovo Force (KFOR) had arrived, soon to be joined by missions representing the UN, OSCE, and EU pillars, as in Bosnia.

> This decade of intervention reflects a period of transition that is more far-reaching than the end of the Cold War and subsequent adjustments. It can be seen in changes in international organisations' memberships, in patterns of investment and trade, in shifts in domestic governance, and new ways of conceiving security. Before the phrase "human security" gained currency, questions of immigration, employment, and environment had become part of the European security agenda, despite the Cold War. All this increased the impact of the Balkan wars on Europe and on the future of peacekeeping.[3]

Peacekeeping as a form of third party intervention to control violence had evolved during similar periods of transition in the past. Many of the things that we commonly associate with Balkan peacekeeping of the 1990s have precursors in less well-known interventions that date from earlier transitions. The word "peacekeeper" entered modern political discourse to describe the way Bismarck's Germany kept the peace to serve its interests in Europe.[4] Before the UN era, both the League of Nations and coalitions deployed peacekeeping missions. Humanitarian NGOs were a feature of the multinational operations led by the French *Corps d'occupation de Constantinople* in the Dardanelles 1920–1923.[5] The precursors of today's election monitors, military observers and multinational forces can be found in plebiscite and supervision missions sponsored by the League of Nations between the wars. The first UN military observation missions – in the Balkans, Palestine, and Kashmir – were adaptations by the UN system in response to emerging East-West confrontation. The next significant innovation, the use of armed UN forces with the consent of the belligerents, appeared as an adaptation to another transition in international affairs. In 1956, the Suez crisis was complicated not only by the East-West conflict, but also by the emerging North-South confrontation over colonialism and self-determination. In the following decade, UN peacekeeping was to include enforcement elements in the Congo, inter-communal policing in Cyprus, and transitional civil administrations and policing in West New Guinea. What has the

Balkan experience brought us beyond the adaptations and innovations that we may have forgotten from our own past?

Four Stepping-Stones
to Better Peacekeeping

THE FOUR stepping-stones to better peacekeeping that I have chosen to highlight are not entirely self-evident. Some might suggest that they are counter-intuitive.

First, some might focus on the belated but decisive action of NATO as a regional security organization, bailing out a failing UN.[6] I suggest, on the contrary, that the extended period of international inaction, containment and observation from 1991 to 1995 was an important experience. Dithering over war in the Balkans in that period allowed the evolution of mechanisms to develop an international consensus about regional action to manage conflict. The Balkan experience helped Europe to delay and resist the American rush to war with Iraq in 2003. The jury is still out concerning how that effort will affect NATO and the UN as conflict management institutions.

Second, much ink has been spent on highly visible military strategies, but I am convinced that these actually brought little new to the management of conflict. We focus on air strikes and troop movements for the same reason that there are more coffee-table books about eagles than about earthworms – it's all about image. I suggest, rather, that the relatively invisible actions of thousands of people working for NGOs developed important new tactics for the reconstruction of societies after conflict. I also show some of the pitfalls encountered in applying these tactics.

Third, did the five-nation Contact Group and the PIC so eclipse the strategic initiatives of the International Conference on the Former Yugoslavia (ICFY) and the UN Security Council from 1991 to 1995, that they should be considered an important innovation? I think not. The Contact Group and the PIC have their precursors in diplomatic history as old as the Concert System and the Conference of Powers settling the Cretan question in 1898, or the Conference of Ambassadors in the League of Nations era.[7] The really striking innovation in the Balkans was an enhanced understanding of the essential connection between top-down diplomatic initiatives and bottom-up initiatives at community level. I believe it was this new understanding of the synergy necessary between low-level and high-level initiatives, and the fundamental importance of grass-roots reconciliation, that represents a quantum improvement in the way third parties look at intervention in protracted conflict.

Finally, the initial containment strategy has not been perpetuated. One of the important steps in managing the conflict has been the successive incorporation of potentially unstable regions into the political and security structures of Europe. The understanding that unstable peripheral areas can eventually be incorporated into the core, with accompanying benefits and responsibilities, has been matched by a careful assessment of how much political instability a political structure can absorb. In this sense, Europe's dealings with the Balkans have followed some of the same debates that NATO and the EU have had over organisational enlargement. They are debates that speak to a measure of diplomatic sophistication that has yet to come to the Western Hemisphere, with its relatively impoverished institutional infrastructure. It is important to draw a sharp distinction here between raw neo-colonial incorporation of a powerless peripheral area, which makes markets and resources available, and full political and social partnership that gives peripheral areas a stake in the decision-making of the institutions of the core.

Each of these four developments of the Balkan conflict has the potential to be a stepping-stone between the way that conflicts have been managed in the past, and the way in which they may be managed in the future. Each has implications for the future of efforts to keep the international peace.

Containment and Observation

THE DEVELOPMENT of a regional containment strategy using observer missions with new functions was slow to show its promise, but had begun to pay dividends by the end of the UNPROFOR mandate. Although the strategy may have been as accidental as it was inevitable, the common need for both accurate information and mechanisms to take common action helped to shape European institutions during the early course of the Balkan conflict.

Western governments are criticised for their response to the crisis in Yugoslavia on two counts: that they acted to precipitate the crisis, and that they did not act to mitigate its consequences.[8] Susan Woodward blames international financial institutions and western government representatives in the Paris Club for creating the conditions of

Yugoslav collapse by making it impossible for the financially strapped government to continue the shell game of regional equalisation payments.[9] The richer regions of Slovenia and Croatia were only too ready to give this up. Early recognition of Slovenia and Croatia, first by Germany and then perforce by its neighbours is also held by many to have contributed to the civil war. So is delayed recognition of Bosnia, which stimulated the referendum, its boycott by Serbs, and the race into civil war over control of territory.[10]

I think much of this criticism is unfair. In the United States, there was a strong lobby to stay out of the Balkans altogether, epitomised intellectually by the Cato Institute. The heart of these arguments was that violence in Bosnia did not touch on US national interests, and was therefore not worthy of any expenditure of American blood and treasure.[11] Opinion in Europe was much more divided. While there was strong support for intervention on humanitarian grounds as early as 1992, there was never support for international occupation, and no consensus on overt support to any of the parties to the conflict. Above all, it is clear from the memoirs of Lord Owen and the commentaries over the war years – so frequently proven wrong by events – that foreknowledge was in short supply. The ICFY was hopelessly optimistic about rational and civilised behaviour by the parties to the conflict. The parties were hopelessly optimistic about their military prospects and about the powers of the "international community."

It was probably the absence of a coherent "international community" that made collective action impossible in 1992. Writing cables in the UN Peace Force Headquarters in 1995, I was struck by how the same nations could take different positions in the ICFY, the North Atlantic Council, and the Security Council. There was not one international community, but several separate communities, in which states pursued different interests. But by 1995 NATO and the UN at least achieved understanding on the use of force, and closely co-ordinated civil and military implementation while sharing operational space in Bosnia. This illustrates how much the separate communities had evolved during the course of the Bosnian conflict. The driving force in that evolution was the emergence of a common regional strategy; a coherent flow of information from the conflict was necessary to develop that strategy. Absent a consensus, observation and containment were necessary precursors to intervention. The process of observation and reporting helped to develop the consensus necessary for subsequent action. The shortcomings of the observation efforts helped to develop the institutions necessary to develop common policies.

At a meeting in Zagreb in 1995, Thorvald Stoltenberg noted that the containment strategy for the Balkans had arisen by default from the failure of the ICFY's members to agree on a more assertive approach.[12] The outcome of assertive action was also highly uncertain, making it difficult to achieve consensus. Andrew Bair, an American political officer with UNPROFOR in 1995, has written on the evolution and application of the wider regional containment strategy.[13] He described the importance of two ends of the strategy: consistent and reliable information had to originate in the area of the conflict, and it had to be digested and understood by bodies that could conveniently co-ordinate a common response. In December 1991, the UN authorised the deployment of military observers to Croatia, and by January, the first had arrived. The UN Secretariat and the Security Council almost immediately had a moderately reliable and consistent flow of common information with which to supplement the national sources available to the members of the Security Council. Europe, in contrast, had no mission to generate information and no coherent body to discuss it. NATO had no mandate for out-of-area operations. The EC had an interest, but no common forum on security matters and no mechanism for launching field missions. As fighting broke out in Slovenia in June 1991, the CSCE (renamed the OSCE in 1994) was still finding offices, and the shape of its future institutions as mandated by the 1990 Paris Charter was not yet clear.[14] There was not yet a Permanent Council, no Forum for Security Cooperation, and no Chairman in Office. The first Commissioner on National Minorities would take office in 1993. The second Commissioner, Max Van Der Stoel, has described the crucial evolution of European conflict management from the era of the Helsinki process to the new era of Europe as a community of shared values and responsibility for the prevention of intrastate conflicts.[15]

A Belgian university study for NATO in 1994 highlighted the new conflict resolution role of the CSCE: "The most impressive progress has been made in what could be called the 'lower end' of conflict management. So-called 'soft' measures, such as sending fact finding, rapporteur and long-term missions, are combined with a close political consultative follow-up." The academics noted that flexibility remained the key to CSCE success in consultation and reaction, despite the institution of procedures such as the Moscow mechanism on the human dimension and the Berlin mechanism for crisis situations.[16]

In 1995 the OSCE deployed its first major field mission to Bosnia. By then, the OSCE structure included regular summits, a Ministerial Council and periodic Senior Council meetings, a body meeting weekly on confidence and security building measures, a Parliamentary Assembly, Secretary General, Secretariat, administrative apparatus for field missions, High-Level Planning Group, and Joint Consultative Group, amongst others. By 1999, the OSCE employed almost as many people as UN headquarters in New York.

In 1991, a CSCE mission was out of the question. The alternative was the European Community Monitoring Mission. Monitors were seconded individually from their governments to the ECMM, which established a headquarters in Vienna in July 1991. Administrative support was minimal and provided *ad hoc* by contributing governments. The skeleton headquarters in Vienna was in no position to screen or analyse field reports, and the practice was to forward all reports to the capital holding the EC presidency. Drawing on interviews with Canadian officers, Sean Maloney describes the first rotation of the operation. Reports were sent to Lisbon, where they were "sanitised and massaged" and forwarded to Brussels and Geneva after some delay. This early experience may account for the later insistence that reports be forwarded directly to all national capitals without any intermediary or editing.[17] Even after four years of operation, when headquarters in Zagreb and Vienna were hiring academic analysts and writing lengthy reports, the reports of field teams were still transmitted directly from the field office to foreign ministries, with only two intermediate steps (the regional office and Vienna) and no editing. In 1994, then, governments were receiving detailed, unedited first-hand accounts of events in the former Yugoslavia and the surrounding region, within 24 hours of the events being observed.[18] The quality of the reports varied, as did the handling of reports in national capitals. Many states initially used the same criteria for EC monitors and UN military observers – mid-ranking (and sometimes quite junior) military officers. By 1994, higher standards had been set, and political and economic acumen was more frequently demonstrated in assessments of the situation. European foreign ministries began to refer more frequently to EC monitors' reports in their communications with their representatives in New York and Brussels, and a common perception of the conflict began to emerge.[19]

The first of the white-clad EC monitors arrived in Croatia on day trips from Vienna in August 1991. The first UN military observers deployed to the UN Military Liaison Office (Yugoslavia) pursuant to Security Council Resolution 713 in September 1991. They established offices initially in Belgrade. By 1995, a network of UN and European observers covered the conflict area, with overlapping areas of responsibility, and multiple military and civil contacts at every level from village informers to the presidents of the entities and republics. The growth and spread of the observer missions, and the way in which they interacted with the diplomatic efforts and with events on the ground is one of the most significant developments of Balkan peacekeeping. A more sophisticated theatre headquarters and direct communications with member-state foreign ministries began to pay off in greater credibility and impact on decision-making.[20] The mission expanded by sending two teams to Bulgaria in November 1992 and four to Albania in December 1992. The mission expanded because the international community needed penetrating information about the conflict. The information that monitors provided forced European states to develop new institutions to handle the information and act upon it in concert. Mass media and public opinion played a role in this, too.[21] But it was the integration of multinational observers in a conflict area with multinational means of response that both helped to construct the international sense of community, and helped the international community to respond to an ambiguous conflict.

Observer missions have three basic characteristics that helped them to shape international perception of the conflict. First, they deploy in multinational teams, reducing or eliminating the perception of national bias from their reports. Second, they are unarmed and have the status of diplomats on mission, allowing them (in theory) free movement, broad powers of inquiry, and appropriate status with national and local authorities. Finally, although mandates vary, they typically include both "monitoring" (passage of information upwards) and "assisting" (implying some intercession with the parties to the conflict). This last characteristic in particular makes observer missions important players in conflict management. By passing information up to international bodies like the Security Council or to individual foreign ministries, observers help states and international institutions manage conflict from the top down, responding to events and putting pressure on governments and non-state actors. By interceding directly with parties to the conflict at the lowest level, observers can help to manage conflict from the bottom up. Although this was clearly the intent of the first UN Special Commission on the Balkans in 1947, the mandate was foiled by the observers' inability to deploy beyond Greece's borders to deal with problems in Yugoslavia, Albania, and Bulgaria.[22]

The challenges facing both EC monitor and UN observer missions can be described in five categories: mandate, personnel, equipment, focus and diplomacy. In each category, significant advances were made over the course of Balkan operations, resulting in generally better performance in Kosovo than in the early stages of Bosnia.

The mandate of the UN mission permitted deployment in Yugoslavia and all its former Republics – states whose successor status would not be determined during the life of the mission.[23] Offices were established in Slovenia (largely for logistic support purposes), Croatia, Bosnia, Serbia, and Macedonia. Observers were not well placed to monitor the borders with neighbouring states, however. Although UN representatives were accredited to Tirana, Athens, and Sofia, and there was a considerable UN presence in Austria and Italy, there were no field teams with the capacity or mandate to monitor sensitive border regions, nor investigate flows of refugees, embargoed goods, or suspicious activities. The ECMM was more broadly constituted, and its monitors travelled comparatively freely in the border regions of Albania, Bulgaria and the Danube. The advantages of a regional rather than strictly national approach to monitoring and crisis prevention have been noted in several UN reports and acted upon by the successor European Union Monitoring Mission (EUMM) in the Balkans.

Both the EC monitor and UN observer mission experienced the frictions of a multinational deployment. UN observers did not always meet the minimum requirements of fluency in English and ability to drive.[24] It would normally take several months from a six, eight or 12 month tour before observers understood the local situation sufficiently to provide useful reports, but this could often be managed effectively by mixing old and new hands. More serious was the problem of "confessional affiliation" – the practice of ensuring that observers of different faith groups were represented in each region to ensure balance. The practice developed in 1992 as a response to objections each party to some of the mission participants. For observers in small mixed-nationality groups, it should have worked better than for formed units working across ethnic lines, and often did. Problems arose when there was a clear ethnic political bias or agenda on the part of some nations.

In 1993 as the fighting expanded the EC monitors were the best-equipped observers in the region. With encoded satellite communications and armoured Land Rovers, they were positioned to monitor the worst of the fighting. They were accused, however, of being overly cautious and standing on diplomatic status to stay clear of the worst situations, which went unreported.[25] UN military observers, on the other hand, had no secure communications, and frequently had inadequate communications for the terrain and distances they were required to cover. The woeful shortage of good vehicles, and the tendency for the best vehicles to concentrate at headquarters, or be stolen at illegal checkpoints reduced the effectiveness of many UN teams. These problems were overcome for the 1998 multinational Kosovo Verification Mission (KVM) which deployed with experienced monitors, armoured vehicles, satellite communications, and a well-planned infrastructure.[26]

Both the EC monitors and UN observers were pulled in two different directions – upwards towards the strategic level, and downwards to the tactical level. In the first two years of the mission, where they focused their efforts seemed to depend as much on individual preference and experience as on the needs of the mission. In 1994 the Chief Military Observer was subordinated to the UN Force Commander in Zagreb, and the UN observers became more closely integrated into the operational planning for the force. The mobility and communications of observers, superior as it was to some national contingents, was an important asset to the Force Commander. Observer teams were also assets that could be allocated to subordinate headquarters and moved across national and entity boundaries more readily than formed units subject to Status of Forces Agreements. As they were used increasingly for reconnaissance at the operational level, they were drawn into economic and political reporting, which was particularly valuable at higher headquarters.[27] The quality of this reporting varied. It depended on observers' experience and understanding of the local situation, dynamics within the team (because of the requirement for consensus on any report), quality of local translators and language assistants, and rapport with local population and authorities. In many cases, observer teams delegated to support local units were drawn into the tactics of supporting UN military operations, leaving little time to develop political or economic reports. These tactical tasks could involve liaison between national contingents, monitoring poorly covered or inaccessible areas (in some cases because national contingents lacked transport, fuel, or the will to patrol) or establishing contact for units moving to new positions. Local liaison fully occupied observers in central Bosnia for several months after the Washington Framework Agreement for a Muslim-Croat federation in Bosnia, while UN units repositioned themselves.[28]

Tactical liaison with UN forces was not a factor in the employment of EC monitors, whose range of employment tended more towards operational and strategic questions. Nevertheless, EC monitors were also drawn down into the "tactical weeds" for two reasons. First, they often found it necessary or satisfying to assist locals with personal problems. This helped to open sources of information, or simply to justify what was often dispiriting work. Second, it was often at the lowest level that monitors came into contact with other agencies including the UNHCR and its NGO implementing partners. Most EC monitors I have interviewed admit to stretching diplomatic privilege by transporting locals, carrying parcels, delivering aid, or passing personal information. In fact, most saw this as an important part of their function. The dilemma is that, without engaging in some form of support to solve local problems, monitors are quickly perceived as foreign voyeurs, and it is not worth the risk to locals to provide them with information or assistance. The most successful teams were often those with the most flexible interpretation of the limits on their activities.

To understand the diplomatic functions of observers, we can plot whom they met with and what they discussed. This evolved during and after the UNPROFOR era. The area of operations for a UN observer team was generally smaller than that of an EC monitor team, but within each area of operations, the liaison responsibilities were comparable. In general, UN observers would establish liaison with military units of the factions, and with local civil authorities. When there was a good working relationship with UN Civil Affairs, UNMO contacts would be limited to the military authorities, while EC observers would have more diverse contacts with local military and civil authorities. As the mission matured from the chaotic early days of 1992–93, it became more common to find smoothly operating international teams with well-delineated responsibilities. For example, one might find a UN battalion commander with his own liaison officers to each of the belligerent units in his area of operations. Meetings involving those units might include both the unit liaison officers and the UNMO team. Meetings with the local civil authorities might involve the UN Civil Affairs officer, the EC monitor team, and possibly also the UNMO. At important meetings, international representatives and their language assistants frequently outnumbered the locals!

UNHCR, ICRC, IMG[29] and NGO representatives preferred to meet local authorities separately. One had to have some sympathy with the local authorities attempting to run a war-shattered municipality overrun with refugees, facing constant demands for meetings with people who made frequent requests but could offer little help.

The pressure for meetings with local authorities increased after the Dayton agreement. Although UN observers were no longer in the picture, EU monitors continued to play an important role in both monitoring and assisting. As the implementation of the civilian provisions of the Dayton agreement progressed, the EU monitors found new roles in monitoring and assistance. Their broad areas of responsibility let them "float" from the lowest level up to regional power centres, seeking information and getting other agencies involved as appropriate. Their reports went quickly to decision-making centres in Europe, and could have decisive impact in making resources available or stopping them. As the OSCE mission deployed into Bosnia in 1996 and expanded its functions down to regional level, EU monitors were asked to provide specific information on a wide range of economic, social and political issues. Availability of fuel and fertiliser for the spring planting, patterns in hog and cattle-breeding, barriers to refugee return, the state of municipal infrastructure, capital shortages, and use of public buildings were only some of many questions asked of EU monitors in the early days of the OSCE mission. As the "year of returns" (1998) came and went without an appreciable rise in returnees, operational planners began to look more systematically at the correlates of local violence. Military civil affairs teams, SFOR units, UN International Police Task Force (IPTF) and OSCE field offices were asked to collect a variety of statistics and report on a growing list of factors thought to be relevant.[30]

By 1998, too many stovepipes of information existed for the EU monitors to combine effectively their monitoring and assistance roles. SFOR and UNMIBH had become the dominant agencies with their own webs of operational units down to the local level. The OSCE had established offices down to the regional level, including cities such as Bihac, Mostar, Travnik, Prijedor, and Jajce, and even the Office of the High Representative had hired the International Crisis Group, an NGO, to provide political analysts in each regional centre. By this stage in the evolution of the mission, the EU monitors were relegated to their strategic role of collecting information for European capitals, and the mission was reduced to a presence in Sarajevo, Banja Luka and Mostar. At the same time, however, its regional importance had increased. The EUMM had shifted its focus from gathering and transmitting local information for strategic action to integrating information at the regional level across national boundaries. Over the period from 1992 to 2002, the number of EC or EU teams in each country varied more or less directly with the level of tension. As more robust and comprehensive missions were deployed, the EC/EU missions decreased.

In this light we can see the real innovation of monitoring and observer missions, deployed by the UN or a regional organisation. Accuracy and timeliness of reporting, multinational balance, reporting up for top-down action while taking immediate steps at the lowest level, and sophisticated awareness of military, political, social and economic factors affecting violence are evident in the evolution of observer missions. This is all one end of the social innovation of observation and containment – the end closest to the fighting. The other end is in the capitals and headquarters taking action to contain and prevent violence. It was clearly difficult to achieve an international consensus on how to handle the crisis in Bosnia. Agreements on action in Albania, Macedonia and Kosovo have been more easily achieved, in part because of the accurate, timely and consistent information available from deployed field missions, and in part because of the evolving European mechanisms for managing information and recommending decisions. The EUMM headquarters, for example, now includes finance, logistics, C4 (command, control, communications, computers) and regional desks.[31] From the diplomatic initiative of the Helsinki Accords and the 1975 Final Act, the OSCE has developed into a sophisticated regional mechanism that supports complex confidence building, democratisation and human rights activities, and collaborates with the EU on economic reconstruction and development.

Europe's successful containment and observation strategy demonstrates an old adage from negotiating: if you cannot agree on substance, agree on process. With Europe undergoing dramatic internal changes, and strong isolationist pressures undermining US leadership, it was clear in 1992 that there was no quick fix to Balkan problems. It was also clear in 1992 that involvement would be long-term and costly, and that there were no unequivocal allies or enemies in the affected countries. The scope and objectives of international intervention would therefore be difficult to agree. Reading speeches from NATO, ICFY, and the EU in 1992, it was clear that *something* had to be done, though it was not clear what or by whom. The "muddling through" strategy was to stop it from getting worse. Regional containment implied gathering information, looking for elements of an effective strategy and building a consensus for action. I think that the monitoring and observation missions – linked to decision centres in Europe and New York – were ideally suited for this purpose. Different countries, however, used them in different ways. Some countries treated the missions as "business as usual" – sending a few observers along to get rich on UN or EU per diems. Some countries sent senior officers or civilians with an eye on quality, but failed to learn much from the individual experiences. Between 1993 and 1995 I interviewed 48 UN observers and EC monitors from 17 countries, none of whom had been debriefed by national authorities following their experiences. A minority of countries got high-level briefings from senior officers who had served as UN observers or EC monitors. Monitoring, observation, reporting and debriefing helps policy-makers to understand the conflict. Beyond understanding what is going on, they need to develop an appreciation of the impact of particular policies. What happens to food aid? How do aid convoys affect the conflict? How is organised crime involved? How are refugee communities supporting the conflict? These are empirically difficult questions about cause and effect, and we are still learning from the experience now. Because it takes time to learn, the slow and painful process of containment and observation was, with hindsight, one of the most important contributions of the Bosnia conflict to future conflict management.

NGOs and New Techniques

MANY AUTHORS have focused on the evolution of the use of force in Bosnia, from the UN to NATO, including air power and the tanks, artillery and armed helicopters of the Rapid Reaction Force (RRF) that paved the way for NATO's deployment. I argue, however, that the proliferation of non-governmental organisations and their use of sophisticated field experiments amongst an educated and urbanised population have led to the emergence of new techniques for managing intercommunal conflict at the lowest levels. This quiet work of the "earthworms" in hundreds of small NGOs is less dramatic than highly visible military deployments, but ultimately much more important, because it changes the extent to which communities are receptive to the social and economic changes that underlie long-term peace.

There are several reasons for ruling out the UN-NATO transition as a ground-breaking innovation in the Bosnian case. First, escalation in the use of UN force in a civil war did not occur in Bosnia for the first time, but forty years earlier in the Congo. Second, the shift in command and control between the UN and NATO had little relevance to the tasks actually conducted in Bosnia. Anything possible under NATO command was possible under UN command. The proof of this can be found in the troops, headquarters and tactics deployed during the transition. The RRF was a NATO formation, under UN command and using UN rules of engagement. The RRF headquarters was set up separately in Visoko with a NATO-nations chain of command, but remained a UN headquarters fully responsive to both Commander UNPROFOR in Sarajevo and Commander UNPF in Zagreb.[32] When NATO members of the UN force presented a security risk, such as certain officers suspected of passing information to the factions, they were discreetly removed from the inner circle and the operation continued. Notwithstanding UN rules about apportionment of command positions and passage of information, operational demands gave full latitude to a resolute commander to choose the people and nationalities necessary to execute a delicate task. Finally, operations comparable to those of IFOR were carried out by a robust UN force under the UN Transitional Administration in Eastern Slavonia (UNTAES) during the life of IFOR.

While troop strengths and dispositions are thoroughly documented, it is difficult to say exactly how many NGOs were active in Bosnia or the wider Balkans at any time. The NGO catalogues compiled by each of the missions offer a good indication of the growth and variety of NGO activity, although not all NGOs listed were consistently present for the life of the mission or the catalogue. In 1995, about 1700 NGOs were active working out of Sarajevo, according to the UNPROFOR Civil Affairs catalogue. Most of these were working in humanitarian fields, delivering food, medicine, and hygiene supplies, and providing psycho-social support to displaced persons. A growing number were beginning to deal with shelter and economic revitalisation. By February 1996, the number working out of Sarajevo had risen to more than 2000. Regional centres had fewer NGO participants, and the spread was slower to the Serb Republic. In February 1996 about 70 NGOs were regularly attending the UNHCR coordination meetings in Bihac, while only 12 (four of them local NGOs) were attending the comparable meeting in Banja Luka. By June 1996 this had largely equalized at about 50 regular participants, most foreign, in both

Muslim Bihac and Serb Banja Luka. Numbers of active NGOs in the regions remained high in 1997 and 1998, but dipped in 1999–2000 as some reallocated field resources to Albania, Kosovo, and Macedonia. Nevertheless, the number continued to climb in Sarajevo. The Combined Press Information Center (CPIC) announced in September 1999 that more than 3,000 NGOs were registered in Sarajevo. Many of these were regional headquarters for international NGOs now working in other parts of the Balkans, rather than field offices working the front lines.

The large number of NGOs, the variety of different roles they sought to perform, their diverse expertise and funding sources, and the complex pattern of institutional sponsorships all served to provide a hothouse environment for experimenting. While much has been written about NGOs and the need for coordination, there is also a lot to be said for creative chaos. The character of individual NGOs, their institutional frameworks and international organisations all evolved over the course of the mission. The many academic works on coordination and humanitarian intervention written over the 1990s have drawn more heavily on the Balkan experience than on African, Asian or Latin American cases.

The character of the NGOs in the Balkans has changed over time. While humanitarian assistance had been the largest single category throughout the war, it began to decline as a proportion of the whole with the implementation of the Dayton agreement. By 1996, almost 20 percent of funded NGO activities were conducted by "implementing partners" of the UNHCR. The largest part of this was infrastructure work (sanitation, water, electricity, medical services, and central heating) carried out according to priorities set by the International Management Group (IMG) established by the UNHCR.[33] The sources of funding diversified in 1997 and 1998, to include the World Bank, the EU, and UN Development Program (UNDP). Work conducted by implementing partners shifted from emergency relief towards economic and social development, and the "social component" of return. This included organisation building, psycho-social support for marginalised groups, legal assistance to returnees, and community building. As the focus shifted from assisting individuals to reconstructing communities, it became increasingly important to grant decision-making authority to local employees. The number of local NGOs partnered with international NGOs increased slightly, but the number of local employees of international NGOs increased dramatically. One of the surest signs of evolution was the shift in language of operation.

When NGOs begin to produce their working documents and reports in the local language, the transition to local control is approaching culmination, even if funding remains largely foreign. This started to occur for some NGOs as early as 1997, but the majority are still receiving most funding from outside the country and producing most of their reports in English or another foreign language today. The 2000 Report of the International Council of Voluntary Agencies (ICVA) listed 365 indigenous Bosnian NGOs, but Soros Foundation field reports suggested there were already as many as 1,500 – though quantity was more evident than quality.[34]

A small number of NGOs deal with personal and community security issues. These include the the American Impact Team International, and the multinational Peace Brigades International. Although tactics vary, these NGOs generally use a range of non-violent accompaniment and witnessing techniques, sometimes linked to communications with media or the international police and peacekeeping presence. Their presence is determined both by need and by funding, and their deployment pattern seems to respond to high-profile emergencies. They have kept a presence in Bosnia, Kosovo, and Macedonia, but have moved away from personal interventions to work with international media, human rights reporting, and local authorities. This reflects a general process – the shifting of institutional roles as the situation has changed over the life of the conflict.

Another small but important group of NGOs has sought to manage information and use mass media to support the peace process and inter-communal reconciliation. Broadcasters Without Borders and National Public Radio (NPR) assistance to local broadcasters, for example, concentrated efforts in 1998 and 1999 on generating local capacity to produce for local consumption. The dilemma was that local demands at the time still reflected the fears of the civil war. Beyond escapist Euro-pop music, local stations were not interested in conveying messages of inter-ethnic accommodation.[35] The public information dilemma illustrates the need for linking top-down initiatives to shape the political environment with bottom-up initiatives to improve the capacity for democratically controlled change.

The roles of international institutions changed over the life of the conflict because of the magnitude of the reconstruction task, as they did at the end of the Second World War in Europe itself. The IMG was developed as an umbrella organisation to manage the infrastructure task for the UNHCR. By identifying and employing "implementing partners" who sought funds independently from other donors, additional resources were mobilised for reconstruction. Having an umbrella structure helped to reduce both the security and financial hazard for many smaller NGOs that wanted to work in the theatre. The rules under which they operated, particularly in 1995–1996, gave some directive control to responsible international organisations such as the UNHCR, and brought some discipline to funding and deployment arrangements. As long as they met their programming objectives, NGO implementing partners would receive ID cards, gasoline rations, and funding for some portion or all of the programs they undertook on behalf of the UNHCR. UNHCR certification of an NGO meant that its personnel were included in evacuation plans and security arrangements. The 1995 debates over the status of "internationally protected persons" were resolved by 1996, and IFOR commanders were told to provide sanctuary if necessary to NGO personnel with UNHCR ID cards. BY 2001, however, the IMG had served its purpose and was dismantled. European Union reconstruction offices assumed the co-ordinating role for infrastructure projects. With funding coming directly from the EU, the UNHCR had a reduced role in co-ordination of the effort to support refugee repatriation, but continues to maintain the most comprehensive data-bases related to refugee return.

New techniques and new applications of old techniques for NGOs can be found in four principal areas, though more in governance and psycho-social reconstruction tasks than in the economic and security spheres. In what follows, I shall examine the first two, as they have been given less attention in the literature than the others.

Governance mandates for NGOs are evident in program labels such as "democratisation," "empowerment," "citizen education," and "civil society." A "grass-roots" focus implies that these issues are addressed at community level, usually meaning municipality, neighbourhood or village. The labels began to appear in the reports and funding requests of European NGOs working in the Balkans by 1993, though problems of "governance" were identified by human rights and civil society groups working in the region as early as 1991.[36] The pedigree for this sort of work goes back to initiatives like Moral Rearmament in the wake of the Second World War,[37] the Peace Corps of the 1960s, and European and North-American people-to-people initiatives of the 1970s and 1980s, inspired by the Helsinki accords.

The atmosphere of nationalism, xenophobia, and intimidation in the Balkans from 1991 to 1995 left very little scope for intervention at any level, but NGOs came nevertheless and established bridgeheads in local communities. By 1994 Jan Oberg's Transnational Foundation (TFF), and others were working in Croatia, Serbia, Macedonia, and Kosovo. Three contributions stemmed from this early involvement. First, a pool of foreign nationals emerged with knowledge of local government structures and personalities, which was essential for later interventions. Second, practitioner research techniques evolved for developing and evaluating programs, and later had considerable impact on the ability of major funding agencies to allocate reconstruction resources. Third, funding agencies were sensitised to the need for social and political community-building work, and began to think beyond the provision of relief and long-term development. This was reflected in new work by the Development Assistance Committee (DAC) of the OECD, and by new structures in national development organisations. USAID's Office of Transition Initiatives and CIDA's Peacebuilding Branch are examples, both influenced by the events in Bosnia.[38]

Opportunity to expand the limited NGO bridgeheads came with the Dayton agreement and its comprehensively supported implementation plans. From 1995 to the present we can highlight four major NGO innovations in the realm of governance, which also help to tie together international intervention at the strategic, operational and tactical levels.

As a new institution, Carl Bildt's Office of the High Representative did not have the infrastructure to support information gathering and analysis when he first deployed to Sarajevo in January 1996. Contracting the NGO International Crisis Group helped to fill that crucial gap in political intelligence. Even as the permanent staff of the OHR grew, ICG work continued to be in demand because of its independence and candour – characteristics sometimes in short supply in UNMIBH, OSCE and OHR.

The second NGO contribution to governance was to help mobilise international indignation that led to accountability. Several Bosnian and European NGOs assisted lawyers in documenting war crimes cases, locating witnesses and physical evidence, and publicising crimes to raise support for prosecutions. This independent and public support for the judicial process has reinforced international law and provided additional resources to the prosecution in a number of cases. [39]

If these two NGO contributions to governance are at the strategic level, the other two are at the tactical level of executing specific tasks that affect individuals and communities. Building civil society within communities, and building links between communities are perhaps the two greatest contributions that NGOs have made to the reconstruction process. Civil society is usually described as the network of social and political institutions not under the authority of the government.[40] In critical theory, civil society is described as a social order in which individual rights are proclaimed at the expense of the social bonds of community.[41] Most NGOs, like the Soros Foundation and NDI, are closer to Swift's conception. These non-governmental institutions that give individuals a measure of collective control over their lives are often lacking in post-communist countries, and the stability of new regimes may rest on the ability to build new democratic structures rather than the ability to control old authoritarian tendencies. The Spanish *NGO Movimiento por la paz, el desarme y la libertad* (MPDL) worked with local lawyers and social workers to address pension and property claims. Conflict resolution NGOs have established community centres like *Omladinski Komunikativni Centar* to bring together interest groups and advocate for special needs. More politically assertive, the American NGO National Democratic Institute (NDI) has helped local leaders to organise student unions, pensioners' associations, and a wide variety of interest groups. After three years, NDI reduced direct involvement and began to work with the local NGO Centres for Civic Initiatives (CCI) to prepare for the April and November 2000 elections. Their domestic election monitoring program mobilised more than 5,000 volunteers and 300 NGOs engaged in voter outreach.[42] The Soros foundation has made enormous contributions to public education and the development of civil society with a focus on values and the active engagement of citizens in government. The Foundation has formed partnerships with the Center for Promotion of Civil Society (Sarajevo), the Centers of Civil Initiatives (Banja Luka, Tuzla, Mostar, Sarajevo), and International Forum Bosnia, amongst others. Promotion of values through open media has also been a hallmark of the Soros campaign.[43] Books have been written on the subject of civil-society development by NGOs in Bosnia,[44] so these examples are offered as illustrations only.

What these examples tend to have in common is a focus on the organisational aspects of civil society, though the Soros Foundation's focus on values begins to get to the heart of the second problem – the willingness of communities in conflict to re-establish constructive relationships. As international and local NGOs attempt to forge links across inter-communal lines, they frequently run into the accumulated fear and hatred from the war. This makes collaboration on political parties, pensioners' associations, or media initiatives difficult, even when it clearly serves common interests, or represents a super-ordinate goal. The neighbourhood facilitators project expended considerable effort on psycho-social preparation for intercommunal cooperation – hate reduction, active listening, consensus building, and mutual understanding of divergent stories about wartime experience.[45] Where these efforts have seen success, they have helped build connections between ethnic communities in the sense used by critical theorists: "A good test for the existence of community is to see if one person is able to ignore another's troubles; if so, then the two don't share community."[46] This sense of social solidarity transcending ethnicity is precisely the characteristic that permits large-scale returns of refugees and internally displaced persons, without generating new violence. The breaking of the log-jam for returns in the spring of 2000 reflects well on five years of community development work supported by international NGOs, although the flood created problems of its own.[47]

The NGO contribution to progress on post-conflict governance has been enhanced by the developed and European nature of the federal structure in ex-Yugoslavia, providing fertile soil for many of the ideas about empowerment and citizen activism. Ideas and practices from the Yugoslavia of the 1970s, including worker self-management and direct democracy, have been easier to resurrect than some expected, even to the point of impeding internationally imposed rule of the OHR. This has been particularly evident in efforts by the OHR to force through new legislation on privatisation of national assets, restrictive interpretations of pension laws, and changes to national banking regulations.[48] These difficulties suggest that despite considerable international penetration, democratic impulses and local economic self-interest remain alive. International NGOs have played a role in linking grass-roots mobilisation of pensioners and citizen-shareholders in publicly-owned industry to national assembly opposition to international financial institution controls.

Psycho-social mandates for NGOs are evident in program labels such as "trauma," reconciliation, healing, and post-conflict recovery. Women's, children's, and refugees' issues are also commonly a focus for NGO psycho-social programs. While Bosnia was a unique laboratory for European and North-American governance NGOs, it has been only one of many countries in which NGOs have experimented with extensive psycho-social programs.[49] The largest of the psycho-social programs have been undertaken by multiple implementing partners of the major international organisations sponsoring post-conflict recovery – UNHCR, UNICEF, and ECHO being the three most active. National bodies like USAID, CIDA, and DFID have tended to fund or partner small national players like Canada's McMaster University and

Queen's University medical school programs. But one of the strengths of the smaller programs is that they have tended to be systematic in their documentation and program evaluation. The enormous body of literature now emerging on the psychological and social correlates of violent inter-ethnic conflict owes a lot to the careful collection of data by many of these projects.[50]

I think two major steps forward have been taken as a result of NGO contributions to post-conflict psycho-social reconstruction efforts. The first concerns recognition of the extent of the problem, and its importance for long-term prospects for recovery. A civil war like that in Bosnia affects the entire population, as the Second World War scarred an earlier generation across the continent. Statistical studies of the population, and anecdotal evidence of those receiving therapeutic help indicate the extent and severity of the trauma, and the impact of that trauma on people's ability to reconstruct their lives and communities.[51] This is an old lesson relearned, because the current generation of decision-makers has forgotten the effort required to rebuild Europe after the second world war.

The second step forward has been the recognition that individual therapy is not a solution. Although therapists, psychiatrists and psychologists have made a significant contribution to individual well-being, there are not enough couches in Europe for 4 million people to take the "talking cure" of the middle-classes. Rather some form of cultural revival or regeneration of national values is the foundation on which both individual and collective social recovery will ultimately rest.

We begin to see glimmers of this in the official reports as early as 1996, with the High Commissioner for Refugees, Sadako Ogata, warning that returns would not occur quickly.[52] The International Crisis Group described the role of hard-line obstruction:

> In practice, minority returns have been consistently obstructed by the nationalist political parties in power. After all, the right of all refugees and internally displaced persons to return to areas in which they form a minority conflicts head-on with the explicit war aims of the Bosnian Serb leadership, which were secession and creation of an "ethnically pure" state, as well as with the more covert aims of the Bosnian Croat authorities. In order to prevent minority returns, the media have generated a climate of hostility to returnees, assessment visits have been blocked, and houses systematically destroyed.[53]

But it was not until the disappointing election results of December 1997 – in which hard-line parties were returned in all three entities – that the broad questions of social and political culture began to be addressed. The elections demonstrated that people on all sides had deep-seated reasons for supporting the hard-liners, and that action was needed to loosen their grip. The ICG report dated just a week after the election results reviewed progress, and suggested renewed sources of hope. It referred specifically to the NATO snatch operation in hard-line Prijedor, in which Karadzic's former chief security officer Simo Drlaca was killed while resisting arrest. Removing or isolating hard-liners was a necessary but not a sufficient condition for progress.[54]

Over the next three years, the insights of the NGOs at work in the communities began to filter up to the analysts writing and planning for the OHR and the ICG. These organisations focused on processes and legalities, rather than human psychological dramas being played out in families fearing and hating their neighbours. Articles in *NATO Review* increasingly emphasised the importance of multi-agency co-operation.[55] It was in the detailed analysis of obstacles to return in Drvar, Jajce, Konjic and Travnik that links between the lowest level of family return and the highest level of declared policy began to become apparent in official reports and pronouncements.[56] Tackling specific problems in the unique local conditions of Sarajevo, Mostar, and Brcko brought the senior management of the international community down to neighbourhood level in their daily operations. The Sarajevo declaration guaranteeing safe return was quickly shown to be a hollow promise in Drvar, Konjic and other targeted cities.[57]

After 1998 we begin to see genuinely innovative efforts to incorporate cultural and psycho-social change into the structural solutions to protracted conflict. These efforts appear as exchanges, conferences, mentoring programs, and closer scrutiny of the education system in the entities, including application of UNESCO's culture of peace program to education efforts.[58] The agreement on education of returnees to Vares set a precedent for inter-ethnic accommodation.[59] An independent media commission produced a code of media rules, with NGO assistance, and began issuing provisional licences in 1999.[60] The success of the independent media commission established in 1998 was reinforced by the establishment of the non-governmental BBC School of Journalism in Sarajevo in March 2000. An Anti-corruption and Transparency Working Group began meeting in October 1999, increasing Bosnian involvement in policing corruption and organised crime. This was reinforced by the activities of NGOs like the Soros Foundation and NDI which emphasised civic responsibility to report on crime.[61] After the deadline for claiming socially-owned apartments had been extended several times, a property awareness campaign was launched in May 2000, to address both rights to property and the problems of illegal occupancy.

These collaborative efforts were combined with firm direction from the OHR. In January 1998 the Serb Republic (RS) parliament was moved from its war-time location in rural Serb Pale to the more cosmopolitan city of Banja Luka in the northwest. When the entities were unable to agree on a common currency design, the OHR made the decision for them in January 1998. Common vehicle license plates were similarly imposed in February. Uncooperative police chiefs were removed in Drvar and Mostar, and the mayor of Sanski Most was removed. OHR rulings on social property, pensions and foreign ownership ran into opposition from nationalist and socialist community-based groups, including the representatives in the Federation and national assemblies. Some NGOs have therefore played an important role in providing international support for local ideas of community that are sometimes in conflict with the OHR's interpretation of the requirement for civil society in a liberal international order, defined by international financial institutions including the World Bank and the IMF.

A complete account of the links between NGO-led psycho-social change and OHR-led structural change for peacebuilding would fill many pages. The foregoing discussion, however, demonstrates that the presence of a large number of NGOs with a focus on both governance and psycho-social reconstruction has led to new techniques and practices being incorporated in the work of the OHR, UNMIBH and even NATO forces in Bosnia. This is evident in the convergence of tactical and strategic tools for conflict resolution.

Convergence of Tactical and Strategic Tools

THE THIRD STEPPING-STONE to better peacekeeping in the future is the convergence of tactical and strategic tools for intervening in a conflict. Four years of war and six years of peace implementation have given practitioners at every level a better understanding of the dynamics of inter-communal conflict. This has supported the convergence of strategic (top-down) and tactical (bottom-up) approaches to conflict resolution, some aspects of which are evident in the discussion up to this point. We can find examples of learning from the interface of the tactical (execution of tasks) and the strategic (decisions about goals), both within military organisations and in the political organisations supervising the missions.

From 1993 to 1995, Force Commander's conferences provided a venue in theatre for contributing states to share their insights. About half of all agenda items at Force Commander's conferences in 1994 and 1995 concerned logistics, administrative and procedural matters.[62] Those which concerned operations helped to establish a list of tasks that could be effectively carried out by UN units, and this shaped the limited strategic objectives for the Force Commander. Military staff in both Zagreb (UNPF HQ) and Sarajevo (UNPROFOR HQ) were acutely aware of the limitations of UN forces. For example, it was recognised by May 1995 that UN units did not have the capacity to re-supply or secure UN safe areas in southeast Bosnia. This shaped Commander UNPROFOR's three-layer strategy of passive self-defence by "white" UN forces, active self-defence by the NATO "green" UN forces under UN rules of engagement, and deterrence by NATO air strikes.[63] This strategy in turn determined the options for the UN force in July and August 1995, when planning was conducted by NATO for both NATO-assisted withdrawal of the UN force and NATO reinforcement to assume responsibility for peace implementation. The convergence of strategy and tactics is no more than the normal function of military planning. Other examples represent greater innovation.

The Danish Operations Research Program (DANORP) conducted interviews and questionnaires with senior military and civilian participants in the Balkans, and held two major UN Commanders' Workshops in 1995 and 1996. These workshops helped to confirm the important role of UN military observers as information collectors, mediators and confidence builders at a tactical level, and to refine the role that these functions played in UN strategy.[64]

Part of the evidence for the convergence of means and ends in the role of peacekeepers is found in surveys of UNPROFOR peacekeepers conducted in 1995 by DANORP.[65] Of UNPROFOR officers surveyed, 88 percent agreed that "consent can only be reached through a liaison system on all levels and with direct contact to the parties." Sixty-nine percent disagreed with the statement that "the liaison system can be limited to the leaders of main parties"; 74 percent disagreed with the statement that "consent of national leaders to a peacekeeping mission is enough," and 78 percent disagreed with the statement that "peacekeepers can operate without the consent of the local population." More than 90 percent of UNPROFOR officers surveyed agreed with statements about the importance of impartiality, and 70 percent or more felt that media, national interference, and contradictory UN mandates had made their job as peacekeepers more difficult.[66] The necessary condition of "consent" could only be built from the bottom up, and the conditions imposed from the top down, including national interference and contradictory mandates, often conflicted with the tasks on the ground.

The surveys of peacekeepers were shared with commanders, who subsequently made recommendations. Frustration with impartiality and reliance on consent led directly to recommendations for greater assertiveness in the execution of mandates. The overlap between NATO participants in UNPROFOR and in IFOR helped translate this to robust execution of tasks by IFOR. Of course, the sense of frustration and impotence under the UN was so widespread amongst military participants that it did not require survey results to bring about a convergence of firm resolve in the execution of tasks at the tactical and strategic levels. Already in January 1996, there was grim resolve no less in Sarajevo than in Brussels that the provisions of the Dayton agreement would be executed to the letter and according to the timeline agreed.

Academic analysis contributed to military understanding of the role of force. Canadian political scientist Frank Harvey spent time with the International Military Staff in Brussels, analysing NATO use of air power in deterrence and compellence and produced both reports for NATO and scholarly work detailing the conditions under which each would work.[67]

The separation and cantonment of forces might be seen as peace enforcement, in which the peace force had primary responsibility for meeting the targets of the agreement. But it was clear even during the Copenhagen conferences that subsequent phases of peace implementation could not be enforced, and would depend on the willingness of the parties to implement the agreement.[68] This recognition on the military side brings us back to many of the issues discussed above. It is not possible to frame strategic objectives that could be achieved by the application of existing military tactics – soldiers could not coerce the population to peace, and had only limited capacity for mediation and confidence-building tactics.

This brings me to the convergence of strategic and tactical tools for conflict resolution on the civilian side. In the previous section, I argued that the involvement of many NGOs brought new skills and perspectives to peace implementation, particularly in the fields of governance and psycho-social reconstruction. Although the NGO work was conducted mainly at the grass-roots or community level, the OHR picked up much of this progress and supported it with institutional change, removal of hard-line leaders, and reinforcement of success through local funding. These came together well in some cases like Brcko, where a supervisory order on multiethnic administration in 1997 was followed by establishment of multiethnic police and municipal offices in 1998, European and non-governmental reconstruction funding, and removal of hostile Serb leaders in the Serb Republic.[69]

The table below summarises some of the options for conflict resolution between states (top-down) and between individuals and groups (bottom up). Those on the left, drawn from the *UN Handbook on the Peaceful Resolution of Disputes Between States*, have evolved mainly to address conflicting interests within an instrumental framework. Those on the right include tools and skills that help to change perception of the conflict and the relationship between parties, acknowledging that interpersonal relationships are emotional as well as rational. The tools on the left tend to be the preserve of diplomats, while those on the right tend to have more diverse practitioners, including psychologists and community activists.

Tools for resolution of conflict between states[70]	Tools for resolution of conflict between individuals[71]
Negotiation and consultation	*Support and networking*
Inquiry	Facilitating meetings
Good Offices	Developing group leaders
Mediation	Group decision-making techniques
Conciliation	*Encouraging and supporting action*
Arbitration	Business acumen and entrepreneurial skills
Judicial settlement	Leadership and teaching
	Rebuilding relationships across boundaries
	Interpersonal communications
	Group facilitation
	Managing psycho-social dynamics of conflict

Items in italics require some therapeutic as well as organisational skills to complete successfully.

There is academic evidence to support the concept that building interpersonal and intercommunal relations from the bottom up must be accompanied by institutional reform from the top down. Books written about Yugoslavia in the 1980s were increasingly pessimistic about the prospects for accommodation: *Political Cohesion in a Fragile Mosaic* (1983), *Yugoslavia: A Fractured Federalism* (1988), *The Improbable Survivor* (1988), *Yugoslavia in Crisis* (1989), *Descent into Chaos: Yugoslavia's Worsening Crisis* (1989).[72] Throughout these years, Yugoslavia's political institutions became less effective at dealing with the conflicts between republics. Although structural explanations account for the break-up, they did not seem to account for the ferocity of the violence between neighbours. A large amount of research in the 1990s seemed to confirm the instrumental origins of the conflict, rather than ancient hatreds that might be associated with the visceral violence actually observed.[73] But what is striking about these works is that all of them rely to some degree on accounts at communal level. Whereas studies in the 1980s concentrated on constitutions and institutional structures, those in the 1990s sought to understand the level at which the violence was occurring – in the villages and neighbourhoods of the mixed communities of the former Yugoslavia. First hand accounts of the violence and of relationships in the communities become more common in descriptions of the conflict and prescriptions for resolution. This is not just prurient interest in violence; I think it reflects the understanding that the national and local scenes must be addressed together in any prescription for recovery from violence, using conflict resolution tools that are appropriate to each level. While this makes intervention planning more complicated than it has often been in the past, it should lead to better results – another step towards improved peacekeeping.

Encompass to Stabilise

THE FINAL STEPPING-STONE to better peacekeeping is a lesson of the past that the Balkan experience of the 1990s has led us to relearn. Incorporating unstable areas in an existing structure may be the best way of stabilising them.

Proximity, contiguity and the long history of European involvement in the Balkans probably precluded any strategy of isolation for the Balkan imbroglio. But the timing for incorporation was not self-evident. The subject of NATO expansion into Eastern Europe was discussed as early as 1990 within the International Military Staff in Brussels. It took another three years before the discussion moved to acceptable public debate of timing and modalities for incorporation. NATO's Assistant Secretary General for Political Affairs, Gebhardt Von Moltke described how the strategy for building the Partnership for Peace was initiated at the Brussels summit of January 1994, targeting former Warsaw Pact members but not ex-Yugoslavia:

> Partnership for Peace is an invitation to these countries to deepen and intensify their ties with the Alliance through practical cooperation. Much of this will be in the military sphere, and will concentrate on fostering the ability to work together in such fields as peacekeeping and humanitarian assistance. In addition, the Partnership has a wider, more political dimension to it, which is the promotion of, and commitment to, democratic principles, thereby increasing stability and diminishing threats to peace.[74]

A year later the American Permanent Representative to NATO was writing about moving eastwards the "thrilling experiment" of NATO's elimination of war between western European nations, but the Balkans were not yet on the agenda.[75] By 1997, NATO's Deputy Secretary General, Sergio Balanzino, referred repeatedly to the Bosnian experience of multinational collaboration as a test for NATO's new partnership institutions.[76]

After almost two years of work towards implementation of the Dayton framework for peace, Balkan specialist Zlatko Isakovic concluded that the key issue for Bosnia would be whether NATO troops would remain long enough to see the region incorporated into European institutions, or whether withdrawal of the peacekeeping forces would lead to permanent ethnic division.[77] What we can distinguish in the changing tone of the international debate from 1995 to 2002 is the gradual realisation that the costs of withdrawal and return to ethnic separation and possibly to violence are likely to be higher than the price of engaging and transforming the conflict in the former Yugoslavia. As Richard Ullman, of the US Council on Foreign Relations notes, "The conflict already has imposed significant costs not only on the neighbours of the former Yugoslavia but on the wider international community."[78] The optimism that it might be possible to reduce these costs through incorporation stems partly from the other steps to improved peacekeeping discussed above.

Implications for the Future

THESE FOUR developments suggest some conclusions about the nature of and requirements for peacekeeping in the future. Of course some aspects of the Balkan experience are idiosyncratic, and these deductions are necessarily generalisations. The many volumes of lessons and summaries of the Balkan experience seem to converge on three implications for future operations: states will need more diplomatic sophistication to manage conflict, more organisational sophistication to deploy and manage resources, and greater clarity in their partnership objectives (if only for themselves, because obscurity can be useful in public).

The international community will find ways to share burdens and minimise risks in an anarchic international order, but this will require more diplomatic sophistication than was evident during most of the Balkans conflict. A lot of attention has been focused on the difficulty that the US had during the 1990s in committing to a long-term strategy. In fact, all democratic states are constrained by domestic considerations – even those like Canada or the United Kingdom enjoying majority governments with extensive executive powers. In his apologia for Germany's role at the outset of the long Balkan crisis, Ambassador Michael Libal makes it clear that Germany's history and domestic politics shaped its policy, even while he rejects the accusation that Germany was condemned by its history to an odious role.[79]

In the US, concern about presidential adventures is part of a long-standing debate about the roles of executive and legislative branches in pursuing strategic interests. Banks and Straussman argue that congressional prerogative to initiate war remained intact until 1950, and began to erode with Truman's unilateral decision on Korea and subsequent UN and Cold War actions. Despite the 1973 War Powers Resolution, presidents have continued to exercise unilateral spending power in security matters. Banks and Straussman conclude that the Bosnian deployment was an unconstitutional usurpation of congressional power over war making.[80] This view is not uncommon in conservative, isolationist circles, supporting the Jefferson and Madison preference for minimal foreign engagement, rather than Hamilton's vision of a powerful state apparatus.[81] Since September 11, 2001, the dispute seems to have been definitively resolved in Hamilton's favour. Concentrated executive powers might enable firm leadership by the US, but the case of American-led unity over Bosnia needs to be set against the case of American isolation over Iraq. This isolation could seriously damage the institutions needed for sophisticated and concerted response to crises and protracted conflicts.

US unilateralism has pushed the nature of peacekeeping away from consensual conflict resolution towards a more strategic application of third party force. Donald Black provides a sociological framework to understand this evolution, describing the comparative social distance of different types of third party intervention in disputes. He describes support roles ranging from informer, through adviser, advocate, ally and surrogate, each having increasingly partisan roles in intervention. Similarly, the "settlement rules" of friendly peacemaker, mediator, arbitrator, judge, and repressive peacemaker, exhibit increasingly authoritative intervention.[82] The "Americanisation" of peacekeeping illustrated by Joel Sokolsky's[83] and Jane Boulden's descriptions of mandate enforcement both reflect the increasing social distance of intervenors from the parties to the conflict, as they move to more coercive strategies.[84] Although the US often plays a variety of third party roles across the full spectrum – from friendly to repressive peace-maker – the roles of international organisations still tend to concentrate at the lower end of partisanship (informer and advisor, as in observer missions) and of settlement rules (friendly peacemaker and mediator). More assertive roles of NATO, the OSCE and even ECOWAS (under Nigerian leadership) have been associated with the interests of powerful states, rather than communities of interest. Nevertheless, new roles and rules for third parties call for greater diplomatic sophistication, because each form of support and settlement implies new combinations of third party action.

At the time of the Dayton accomplishment, Professor Alan Henrikson, director of the Roundtable on a New World Order at the Fletcher School of Law and Diplomacy, wrote that America's unique moment as sole superpower was already fading, and the model of lead nation – the American model – might be seen as an artefact of the twentieth century:

> In its place, a new pattern of international participation is emerging. Its distinguishing feature is cooperation, or willingness on the part of individual states, whether large or small, to join together to perform urgent and important international tasks, on the assumption that most other states will do so as well.

Historically, it has tended to be the middle powers, Canada being the exemplar, that have shown the greatest readiness to offer their international services in this forthcoming way. Accordingly, it will here be called the 'Canadian model.'[85]

With seven years of hindsight, as Gulf War II looms, this pronouncement may seem premature. Even as Henrikson wrote, strong forces in think-tanks like the Council on Foreign Relations and the Cato Institute resisted American participation in anything resembling the "Canadian model."[86] Nevertheless, Henrikson's optimism reflects the diplomatic sophistication that contributed both to the Dayton solution and the efforts to implement it since then.

In implementing the Dayton agreement, organisational sophistication in the combination and deployment of tangible resources has been vital. It will be important in peacekeeping and post-conflict reconstruction in the future to integrate top-down (diplomatic-political and interstate) and bottom-up (psycho-social and inter-communal) means to control violence and rebuild stable peace. The practicability and feasibility of mandates like those of the UN, NATO, and OSCE missions now in Bosnia are difficult to determine in advance, and field headquarters often have to stretch to accomplish new mandates.

Finally, the effort to create rules-based regimes to manage protracted conflicts will continue to coexist with unilateral actions by powerful or desperate states and their regimes. Peacekeeping will therefore continue to be a strategic tool for the powerful (Henrikson's "American model"), but also represents enlightened self-interest for the international community (Henrikson's "Canadian model"). This demands more clarity in identifying the willing and the able for coalitions and UN missions. To facilitate this clarity, an alternative view of amorphous "international community" involvement in the Balkan conflict is possible. Rather than seeing the intervention as unambiguous third party assistance to the belligerents, this alternative view sees the intervention as self-serving at several levels. International organisations make work for themselves. Individuals gain prestigious and lucrative employment. Commercial interests break down state barriers and open assets for purchase, while eliminating competition. States and alliances find mechanisms to control peripheral areas for less than the cost of an outright war to defeat the target. Taken together, this self-interested behaviour looks like a Euro-American approach to colonisation – start with a treaty to disarm opposition, then push the treaty aside when it suits. When we are honest as well as clear about the intent and effect of our interventions, this neo-colonial critique might be put to rest.

Conclusion

ONE OF the accomplishments of twentieth-century academics has been to shift the spotlight from kings and battles to some of the mundane determinants of the future – birth rates, disease, social relationships, and the dynamics of trust and cooperation, to list a few examples. The Balkan experience has cast such a long shadow on so many fields of research that we would be wrong to concentrate on its obvious battles and champions. With the benefit of 10 years of hindsight, it is not NATO's charge to the rescue, but the patient floundering of regional institutions that offers new hope for conflict resolution. It is not the robust parading of thousands of soldiers, but the quiet tending of hundreds of NGOs that is changing conflict attitudes and behaviours. It is not the highly visible Peace Implementation Conferences, but the almost invisible web of ties between the highest decision-makers and the lowest implementing agencies that has changed the way peacekeeping works. Finally, it is not containment and coercion, but incorporation and cooperation that provides a path to a peaceful Balkan community in the future.

Notes

1 Ivo Andric, "A Letter from 1920," *Three Stories About Bosnia, 1908, 1946, 1992* (Belgrade: Association of Yugoslav Publishers and Booksellers, 1995), p. 39.

2 Susan Woodward, *Balkan Tragedy: Chaos and Dissolution after the Cold War* (Washington: Brookings, 1995).

3 One could argue that this was the beginning of the end of the distinction between peacekeeping and international policing in the interests of a globalised liberal economic order. Though Duffield concentrates on wars more peripheral to the liberal economy, I would argue that the incorporation of the immediate hinterland might have been more significant. Mark Duffield, *Global Governance and the New Wars: The Merging of Development and Security* (London: Zed Books, 2001).

4 *Compact Oxford English Dictionary*, 2nd Edition (Oxford: Clarendon Press, 1991), p. 1292.

5 Olivier Forcade, "Interpositions françaises dans le cadre des traités de paix en Hongrie, Haute-Silésie et Turquie de 1918 à 1923," *Peacekeeping 1815 to Today*, Proceedings of the XXIst Colloquium of the International Commission of Military History (Ottawa: International Commission of Military History, 1995), pp. 166–168.

6 Thomas G. Weiss, "Collective Spinelessness: U.N. Actions in the Former Yugoslavia" in *The World and Yugoslavia's Wars*, ed. Richard H. Ullman (New York: Columbia International Affairs Online, 1995).

7 Britain, France, Italy, and Russia intervened in Crete 1998–1906 with military forces, *gendarmes* and *carabinieri* to impose a settlement after the Greco-Turkish war of 1896. They appointed a single High Commissioner with whom their four Consuls General communicated on matters for coordination. *The Cretan Drama: the life and memoirs of Prince George of Greece, High Commissioner in Crete 1898–1906*, ed. A.A. Pallis (New York: R. Speller, 1959).

8 Michael Libal, *Limits of Persuasion: Germany and the Yugoslav Crisis, 1991–1992* (Westport, CT: Praeger, 1997), responds to these criticisms.

9 Woodward, 1995; see also Lee Bryant, "The Betrayal of Bosnia," Centre for the Study of Democracy, University of Westminster, Autumn 1993.

10 Sabrina Petra Ramet, *Balkan Babel: The Disintegration of Yugoslavia from the Death of Tito to Ethnic War*, second edition (Boulder, CO: Westview, 1996).

11 Ted Galen Carpenter, "Foreign Policy Masochism: The Campaign for U.S. Intervention in Yugoslavia," The Cato Institute, Foreign Policy Briefing No. 19, 1 July 1992; "Resolving Intra-National Conflicts: A Strengthened Role for Intergovernmental Organizations," February 1993; "Holbrooke Horror: The U.S. Peace Plan for Bosnia," The Cato Institute, Foreign Policy Briefing No. 37, 27 October 1995 – Carpenter's tone never changes.

12 Meeting attended by the author in Zagreb, September 1995.

13 Andrew S. Bair, "Managing the Crisis in the Former Yugoslavia," in *Peace Support Operations and the US Military*, ed. Dennis J. Quinn (Washington DC: National Defence Univeristy Press, 1994), pp. 217–234.

14 Centre for OSCE Research (CORE), *The OSCE Yearbook*, 1995–1996 (Baaden-Baaden: Institut fur Friedensforschung und Sicherheitspolitik, 1996), np.

15 Max Van Der Stoel, "Preventing Conflict and Building Peace: a Challenge for the CSCE," *NATO Review*, web edition, 4/42 (August 1994), 7–12. His vision of the Commissioner and CSCE role foreshadows that spelled out in the International Commission on Intervention and State Sovereignty, *Responsibility to Protect* (2002).

16 Werner Bauwens, Bruni Colson, Wim De Haar, Koen De Feyter, Olivier Paye, Nico Vertongen, "The CSCE And The Changing Role of NATO and the European Union," *NATO Review*, web edition, 3/42 (June 1994), 21–25.

17 Sean Maloney, *Canada and the European Community Monitor Mission in the Balkans, 1991–1994*, The McNaughton Papers, No. 10 (Toronto: Canadian Institute of Strategic Studies, 1997), 16.

18 Interviews, Prijedor, Jan Schunk (Denmark, ECMM) and Oyvind Hoel (Norway, OSCE), May 1996.

19 David Owen, *Balkan Odyssey* (New York: Harcourt Brace, 1995), pp. 75–79, 223–254.

20 Maloney, 1997, p. 33.

21 Kevin Avruch, James L. Narel, Pascale Combelles Siegel, *Information Campaigns for Peace Operations* (Washington, DC: CCRP, 1999).

22 Alan James, *Peacekeeping in International Politics* (London: MacMillan, 1990), pp. 87–92, and Amikam Nachmani, *International Intervention in the Greek Civil War: The United Nations Special Committee on the Balkans, 1947–1952* (New York: Praeger, 1990), pp. 143–164.

23 Although plenary sessions on successor state status were held in 1996, 1997, and 1998, the Serb Republic (RS) continued to dispute the finding that it was not entitled to successor state status.

24 Discussions with Chief Military Observer, Zagreb, December 1995.

25 David Last, "Early Warning and Prevention of Violent Conflict: The Role of Multifunctional Observer Missions," *Conflict Prevention: Path to Peace or Grand Illusion?*, eds. David Carment and Albrecht Schnabel (Tokyo: United Nations University Press, 2003), pp. 157–181.

26 General Michel Maisonneuve, Report to National Defence Command Centre, attended by author, November 1998.

27 UK commanders in MND SW found this role particularly useful, and after the Washington Agreement of February 1994 deployed teams of "Joint Commission Observers" (JCOs) in an armed observer role that complemented EC Monitors and UNMO deployments, but responded directly to the MND commander.

28 Interviews, Dubrovnik, May 1994, reported in "Cooperation between Units and Observers," *News From The Front!* (The Centre for Army Lessons Learned, September/October 1994), pp. 1–2, 5, 7. Also published in *Peacekeeping and International Relations*, September–October 1994, p. 4.

29 The International Management Group (IMG) was established by the UNHCR in 1993 as an umbrella organisation to co-ordinate assessment of infrastructure needed for displaced and refugee populations, including water, sewage, electricity, central heating, medical clinics, schools and housing. The reports generated during the course of the war were used by the repatriation task forces and reconstruction working groups after the Dayton agreement was signed.

30 Interviews, NC3A Assessment Cell, Sarajevo, March 1998.

31 EUMM HQ, EUMM SOP 1/2B, dated 1 April 01.

32 Meeting, Admiral Leighton Smith, General Rupert Smith, General Bernard Janvier, Pleso, July 1995, attended by author.

33 This figure is from statistics at a UNCHR presentation attended by the author in Sarajevo in February 1998.

34 Soros Foundation, "State Of 'The Third Sector' in Bosnia and Herzegovina," *2001 Report – Civil Society* (Zagreb: Open Society Fund, Bosnia and Herzegovina, 2002), np.

35 Jonathan Steele, "Peacekeepers Seize Hard-line Bosnian Serb Transmitters," *Manchester Guardian*, 2 October 1997, p. 12. Kevin Avruch, James L. Narel, and Pascale Combelles Siegel, *Information Campaigns for Peace Operations* Washington, DC: DOD C4ISR Cooperative Research Program, 1999, 42.

36 Marta Henricson-Cullberg, Sören Sommelius, Carl-Ulrik Schierup & Jan Øberg, *After Yugoslavia – What?* (Stockholm: TFF, 1991). This small book includes more than 70 proposals for non-violent conflict-mitigation between Serbia and Croatia, based on observations from field visits and local knowledge.

37 Cornelio Sommaruga, "CAUX Initiatives of Change: can an individual make a difference?" Initiatives of Change, Caux, Switzerland, 29 January 2002, on Moral Rearmament (MRA) and the Caux conferences in seeking Franco-German reconciliation from 1946 to 1952.

38 Susan Brown, Director of CIDA's Peacebuilding Branch, and Johanna Mendelson-Forman, a former director of the Office of Transition initiatives, both acknowledge the importance of response to Bosnia in shaping organisational objectives. USAID's OTI, however, was probably more influenced initially by the experiences of Haiti.

39 James Luko, Operations Officer, ICTY, 10 June 2001.

40 Jamie Swift, *Civil Society in Question* (Toronto: Behind the Lines, 2001), p. 4.

41 T.R. Young and Burce A. Arrigo, *The Dictionary of Critical Social Sciences* (Boulder, CO: Westview, 1999), p. 45.

42 National Democratic Initiative for International Affairs, "Europe: Central and Eastern: Bosnia and Herzegovina," www.ndi.org/worldwide/cee/bosnia/bosnia_pf.asp updated June 2002.

43 Soros Foundation, op. cit., "Our Approach."

44 For example, Jason Aplon and Victor Tanner, *Civil Society in Bosnia: Obstacles and Opportunities for Building Peace* (Washington, DC: The Winston Foundation for World Peace, Conflict Prevention Resource Site, http://wf.org/aplontoc.htm, 2002).

45 David Last, "Defeating Fear and Hatred through Peace-Building: Multiplying the Impact of a Military Contribution," *Canadian Foreign Policy*, January 1998.

46 Young and Arrigo, op. cit., p. 53.

47 ICG, "Bosnia's Refugee Logjam Breaks: Is the International Community Ready?" (Sarajevo: International Crisis Group Report, 31 May 2000).

48 The BiH House of Peoples rejected the Framework Law on the Privatisation of Enterprises and Banks, July 1998. The High Representative decided to impose the Framework Law on the Privatisation of Enterprises and Banks. HR was forced to remove the Bosnian head of the Privatisation in May 2000 (OHR report), and in Sept. 2000, OHR, WB and IMF warn BiH to adopt pension reform law or lose $150M in funding.

49 Barry S. Levy and Victor W. Sidel, "The Impact of Military Activities on Civilian Populations," in *War and Public Health*, eds. Barry S. Levy and Victor W. Sidel (New York: Oxford University Press and American Public Health Association, 1997), pp. 149–167.

50 Johanna Santa Barbara, "The Psychological Effects of War on Children," in *War and Public Health*, eds. Barry S. Levy and Victor W. Sidel (New York: Oxford University Press and American Public Health Association, 1997), pp. 168–185, for example.

51 ICG, "Going Nowhere Fast: Refugees and Internally Displaced Persons in Bosnia and Herzegovina," International Crisis Group Report, 1 May 1997. Paula Green, "A Tale of Two Cities – Dialogue and Community Building in Bosnia: Educators' Workshops – November, 1998," A Joint Project of Karuna Center for Peacebuilding and The Foundation for Community Encouragement (Leverett, MA: Karuna Center Report, 1998).

52 Sadako Ogata, "UNHCR in Bosnia: an uphill struggle 11 months after Dayton," *Nato Review*, 1996:6

53 ICG, "Going Nowhere Fast: Refugees and Internally Displaced Persons in Bosnia and Herzegovina," International Crisis Group Report, May 1997.

54 ICG, "A Peace or just a Cease-Fire? The Military Equation in Post Dayton Bosnia," International Crisis Group Report, 15 December 1997.

55 Gregory L. Schulte, "Bringing peace to Bosnia and change to the Alliance," *NATO Review* (1997:2); Volker Rühe, "New NATO, new Bundeswehr and peace in Bosnia and Herzegovina," *NATO Review* (1997:3); Thierry Germond, "NATO and the ICRC: A partnership serving the victims of armed conflicts" (1997:3).

56 In addition to the ICG reports, see UN Secretary General's reports, S/1997/468 dated

19 June 1997. For the period from 15 March 1997 to 19 June 1997, S/1997/694 dated 8 September 1997. For the period from 16 June 1997 to 8 September 1997, and S/1997/966 10 December 1997. For the period from 8 September 1997 to 1 December 1997.

57 ICG, "Brcko: What Bosnia Could Be" (10 February 1998); ICG, "A Hollow Promise? Return of Bosnian Serb Displaced Persons to Drvar" (19 January 1998); ICG, "Impunity in Drvar" (20 August, 1998); ICG, "The Konjic Conundrum: Why Minorities have failed to return to Model Open City."

58 UNESCO, *Culture of Peace Program* (New York: Department of Public Information, 1999).

59 17th Report by the High Representative for Implementation of the Peace Agreement to The Secretary-General of the United Nations (Sarajevo: Office of the High Representative, 17 October 2000), paragraphs 5, 45, and 49–52.

60 14th Report by the High Representative for Implementation of the Peace Agreement to The Secretary-General of the United Nations (Sarajevo: Office of the High Representative, 16 July 1999), paragraph 91.

61 Soros Foundation report, op. cit., 2001.

62 Review of agendas conducted by the author for Deputy Force Commander UNPF, October 1995.

63 I have described this in greater detail elsewhere, David Last, "Peacekeeping in Divided Societies: Limits to Success," *Low Intensity Conflict and Law Enforcement*, Winter 1997.

64 Soren Bo Husum, "UN Military Observers in De-escalation of Local Conflict," Chapter 21 in *UN Peacekeeping in Trouble: Lessons Learned from the Former Yugoslavia*, eds. Wolfgang Biermann and Martin Vadset (Aldershot: Ashgate, 1998), pp. 318–329.

65 Wolfgang Biermann and Martin Vadset, *Lessons Learned from Former Yugoslavia*, Copenhagen Peace Research Institute, Report of Conference, held in Copenhagen, Denmark, 12–14 April 1996. Annex A.

66 Biermann and Vadset, op. cit., Annex A.

67 David Carment and Frank Harvey, *Using Force to Prevent Ethnic Violence: An Evaluation of Theory and Evidence* (Westport: Praeger, 2001).

68 Comments by Commanders, "From UNPF to IFOR," in Bierman and Vadset, 1996, p. 64.

69 ICG, "Brcko: What Bosnia Could Be," International Crisis Group Report, 10 February 1998.

70 *UN Handbook on the Peaceful Resolution of Disputes between States* (New York: United Nations, 1992).

71 David Last, *From Peacekeeping to Peacebuilding: Theory, Cases, Experiments and Solutions*, Politics and Economics Working Paper 99/01 (Kingston: Royal Military College of Canada, 1999), table 5, developed from a survey of grass-roots conflict resolution activities and interviews with practitioners.

72 Beverly Crawford, "Explaining Cultural Conflict in Ex-Yugoslavia: Institutional Weakness, Economic Crisis, and Identity Politics," in *The Myth of "Ethnic Conflict,"* eds. Beverly Crawford and Ronnie D. Lipschutz, International and Area Studies Research Series, Number 98, University of California, Berkeley, 1998. Crawford's and Lipschutz's extensive review of research on ethnic conflict has informed this section.

73 Examples of the instrumental explanations of violence include Djilas, "The Breakup of Yugoslavia"; Sumantra Bose, "State Crises and Nationalities Conflict in Sri Lanka and Yugoslavia," *Comparative Political Studies*, 28/1 (April 1995), 87–117; Warren Zimmerman, "The Last Ambassador: A Memoir of the Collapse of Yugoslavia," *Foreign Affairs*, 74/2 (March–April 1995), 2–21; Bette Denich, "Dismembering

Yugoslavia: Nationalist Ideologies and the Symbolic Revival of Genocide," *American Ethnologist*, 21/2 (May 1994), 367–394; Milica Bookman, "War and Peace: The Divergent Breakups of Yugoslavia and Czechoslovakia," *Journal of Peace Research*, 31/2 (May 1994), 175–188; Bogdan Denitch, *Ethnic Nationalism: The Tragic Death of Yugoslavia* (Minneapolis: University of Minnesota Press, 1994); Obrad Kesic, "Serbia: The Politics of Fear," *Current History*, 92/577 (November 1993), 376–381; Vesna Pesic, "A Country by Any Other Name: Transition and Stability," *East European Politics and Societies*, 6/3 (Fall 1992), 242–260; Anton Bebler, "Yugoslavia's Variety of Communist Federalism and Her Demise," *Communist and Post-Communist Studies*, 26/1 (March 1993), 72–87; Juan Linz and Alfred Stepan, "Political Identities and Electoral Sequences: Spain, the Soviet Union, and Yugoslavia," *Daedalus*, 121/2 (Spring 1992), 123–140; Ivo Banac, "The Fearful Assymetry of War: The Causes and Consequences of Yugoslavia's Demise," *Daedalus*, 121/2 (Spring 1992), 141–175; V. P. Gagnon: "Serbia's Road to Democracy," *Journal of Democracy*, 5/2 (April 1994), 117–131; and "Ethnic Nationalism and International Conflict: The Case of Yugoslavia," *International Security*, 19/3 (Winter 1991), 130–167; Branka Magas, *Destruction of Yugoslavia* (London: Verso, 1993).

74 Gebhardt Von Moltke, "Building A Partnership for Peace," *NATO Review*, web edition, 3/42 (June 1994), 3–7.

75 Robert E. Hunter, "Enlargement: Part of a Strategy for Projecting Stability into Central Europe," *NATO Review*, web edition, 3/43 (May 1995), 3–8.

76 Ambassador Sergio Balanzino, "Deepening partnership: The key to long-term stability in Europe," *NATO Review*, web edition, 4/45 (July–August 1997), 10–16.

77 Zlatko Isakovic, "The Dayton-Paris Peace Accords: Failure or Success?" Institute of International Politics and Economics, Center for Peace and Conflict Research, Belgrade, Yugoslavia, paper presented at the International Studies Association, March 1998.

78 Richard H. Ullman, "The Wars in Yugoslavia and the International System after the Cold War," in *The World and Yugoslavia's Wars*, ed. Richard H. Ullman (Washington, DC: Council on Foreign Relations, February 1998), unpaginated electronic version.

79 Michael Libal, *Limits of Persuasion: Germany and the Yugoslav Crisis, 1991–1992* (Westport, CT: Praeger, 1997). See pp. 3–10 and pp. 103–105 on Germany's history and values, and 113–119 on Libal's rejection of historicist accusations.

80 William C. Banks and Jeffrey D. Straussman, "A New Imperial Presidency? Insights from U.S. Involvement in Bosnia," in *The New American Interventionism: Essays from Political Science Quarterly*, ed. Demetrios James Caraley (New York: Columbia, 1998), np.

81 Gary Wills, *James Madison* (New York: Times Books, 2002). See also review by Gordon Wood, *New York Review of Books*, 9 May 2002.

82 Donald Black, *The Social Structure of Right and Wrong*, with M.P. Baumgartner (San Diego: Academic Press, 1993), pp. 95–124.

83 Joel Sokolsky, *The Americanization of Peacekeeping: Implications for Canada*, Martello Papers, No. 17 (Kingston: Queen's University Centre for International Relations, 1997).

84 Jane Boulden, *The United Nations and Mandate Enforcement: Congo, Somalia and Bosnia*, Martello Papers, No. 20 (Kingston: Queen's University Centre for International Relations and Institut quebecois des haute etudes internationales, 1999).

85 Alan K. Henrikson, "Leadership, Cooperation and the Contribution Principle," NATO Review, web edition, 6/42 (December 1994), 1/43 (January 1995), 17–21.

86 Jonathan G. Clarke, "The United States and Future Bosnias," The Cato Institute, Foreign Policy Briefing No. 36, 8 August 1995; Gary Dempsey, "Rethinking The Dayton Agreement: Bosnia Three Years Later," Cato Institute, 14 December 1998.

A. WALTER DORN

JEREMY KING

Taking Stock of Security Sector Reform in Bosnia 1995–2002

I Introduction[1]

A FTER FOUR YEARS of bloody internecine fighting, the war in Bosnia and Herzegovina (BiH) was finally brought to an end with the signing of the Dayton Peace Accords (DPA) in December 1995. The international community, having invested so much in the peace process leading to the Accords, became intimately involved in implementing them as part of an unprecedented effort at post-conflict peace-building. The goal was to prevent a rapid relapse into warfare and to build the infrastructure for a future peaceful nation. At the outset, this meant dealing with the three belligerent *ad hoc* wartime armies – the Bosnian-Muslim forces (ABiH), the Bosnian-Croat Croatian Defence Council (HVO), and the Bosnian-Serb Army (VRS) – that had caused so much damage in the country. Slowly efforts expanded to cover other parts of the security sector and, even more broadly, to democratic governance across the spectrum of security and non-security agencies in the two DPA-established entities, the Federation of Bosnia-Herzegovina and Republika Srpska (RS), which together form the state of BiH.

A. WALTER DORN is a Research Professor with the Department of Politics and Economics at the Royal Military College of Canada and a faculty member of the Pearson Peacekeeping Centre.

JEREMY KING is a UN Political Officer who served in 2000–02 with the United Nations Mission in Bosnia and Herzegovina, working in the office of the Special Representative of the Secretary-General.

The need to reform all the BiH agencies that deal with security, which collectively form the "security sector," was increasingly recognised as essential for the success of peace-building. During the conflict, the military forces became habituated to egregious human rights violations, as had a number of ruthless paramilitary bodies that fell outside the normal chain of command. Law enforcement agencies routinely overstepped their bounds and engaged in widespread abuses and corruption. The courts were partial to ethnic identity and ignored due process in the name of wartime expediency. The corrections system was in utter disrepair, as enemy soldiers had displaced legitimate criminals in decrepit prisons run under sub-human conditions. Borders were porous as customs officials participated in illegal trafficking of persons, weapons and goods. The intelligence agencies wielded tremendous power as tools of ultra-nationalist political parties, including those in neighbouring capitals. In short, the entire system of government had become warped to meet the dictates of the war and the ruling elites.

Hence, in post-Dayton BiH the international community found itself engaged in an unprecedented effort, both in scope and cost, of security sector reform (SSR). SSR is a holistic concept that recognises the strong interrelationships between security agencies. Without a comprehensive approach, one unreformed body might continue playing by the old "dirty rules" and undermine efforts to transform not only itself but also the other agencies. So despite the absence of guidance on SSR in the DPA, many innovative programmes were begun.

Not since the end of the Second World War had the United States, the nations of Europe and the world (through the UN) committed such great resources to reform the security sector of a state. While it is too early to judge the final impact of the many SSR initiatives, it is important to take stock of them and to identify the successes and limitations that are already apparent in this crucial Balkan experiment. This chapter endeavours to provide an overview of the initiatives and international actors conducting SSR in BiH in each element of the security sector: military, police, customs and border service, judicial, corrections and intelligence. It also looks at another important security measure: disarmament of the general population. Successful instances and synergies among the international actors are illustrated, as are some of the failures and the many challenges that have impeded reform. Finally, some of the lessons learned from this great experiment are explored in the context of newer peacekeeping and peacebuilding operations.

II Military Reform

(a) Demobilisation and Reintegration of Former Combatants

A critical issue for post-war BiH was what to do with the 400,000 soldiers in the three armies. The UN peace operations in the early 1990s, supported by substantial academic and policy research,[2] had yielded an important lesson: demobilisation and reintegration of combatants must be an integral part of post-conflict peace-building. Despite this, the DPA failed to incorporate a strategy to guide national and international actors. The result was minimal activity at first and uncoordinated project delivery later. The NATO-led Implementation Force (IFOR) considered the "demobilisation of remaining forces" a primary military task[3] but offered little more than security advice on the proposed locations of military barracks. The brunt of responsibility for employing a limited degree of emergency demobilisation and reintegration support fell first to the devastated local governments responsible for the armies and second to the international community, which reacted with varying degrees of effectiveness.

Two factors are largely responsible for the neglect of demobilisation and reintegration processes. Firstly, political tensions between the belligerents during the DPA negotiations hindered agreement on the very sensitive security issues surrounding demobilisation. Parties were unwilling to give up their fighting forces, which they felt might be needed if the peace were to fail again. Secondly, it would appear that NATO, in its peace-keeping infancy, lacked the experience in civil-military co-operation to manage such ambitious tasks, which go well beyond traditional military security functions. IFOR's concerns that its primary role be the military function of "separating armies from fighting one another" and "protecting civil populations from the actions of the military forces," ensured that the institutionalised knowledge of the UN in disarmament, demobilisation and reintegration (DDR) was initially resisted by NATO in BiH. In an April 1996 statement concerning the alliance's assistance to demobilisation and reintegration, IFOR Commander Lt Gen Sir Michael Rose stated that IFOR would "do whatever it can to try and help [demobilisation]," but IFOR is "not the best organisation for doing it."[4] With the absence of local government co-operation and capacity, no official demobilisation and reintegration assistance was provided immediately following the cessation of hostilities.

Reintegration was also a major impediment in the process, as ex-combatants needed to reintegrate not only into a divided state, but also into a post-communist one. The struggle for democracy and a free-market economy compounded the difficulties. The lack of adequate reintegration has undoubtedly contributed to organised crime, weapon smuggling, violence towards minority returnees and an export of mercenaries to other parts of the world. Some specific examples of the latter include:

- Bosnian Muslims fighting in Chechnya; two were killed by Russian troops in April 2000 after joining Chechen fighters six months previously;[5]

- Demobilised ABiH soldiers assisting the Kosovo Liberation Army (KLA) with military equipment and training in 1999;[6]

- Bosnian-Serb "volunteers" made up of demobilised VRS soldiers assisting Yugoslav security forces in Kosovo in 1998;[7] and

- The exportation of Bosnian-Serb mercenaries to Zaire in a failed attempt to prop up the regime of President Mobutu Sese Seko in 1996.[8]

The demobilisation, or rather "disintegration" of the armed forces, came about in three distinct phases: first as an emergency demobilisation phase in late 1995/1996; second as part of an intermediate professionalisation of services in 1997/1998; and then, in the country's pursuit of a peace dividend, while continuing the professionalisation processes in 1999/2000. Of the estimated 400,000 soldiers in 1995, an estimated 370,000 soldiers were demobilised over the five-year period.[9]

International community support for demobilisation came largely in the form of project funding from the World Bank. In mid-1996, in response to a request from the government bodies of BiH, the World Bank's International Development Association provided the BiH government with a credit of US $7.5 million for an Emergency Demobilisation and Reintegration Project to help reintegrate displaced workers, especially soldiers, into the civilian workforce.[10]

The World Bank established Project Implementation Units (PIUs) for the Federation and RS. Both PIUs were operated as Employment and Training Foundations (ETF) with tripartite governing boards (ie, with Bosnian Serbs, Bosnian Croats and Bosnian Muslims as members). The Foundations were responsible for issuing funds based on competitive project proposals, with the Federation receiving two-thirds of overall project resources. According to the World Bank, the programme focuses on counselling, employment and training. These "finance demand-driven reintegration services ... include support for employment, micro-enterprises, farming, skills enhancement, and higher education." [11] "Comprehensive information and counselling services" are offered to all ex-soldiers in areas such as pre-discharge orientation, professional orientation, (self-) employment opportunities, and "as needed post-traumatic stress disorder."

The World Bank has regarded the programme, which ended in the summer of 1999, as a success. Several problems have however been identified. Individuals associated with the project made allegations concerning misappropriation of funds, the generally poor quality of programme proposals, funding preference to international NGOs, and partiality towards funding projects that were labour intensive, which while reducing unemployment in the short-term did nothing to address underlying psychological tensions and post-traumatic mental illness.

The reintegration of demobilised soldiers in BiH was an urgent practical need which shifted international efforts away from longer-term reconstruction assistance to more immediate projects for job creation, education, and counselling. Demobilised soldiers, especially those without work, represented a powerful political lobby, often manipulated by extremists and nationalist parties, and posed a physical threat to the peace process. The dangerous mixture of high unemployment, weapons proliferation, hopelessness and mistrust between the ethnic communities remains combustible, countered only by the presence of the international community.

During the first quarter of 2002, the harsh reality of depleted entity budgets and the increasing inability to pay soldiers' salaries required a "radical and fast reduction of the army." [12] Speaking frankly to government officials in February 2002, the Special Representative of the UN Secretary General (SRSG), Jacques Paul Klein, warned that "the current excessive spending on the three armies is bankrupting the state, preventing economic growth and delaying BiH's entry into the European family of nations." He went on to say that

BiH cannot pay police salaries and pensions with machine guns, or buy school textbooks and medicine with bullets... The time has long come to take a bold step into reality. The future that is being squandered by excessive defence spending is yours and your children's.[13]

NATO Secretary General Lord Robertson echoed this message in his April 2002 visit to Sarajevo when he said that "it is scandalous that 10 percent of the state budget in BiH is being used for the military."[14]

Considerable defence downsizing took place in 2002, pushed by the NATO-led Stabilisation Force (SFOR) on the military side and the Organisation for Security and Cooperation in Europe (OSCE) on the civilian side. In April 2002, entity army chiefs of the general staff/joint command informed the Joint Military Commission that on the Federation side, 8,900 out of the current 22,400 professionals had accepted termination of their employment. In the RS, the 8,300 military professionals were to be reduced to 6,600 by October 2002. RS Army Commander Simic stated that its strategic goal was simply "to survive (in budget terms) at least until the end [of] 2002." However, as severance payment was not on the agenda in the RS, the reduction is expected to be completed without major budgetary implications.

Although the RS defence reductions do not go as far as affordability requires, they are very likely to be completed as planned and even faster than originally scheduled (2005). The Federation made a request to the International Monetary Fund (IMF) for commercial loans to fund its KM100 million (US$ 45 million) redundancy package, but concerns remain over the ability of the Federation to secure the loan and then to pay it off on time. More military reductions are expected in 2003, however, enabling the entities to reach the European average defence budget spending of two to three percent of GDP.[15]

(b) Military Professionalisation

At the end of the civil war, it was clear that the military forces needed not only to be reduced but also restructured and professionalised. Military professionalisation measures in BiH, as elsewhere, are intended to instil an understanding of the appropriate roles and behaviour of military forces in a democratic society in all ranks. At a minimum, firm restrictions are placed on the military's political role and clear boundaries are delineated between civilian and military power. Specific professionalisation processes have included: restructuring the forces and/or re-vetting personnel and disbanding irregular forces; training at the strategic, operational and tactical levels; encouraging higher professional standards; increasing technical capabilities; establishing greater efficiency in administrative structures; and establishing external civilian oversight.

The first problem encountered was as fundamental as it was obvious. The DPA recognised the existence of two separate armies in Bosnia-Herzegovina: the Federation Army, a predominantly Bosnian-Croat and Bosnian-Muslim force, and the Republika Srpska Army, a predominantly Bosnian-Serb body. As defence analyst David Lightburn explains, "[d]e facto, however, there were and remain, three armies, since the [Bosnian] Croat and Bosniac [Bosnian-Muslim] forces have not been integrated either in structure or in practice and co-operation between the two is minimal and superficial."[16]

The international community developed a series of initiatives designed to build confidence between the former belligerent armies and create conditions in BiH in which an appropriate, common, cost-effective and durable security framework could evolve.[17] Cost has remained a major concern, particularly since until 2000 the state allocated as much as 40 percent of its total annual budget to defence spending.

The primary actors engaged in military professionalisation efforts, described below, have been: the private US-based company Military Professional Resources Incorporated (MPRI), SFOR, the OSCE, the Office of the High Representative (OHR), and the United Nations Mission in Bosnia and Herzegovina (UNMIBH).

Shortly following the signing of the DPA, MPRI arrived in Sarajevo armed with a US State Department-brokered contract with the Federation to assist with "the development of their military structure, the fielding of military equipment and the conduct of a broad-based individual and unit training programme."[18] The use of a private military company raised eyebrows in many parts of the peacebuilding community. In addition, MPRI's Military Stabilisation Programme has received a great deal of criticism from defence planners, politicians and academics, who see the programme as counter-productive for long-term peace.

One criticism is that MPRI only provides military training to one half of the military equation, the Federation Army, thus polarising the state militarily. Despite the criticisms and a downsizing of personnel and training, MPRI obtained a series of lucrative contracts to continue training the Federation Army. In response, since 1998, a great deal of effort has been exerted by the other international actors to counter the effect of MPRI training and bring the two recognised armies together to encourage the development of a common defence doctrine. There is a further possibility that MPRI will extend training to the Republika Srpska Army as mechanisms for centralised command and control at the state level develop further. However, it is unlikely that such a training programme would include an equipment component.

(c) The Evolving Role of NATO: From Peace-keeping to Peace-building

Peace-keeping in BiH encouraged the evolution of NATO from purely a defensive alliance to a significant, if sometimes reluctant, peace-keeper and peace-builder. In addition to NATO member states, non-NATO nations have contributed in sizeable numbers.[19] IFOR experienced growing pains, as it tried to adapt to its new role in BiH, but its successor, SFOR, has matured to the level of involving itself deeply in civil-military co-operation, including questions of internal BiH defence policies. NATO launched a Security Co-operation Programme in 1998 between the alliance and BiH to stimulate dialogue and to begin the process of internal co-operation between Federation and RS defence authorities. The initiative sought to promote confidence and encourage transparency and accountability in the military forces, de-politicisation, a central defence structure, and the development of democratic practices. The programme included courses and seminars in BiH and abroad. By November 2000, more than 450 BiH defence personnel including defence ministers and their deputies, chiefs of staff, and other senior political and military personnel had participated in NATO-run professionalisation courses. Junior commanders and staff from other government ministries have also attended.[20]

A significant goal in NATO professionalisation assistance is to encourage BiH to join the NATO Partnership for Peace (PfP) programme. Among the conditions for the accession of BiH to PfP are: a common security policy; democratic parliamentary oversight and control of the armed forces; the provision at the state level of command and control of the armed forces, including the state level ministry responsible for defence matters; full transparency for plans and budgets; and the development of a common doctrine and common standards to train and equip the armed forces of BiH. In July 2001, NATO's Secretary-General, Lord Robertson, stated: "Our message to the members of the BiH Presidency is clear – show leadership, lead on overcoming the internal divisions, strengthen the state-level institutions and promote co-operation and reconciliation."[21] In his April 2002 visit to Sarajevo, he declared "that BiH was not yet ready to join Partnership for Peace."[22] PfP membership is a carrot that is being dangled in front of the BiH government to encourage reform.

(d) OSCE and OHR:
Civil Control, Accountability and Transparency

Complementary to NATO efforts are those of the OSCE Regional Stabilisation Office and the Military Cell of the OHR. The OSCE agenda seeks to develop budget transparency and parliamentary oversight of the militaries, elimination of conscription practices, creation of a joint staff college, support for balanced reductions of military expenditure and BiH military association with the European Union (EU) and NATO's PfP programme. The OSCE, like NATO, also consults with the Standing Committee on Military Matters (SCMM), which is made up of the joint presidency and their military advisors.[23] The SCMM is designed to serve as the country's civil control mechanism over the militaries. The Military Cell of the OHR, which is responsible for overall coordination of the international community's military professionalisation efforts, consults and provides material support to the SCMM.[24]

(e) UNMIBH:
Training the "Peace-kept" to Peacekeep

While the main work of UNMIBH is to work with local police, it has also assisted with military reform. It has facilitated overseas training for deployments of RS Ministry of Defence and Federation Ministry of Defence personnel for UN operations. In January 2001, BiH inaugurated its first multi-ethnic contingent to serve abroad as UN military observers. A nine-strong multi-ethnic unarmed contingent of military officers deployed to serve with the UN Mission in Ethiopia and Eritrea (UNMEE). A second rotation commenced in June 2001. The initiative is seen as an important step toward building better co-operation between the three Bosnian communities, which retain fresh memories of their 1992–95 conflict.[25] Building on the success of this initiative, UNMIBH established a BiH composite, non-combat, transport/logistics unit to contribute to international peace and security under the UN flag. The BiH State Ministry of Foreign Affairs now coordinates directly with the UN's Department of Peacekeeping Operations to plan deployments of the unit in UN operations.

(f) A Way Forward?

International planners hope for a convergence of defence policies into a common state-level approach by 2005. However, events such as the desertion of Bosnian Croats from the Federation Army (later rectified), and recent assertions in the RS that a single army is in no way an option, make it highly unlikely that BiH accession to the PfP, or even a convergence of defence policies will occur in the medium term. Nevertheless, progress has been made. According to former SFOR General Hilliard, Commander of Multi-National Division South West, "the armies in Bosnia are compliant forces which have moved from phases of inspection to compliance to that of consensus."[26] There is also clear evidence of a genuine commitment to downsizing military structures, albeit separate ones in the entities, to more affordable levels.

However, until the international community resolves the problem of three armies in one state, everything that is achieved in civilian implementation will be fragile and uncertain. This structural defect imperils the entire international effort in BiH. As long as there are formed military brigades ready to mutiny and defect in a matter of hours (as the Croats did *en masse* in 2001 despite nearly six years of "confidence-building measures"), SFOR must maintain a presence that is capable of defending weapons storage sites and remaining loyal troops. The situation is even more dangerous at present because the RS Army risks imploding through lack of finances while the Federation Army (both Bosnian-Croat and Bosnian-Muslim components) is becoming more confident.[27]

It is abundantly clear that the issue of mistrust between and within the forces must be addressed. Left alone, it is highly unlikely that they will reorganise themselves. For SRSG Klein, the future is clear:[28]

The time for war is over. Even if there remain differences and issues that are yet to be resolved, the leaders that led you into war are largely gone; the borders of BiH will not be changed, and it is inconceivable that the international community will allow your armed forces to go back to war.

The OHR, as the only international body in BiH with executive political powers to impose decisions and make legislative changes, has forced the government to adopt contemporary defence tasks and functions consistent with modern European armed forces. The message is being conveyed clearly: if BiH wants to take on the normal functions and roles of a Western democracy, it must develop a state level defence instrument which is non-threatening, affordable, and contributes to the development of domestic security for all BiH citizens in a European security construct.

Once consensus is reached on this issue, there is a substantial role for NATO to play in the technical aspects of reform and restructuring. NATO is the only organisation with the expertise and knowledge to address this task. This will entail three components. First, in terms of force reduction, professionals should be reduced and conscription eliminated, or at the very least their numbers shaped to a balanced and affordable level. Second, training and education will have to be redirected to correspond to the required tasks of the European security environment (peace-keeping, disaster relief, collective security, etc.). Serious consideration must be given to joint staff colleges, joint officer academies, common instruction for non-commissioned officers (NCOs), and linked reserve officer training. Third, equipment must be appropriate to the tasks at hand and meet the requirements of affordability, compatibility and interoperability.[29]

For more than six years various options and policy plans have been floated to deal with the segregation problem. Almost all of them are directed towards some form of joint or unified army to be formed in a time scale that is constantly receding. Some even feel that the time has come to recognise that the BiH entities are a reality whose separate interests (and armies) must be accommodated. An objective analysis should be undertaken of what actions are politically feasible within the Dayton framework for both the single and multiple army options.[30]

III Police Reform and Restructuring

POLICE FORCES often assume military roles during armed conflicts. With the cessation of conflict, they are characteristically slow to return to the required standards of professional policing, often inept in standard procedural and technical skills and sometimes continuing to carry out human rights abuses while trying to hide their previous atrocities. In addition, they usually retain strong loyalties of political or ethnic affiliation and resist a loss of power. Post-conflict police reform is intended to concentrate on strengthening the management capacity of the police force to implement change and foster understanding of what it means to be a police officer in a democratic society, distinguishable from the military. The overall aim is to establish effective and humane services to uphold law and order. New structures are required to assist the state in managing competition between groups, settle disputes and grievances and protect rights and interests. In the words of Laina Reynolds, editor of the *UN & Conflict Monitor*, "[t]he creation of a democratic police force cannot, by itself, create a democratic system of governance in a country. However, the lack of effective and accountable policing can certainly undermine even the most stable government."[31]

To create a new professional police force, the DPA provided an ambitious mandate for force restructuring to the UN. In accordance with the DPA, the UN created, as part of UNMIBH, the International Police Task Force (IPTF). The IPTF, in turn, developed a three-point plan concentrating on: (1) restructuring a post-communist and post-paramilitary police force; (2) reforming the police through training, selection, certification and de-certification procedures; and (3) democratising the police forces by establishing a de-politicised, impartial, accountable, multi-ethnic police force that abides by the principles of community policing.[32] As with the army, a large demobilisation effort was needed.

Michael Dziedzic and Andrew Bair's (1998) study on the IPTF determined that although there were concerns that demobilised police personnel would cause "social disruption and thus threaten the peace process," there is no significant evidence that this has occurred.[33] According to Dziedzic and Bair:

[T]hose policemen who were dismissed from service were not career policemen in the first place, but rather the minimally skilled recruits added to police ranks during the war. This outcome is probably in line, therefore, with what most of those involved expected to happen. To the extent these vetted individuals had a previous skill or trade, they presumably have attempted to return to that; this would undoubtedly include those who had been involved in criminal activity as well.

Of the approximate 44,000 police officers active in both the Federation and the RS in December 1995, some 26,000 have been demobilised. Of this number, over 200 officers have had their police powers withdrawn for involvement in wartime criminal activities or unprofessional conduct (according to UNMIBH internal reports).

Experience has shown that by using stringent selection criteria with effective oversight units and broad public education on community policing, the number of unprofessional or criminal recruits can be minimized. Still, even the most technically sound and careful selection procedures may not resolve deep legitimacy problems – a sense of unjust discrimination and lack of alternative job opportunities may facilitate the transformation of some demobilised police personnel into criminals and perpetrators of violent crime.[34]

The Bonn-Petersberg Declaration of April 1996 obliged the Federation to reduce its police personnel to 11,500 from the estimated 32,750 police officers who were active at the end of the war. Although this left a ratio of police officers to citizens of nearly double the European standard, it nevertheless reduced their forces by almost two-thirds. Progress was slow, however, because RS police remained unwilling to submit to the IPTF restructuring formula until late 1997, rejecting the IPTF limit of 6,000 policemen, and insisting on a force equal in strength to that of the Federation's.[35]

The US Department of Justice International Criminal Investigation Training Assistance Programme (ICITAP) has provided training to the IPTF itself and to local police forces. Other actors engaged in police reform have included the European Union and a number of bilateral initiatives undertaken mostly by EU countries.

While police advisors and trainers have made sizeable gains in technical capacity-building over the first five years, the results of efforts to establish police forces that respect human rights and the rule of law have been uneven, as the positive compliance record in some areas of the country and resistance in others shows. One important lesson has been the realisation that while technical capacity can be achieved in a short period of time and attitudes changed in the medium term, the success of long-term reform and restructuring is jeopardised if the responsible international organisation lacks the authority to remove elements of politicisation or lacks the mandate to ensure that law enforcement officials receive adequate salaries on time.

To encourage longer-term professionalisation and greater cohesion between RS and Federation police forces, UNMIBH established a BiH civilian police (CIVPOL) capability to undertake international peace-keeping activities. In February 2000, the first BiH CIVPOL training contingent, comprised of 16 police officers from both the Federation and RS, representing all three ethnic groups, successfully completed background checks and a two-week training course provided by the IPTF. The groups deployed to the United Nations Transitional Administration in East Timor (UNTAET) peace-keeping operation in April 2000.[36] Subsequently, a second contingent has deployed to that same mission. Proponents of BiH involvement in peace-keeping operations have argued that the endeavour is more than an empty gesture, as these officers will not only contribute to a peace-keeping mission in a part of the world where their services are needed but they will also gain invaluable international experience which they can bring to their profession upon returning home. This initiative was heralded as an important symbolic contribution to strengthening BiH state identity.[37]

After nearly seven years of mandate implementation, UNMIBH completed its police reform and restructuring programmes on 31 December 2002. UN Security Council resolution 1396 (2002), adopted unanimously, paved the way for transition planning to establish a much smaller follow-on mission under the auspices of the EU. The European Union Police Mission (EUPM) began on 1 January 2003 with some 500 highly skilled police monitors, plus civilian support. The EUPM's objective is to preserve UNMIBH's achievements while continuing to qualitatively raise police standards, motivation and performance, and sustain existing levels of institutional and individual reform and development.[38]

The EUPM has the advantage of retaining the services of the final IPTF Commissioner, Sven Frederiksen, who will serve as the first EUPM Commissioner. The follow-on Mission will also benefit from a recent decision to bring all of the elements of rule of law (police, criminal justice, judiciary, and prisons) together in one task force, the Rule of Law Task Force. As the international community has learned, yet again, the elements of the rule of law are inseparable and can only be achieved through a holistic, synergistic approach.[39]

IV Customs and Border Services: From Old to New

ALTHOUGH Bosnia's constitution (Annex 4 of the DPA) empowers the state to make customs policy, enforcement was, until recently, delegated to the two (or, in practice, three) entities. This arrangement proved highly ineffective, as the entity governments decided on customs issues in accordance with their narrow passing political and economic interests. Effective, nation-wide border control proved impossible. From 1995 onwards, the vacuum in customs administration and border control has encouraged an illegal migration pipeline transiting BiH into Western Europe.

Organised crime elements conducting human trafficking and smuggling have exploited Bosnia's lax visa requirements and border controls to further their trade. For example, the UN reported that of the 1,298 Iranian passport holders entering BiH on one-to-two week visas in June 2000, only 116 "officially departed" the country.[40] The other 1,182 (91 percent) are suspected of having left BiH and entered Western Europe illegally through the porous south eastern European borders. An estimated 50,000 illegal migrants transited BiH territory in 2000, representing 10 percent of the estimated 500,000 that enter the EU every year.[41] International civilian police and aid workers have also reported an alarming number of incidences in illegal trafficking of women in BiH.

To assist the BiH government, the international community made efforts to assist with capacity-building and material support to fortify the country's various border services. Shortly after the signing of the DPA, the United States Agency for International Development (USAID) established a Customs Training Team to teach Federation and RS customs officers standard law enforcement techniques. Teaching took place in the field as well as in the classroom. Recruits learned searching techniques, including how to identify undervalued shipments and weight fluctuations as well as how to uncover contraband. Smuggling of weapons was a recognised concern during the training period. Corruption was similarly a well-known problem, encouraged by irregular pay and monthly salaries of less than US$ 200 a month.[42]

In 2000 the international community established for the first time a single and uniform customs territory in BiH. This had been one of the major goals of the Customs and Fiscal Assistance Office (CAFAO) programme funded by the EU.[43] The CAFAO programme includes assistance from approximately 30 European customs and tax experts, focusing on the development of customs and tax systems in BiH based on modern European standards. Although the EU-sponsored CAFAO has worked with the OHR and other international agencies to assist the entities' tax and customs authorities to combat evasion, progress has been slow. Still, in the period 1996–99 customs revenues for the entities doubled due to the success of the CAFAO programme.

Bosnia now has regulatory legislation covering its customs administration that, on paper, meets European standards. Drafted and implemented with the assistance of CAFAO, some commendable changes have followed. They include numerous training and technical assistance programs, the introduction of enforcement units in 1999 to improve compliance, and the ongoing installation of two modern customs databases to centralise information and improve the slow and inconsistent exchange of customs information between the entities. Yet the implementation of such legislated reforms in the face of political obstruction and rampant corruption is a difficult task. Allan Jansen, Head of the CAFAO Mission in BiH, has stated that "corruption is still present in both Entity customs administrations. The other deficiency is the fact that many decisions are still being made on the principle of ethnic and party preference." As an example, Jensen cited the Federation government's loss of KM 64 million in 2001 through tax evasion on oil and its derivatives.[44] Encouragingly, the establishment of the BiH State Border Service (SBS) is improving Bosnia's customs track record.

Formation of the SBS was agreed to in the New York Declaration of 15 November 1999 by Bosnia's multi-ethnic tripartite presidency. The Declaration sought to combat widespread smuggling across the country's loosely guarded borders and to encourage efficient customs verification and control. It also aimed to suppress the current double financing of institutions which obstructs the development of the Federation and the BiH state. This ambitious project, undertaken by UNMIBH, established the first multi-ethnic state-level law enforcement institution reporting directly to the presidency. The international community sees the development of customs and border control as a decisive step towards combating crime, building state identity, contributing to state revenues and fulfilling its obligations to protect its international borders. European countries nearby have, of course, an especially strong interest in proper border controls in BiH.

The official establishment of the SBS in June 2000 ended a long-standing feud between Bosnia's two entities. Despite facing repeated upsets and problems with funding, logistics and political foot-dragging, the SBS gradually gained more responsibility for international border control.[45] In July 2002, the SBS covered some 94 percent of the BiH border of over 1,660 kilometres and three international airports in Sarajevo, Mostar and Banja Luka, employing some 1,750 officers. By September 2002 it had responsibility for 100 percent of the border and by the end of the year was expected to employ some 2,700 officers.

The SBS has had immediate impact in two core areas of border security. First, combating pervasive illegal migration: in 2001 the SBS achieved a 66 percent reduction in illegal migrants passing through Sarajevo airport alone – from 24,000 in 2000 to 8,000 in 2001. Secondly, by closing illegal smuggling routes and re-directing commercial traffic to recognised border crossings, the SBS is largely attributed with increasing customs revenues in both entities by at least 20 percent.

The SBS is made up of individuals from the RS, the Federation and the Brcko Special District. They are either former police officers or new recruits. Following subsequent vetting and re-training by the IPTF, they are deployed in multi-ethnic Border Service Units. While soldiers are eligible to join the SBS, they must successfully graduate from the SBS Training Centre, which inaugurated its first class of cadets in April 2002.[46]

V Legal, Judicial and Corrections Reform

THOUGH MILITARY, police and border reform has been slow, change in other elements of the security sector has been even slower. Since the reform of the legal/judicial and corrections system in BiH is dealt with elsewhere in this volume,[47] it is treated only briefly here.

At the end of the war, it was recognized that the creation of an effective legal/judicial system was essential not only to uphold human rights and punish violent offenders, but also to permit the fair and impartial settlement of civil and commercial disputes. The war-shattered system included judges who consistently gave rulings that were blatantly partial to ethnicity and who were engaged in corruption. Furthermore, IFOR's 1996 legal evaluation indicated that approximately 50 percent of judges from the RS and Bosnian-Croat courts were not even aware of the European Convention on Human Rights, nor its fundamental freedoms as incorporated into the legal system.[48] Unfortunately, the DPA did not provide any strategy to train, select and appoint new judges and prosecutors, though the IPTF was given a role in monitoring, observing and inspecting judicial bodies associated with law enforcement.

Leadership in legal reform was assumed by the OHR, in an attempt to coordinate the various scattered efforts. Other actors included UNMIBH (through its Judicial System Assessment Programme, JSAP), OSCE, the American Bar Association (through its Central Eastern European Law Initiative, CEELI) and SFOR. These agencies sought to build a new foundation, including legal education, the strengthening of bar associations and the development of law schools. But the ambitious early efforts to reintegrate the legal systems of the Federation and the RS were unsuccessful. Even reciprocity legislation that would enable lawyers from each entity to practice law throughout BiH was not passed.

A new central organisation, the Independent Judicial Commission (IJC), was created in December 2000 to lead the reform process. The body monitors and assesses court cases as they make their way through the system. The High Representative recognised, however, that domestically-led commissions and councils were not moving swiftly enough to remove corrupt judges and prosecutors. On 23 May 2002, he imposed a package of decisions that moved the IJC and the international community more squarely into the structure of recruiting, appointing and disciplining judges and prosecutors. Common ethics codes for members of the judiciary were introduced. He also imposed the creation of Judicial Training Institutes and legislation reforming the Bar, in effect creating a single, unified Bar association for all of BiH.[49] Legislation is now under consideration at the entity level to provide budgetary independence for the courts.

In summary, the process of judicial reform has been exceedingly slow. Only recently (2002) were judges or prosecutors removed on the recommendation of the councils and commissions created to advance impartiality. Now, there is a stronger expression of political will on the part of both the international community and the Bosnian governments to take more assertive action to establish a judicial branch of government that can perform in accordance with European and international standards.

Like the judiciary, the corrections system was plagued with problems at the end of the war, including destroyed prison infrastructure, corrupt and inadequately trained officials, irregular pay, shortages of food, heating, hygiene, health care, prisoners' clothes, equipment for staff, and in general, "insufficient resources even to meet essential requirements."[50] Once again, the DPA provided no guidance. It only endorsed the right of the International Committee of the Red Cross (ICRC) to inspect and report on the state of prisons. While doing so, the ICRC was able to bring in modest amounts of hygienic supplies, food, and clothing.

Other international community initiatives have included education and training, donation of equipment and the promotion of internationally agreed corrections principles. Emphasis was placed on instilling a respect for the personal integrity and dignity of prisoners, who were previously the subject of violent abuse. Inspections were made by UNMIBH to verify compliance. It reported some positive findings with respect to human rights, and provided reliable statistics on prisoners. In January 2002, there were 2,251 persons in BiH prisons: 1,438 in the Federation and 813 in the RS.[51] However, other than infrastructure reconstruction and the provision of new uniforms, correction officers have not received levels of assistance that compare well with their colleagues in other parts of the security sector.

There is a lack of co-operation and sharing of resources between Bosnian-Muslim, Bosnian-Croat, and RS correctional facilities. On a positive note, on 18 July 2001, the Federation Ministry of Justice in coordination with the UNMIBH Human Rights Office unified the Mostar city prison system. Previously, parallel correctional facilities existed to serve Bosnian-Croat and Bosnian-Muslim communities there. UNMIBH also established a Court Police, which now serves 174 courts in the Federation, with a special unit trained for protection of judges and witnesses. In the RS, Court Police were deployed on 1 January 2003 to serve 151 judicial institutions. Another feather in the UNMIBH cap is the successful state-wide implementation of the Arrest and Custody Project, ensuring that proper records are kept in regard to detainees, and that law enforcement officials follow Council of Europe standards for arrests and detentions.

Still, there is still a long way to go to meet the OHR goal "that the prison/corrections systems of each Entity meet international standards."[52] This goal is unlikely to be achieved without the investment of resources and proper training required to make a significant impact on the corrections system.

VI Intelligence Reform:
Too Tough to Tackle?

AFTER THE WAR, it was essential to deal with the competing intelligence services, but this proved to be a daunting and unenviable task for reformers. Because these agencies wielded power clandestinely, based on the information they collected and the covert operations they sponsored, they were the hardest part of the security sector to tackle. No international organisation had or sought the lead on intelligence reform. As the Norwegian Institute of International Affairs (NUPI) has written:

> ... donors have been reluctant to contribute, as the need for transparency that pervades all other efforts in security sector reform is difficult to reconcile with the development of secret services. To counteract the obvious lack of transparency, the intelligence agencies must be subject to some form of civilian control. A complete detachment of such services from a general process of reform may easily undermine constructive development in other areas.[53]

IFOR, however, did take early action when, on 15 February 1996, it raided a secret police/intelligence training camp in Fojnica, near Sarajevo. There the peacekeepers found documents showing "assassination plans against well-known politicians, ways to cause public panic and methods of releasing compromising information about certain officials."[54]

UNMIBH was later able, due to its influence over the police, to remove intelligence services from police facilities in the Federation. In 1996, a Federation level law was passed, labelling all *ad hoc* intelligence services operating on the territory of BiH as illegal. But this was on paper only. A committee to discuss intelligence reform and restructuring was also called for but was never established.

Details are scant on the activities of the intelligence services. Several are believed to be under the control of various political parties. In addition to the intelligence services of Croatia (SIS) and Serbia that, no doubt, operate in Bosnia, Bosnia's own services include the RS intelligence service, the Bosnian-Muslim Agency for Investigation and Documentation (AID), and the Bosnian-Croat National Security Service (SNS). It is estimated that each of these services has up to 700 operatives.

NATO revealed in December 1999 that these intelligence services were engaged in targeting the international community, in conducting wire-tapping and surveillance of senior international officials.[55] There is media speculation that AID was responsible for murders of Bosnian-Croat returnees, bomb blasts at Catholic sites and politically-motivated assassinations. There are even allegations that agency officials were behind the attempted assassination of Pope John Paul II, which was foiled on 23 April 1997 when 23 anti-tank mines were discovered and defused under a bridge the Pope was expected to travel over. The Federation's public prosecutor has filed charges with the Supreme Court against AID's first director and former interior minister, Bakir Alispahic, and several of his lieutenants for numerous crimes that have rocked the country over the past decade.[56] The trial was expected to begin in the summer of 2002. This is welcome evidence of growing courage to control formerly powerful intelligence officials and agencies.

In March 2002, the Federation parliament passed the Law on Intelligence Service. It establish a Federation Intelligence and Security Service to replace the current ones. It is expected that a Permanent Working Group, to be established by the president and vice-president of the Federation, will coordinate the new service. The service will include the following other bodies: an Inter-Resource Group, also to be established by the Federation Government, and a Working Group for Monitoring and Controlling the work of the service, to be established by the Federation Parliament. In addition to the service director and deputy, the Federation Government will also appoint an executive director (operator of services) and a chief inspector. The service is to operate until the eventual establishment of a state intelligence service. The Federation service will then be obliged to hand over all documentation, materials and equipment to the new state service. As for the current intelligence services – AID and SNS/SIS – they were expected to stop their operations by the end of 2002. Employees of the two agencies will not automatically become members of the new service, but will have to apply to the new vacancies. This is a positive development, but if the process of military integration is an indication, a long protracted process of political obfuscation is likely to follow.

The area of intelligence reform and restructuring clearly requires increased attention, both from the analysts studying the problem and the practitioners working to find solutions. Only through detailed consideration of the challenge can the appropriate balance between the classification of information (secrecy) and its free dissemination (openness) in matters of internal and external affairs be found. In any case, to achieve democratic oversight of the intelligence sector, a select number of government leaders must be allowed a complete overview of the activities of intelligence agencies to ensure accountability. There are now hopeful signs of a move in this direction. Furthermore, with the creation of a new State Information and Protection Agency (SIPA), tasked with coordinating national law enforcement efforts, liaising with the Interpol National Coordination Bureau (established by UNMIBH in 2001), and providing protection to state institutions and VIPs, BiH has all of the requisites for becoming fully integrated into the international police network and facilitating national, regional and international police cooperation. The 400 members of SIPA may also provide the basis for a state-level intelligence service.

VII Civilian Oversight of the Security Sector

A central principle of good governance, applicable to the entire security sector (not just intelligence), is that of democratic oversight and control. Herbert Wulf provided a valuable list of the ingredients for such a capability:

> Civil control and oversight of security sector actors is pre-requisite to those actors playing a constructive role geared to the goals of sustainable development. The basic pre-conditions for democratic control include procurement authorities independent of the armed forces and the police, budgetary control by parliament and thus the creation of transparency, accountability of the top ranks of the armed forces vis-à-vis a democratically elected civilian government, an independent judiciary, etc.[57]

Good governance is proving hard to achieve in the fledging BiH and must be considered as a long-term goal. The DPA brought into being a complicated state structure. The high level of autonomy endowed to the two divided and to some extent competing entities creates inefficient government institutions at the level of the state. The result has been a complex web of administrative structures, lack of experienced civil servants, inappropriately managed public and private resources, high levels of corruption and little attention to the socio-economic needs of BiH citizens.[58]

Since 1996, a number of programmes and projects have been launched to assist or create accountable, efficient and transparent processes and mechanisms in the legal and defence sectors. The establishment of oversight mechanisms is a broad area covering elements of defence, civil society, economic reform and so on. The primary actors engaged in governance projects have been the OHR and the OSCE.

To tackle the widely-recognised problem of government corruption, the Anti-Fraud Unit of the OHR assists local authorities in identifying and prosecuting illegal activities, monitors court cases through all phases of the judicial process, and engages in reform of the legal and judicial systems. Its current priorities are the drafting and enactment of anti-corruption legislation that meets international standards, increases transparency in government procedures, and promotes a far-reaching public awareness campaign.[59] OSCE governance efforts have focused on the transparency, accountability and anti-corruption training of police, judicial personnel and civil society in support of the OHR's economic reform policies.[60]

Similarly private security agencies have been subjected to regulatory legislation following increasing concerns about criminal involvement, ethnically motivated violence and recruitment of disaffected demobilized soldiers and decertified police officers. In October 2002, the Federation passed a Law on Private Security Agencies to regulate the services of an estimated 80 to 100 firms working in Federation territory. Drafted in consultation with the international community, the legislation is intended to address structures, organization, recruitment, weapons and coordination with law enforcement agencies in accordance with European regulations and standards. The Law was put into full effect on 15 January 2003, in conjunction with a new law on weapons and ammunition. While it is unclear at this stage whether the RS will adopt mirroring legislation, it is likely to do so.

VIII Disarmament: Making Bosnia Safe for Itself

DISARMAMENT after a conflict is a reform measure of great importance. Weapons held by former warring parties and the citizenry create a volatile security situation, with the possibility of rapid flare-ups. Many people and groups are easily able to commit revenge killings, crimes at gunpoint and, even worse, large-scale atrocities. But despite the "disarmament impera-tive" shown by academic and policy research[61] and demonstrated in earlier UN missions in the 1990s, the DPA did not incorporate a disar-mament strategy with which to guide the national and international actors. The DPA's *Agreement on Sub-Regional Arms Control* con-cerned only heavy weapons: it placed restrictions on weapon calibres greater than 75mm. It had minimal impact on small arms and light weapons. As one critic observed, policy-makers failed to take advan-tage of the "unique opportunity to institute a comprehensive disar-mament regime" (especially for small arms and light weapons) in the region.[62] The result was a slow *ad hoc* process of disarmament and uncoordinated project delivery over the next half decade. The mix-ture of weapons proliferation, mandatory conscription, high unem-ployment and mistrust between the ethnic communities remains combustible and a serious threat to the peace, countered only by the strong presence of the peacekeepers and the general fear of a return to open warfare.

Small arms were a big problem and remain so. Their predominance in the recent Yugoslav wars and the current abundance can be traced to Tito's total defence policy. Tito's Territorial Defence Forces were trained in guerrilla warfare and armed accordingly with abundant light infantry weapons, land mines and rocket launchers. Weapon saturation coupled with acute levels of unemployment and inefficient state control are a deadly mix. The impact has been significant in many areas in BiH:

- *Humanitarian impact*: Light weapons continue to thwart the return of refugees and internally displaced persons to the homes from which they were "cleansed." Armed attacks on returnees and minorities have been all too frequent in BiH.

- *Socio-economic impact*: Inappropriate planning for the demobili-sation of armed forces, together with unemployment and the easy availability of weapons is likely to increase the incidence of violent crime, including armed robbery, domestic violence and terrorism. The absence of comprehensive small arms control policies along with lax controls of collected surplus weapons has resulted in inevitable black market trading from conflict to con-flict in the Balkan region and abroad.

- *International force protection:* Peace-keeping casualties as a result of attacks with light weapons occurred throughout the UN peace-keeping operations in Croatia and Bosnia-Herzegovina and have continued to be a security concern for SFOR troops in the Balkans.

- *Lack of transparency:* The lack of transparency in light weapons holdings prevents the establishment of a balance of power at the lowest and safest possible level in the region, a conflict prevention measure sought by international security regimes. Any renewed conflict, as witnessed in Kosovo, will be a conventional one that relies on substantial holdings of light weapons.

Feeling a direct threat, NATO peacekeepers conducted light weapons confiscation from the civilian population on an *ad hoc* basis from 1996 to 1998. NATO employed coercive cordon and search techniques that often resulted in increased tension with community members. With these experiences in mind and all too aware of dangers posed by the many remaining small arms, a joint national authority/international community weapons amnesty was established in March 1998, appropriately named "Operation Harvest." The amnesty was accompanied by a campaign to inform communities how they could hand in weaponry without fear of consequences at both mobile and fixed sites staffed by local police forces whose work was supervised by NATO.[63]

This approach proved much more fruitful. During Operation Harvest a large number of weapons were collected despite the absence of monetary or material incentive. In the first month (March/April 1998), over 1,700 small arms, 26,000 hand grenades, and 2,200 antipersonnel mines were collected.[64] Encouraged by these results, NATO troops, UN police monitors, local police and local military units operated amnesties over the next three years. As of July 2002, the Operation had yielded 23,400 small arms and light weapons, 7.5 million rounds of ammunition, almost 100,000 hand grenades, 26,000 mines, 22,100 kg of explosives and 90,931 assorted mortars, rifle grenades and hand-made ordnance.[65] Operation Harvest has continued, albeit on an *ad hoc* basis largely under the discretion of the SFOR Multi-national Divisions in the country. Ironically though, as the disarmament efforts were afoot, an armaments programme was underway, having some of the same sponsors.

IX Armaments Programmes: Going In The Wrong Direction

THE US GOVERNMENT sponsored large programmes to re-arm the Federation Army, giving rise to the danger of arms spill-over to the citizenry and the possible hostile use of the more deadly armaments in future conflicts in BiH and abroad. In particular, MPRI has undertaken, under US sponsorship, a massive military re-armament programme. Under the Military Stabilisation Programme, MPRI provided the Federation army in September 1996 with 46,000 M-16 rifles and over a thousand machine guns.[66] While it may be reasonable in some cases to re-arm professionalized elements of the state security apparatus, the lack of transparency in the re-armament process remains a concern. In 1996, the International Institute for Strategic Studies concluded that the decision "to re-arm warring parties in order to establish a local balance of power ... carries serious risks of destabilisation unless it is clearly understood and accepted as a necessary requirement for overall political and military stability."[67]

Additional controversy has arisen as BiH has begun to sell some of its surplus weaponry abroad. Some weapons have gone to Africa (e.g., Cameroon) via Israel. While such sales are not necessarily illegal, they highlight the important unresolved issues of arms sales and profit-making in BiH where new arms are being imported and where effective oversight mechanisms are lacking. There is the danger of fostering threats to the peace not only internally but also in other parts of the world. In addition, there is confusion within the international community as to how and by whom arms transfers should be approved. SFOR has called for an arms sale policy and noted that arms sales could be an important source of revenue for BiH. Recognising that arms sales are an important political/foreign policy issue, the OSCE has offered to provide guidance on this matter, including texts of relevant laws adopted in other states. A number of conventions and European standards on arms transfers are applicable, as are some existing (UN) arms embargoes. There is agreement on the need for state-level legislation on commercial exports, though some policymakers wonder whether BiH should be in the business of selling arms at all.[68]

Less controversial was the re-armament of the police officers of the Federation, who were equipped with Austrian Glock side arms. The

RS police, in contrast, continue to use their old Yugoslav model (Cervena Zastava CZ99). The Federation programme has been justified on the basis that Federation police officers possessed a "mix of weapons" including the Hungarian Marakov, and various other Eastern European varieties, requiring a range of expensive ammunition.[69] In addition, there were safety issues associated with the often-decrepit police firearms: some had improper magazines that did not fit their weapon, and others were dangerously modified.

Perhaps there is a lesson to be learned from an earlier US military initiative in the region. American military aid to Tito in the 1950s helped funnel an enormous amount of light weaponry into the country, fuelling future civil wars. For example, thousands of the US-supplied Thompson M1A1 submachine guns were used in the war in Croatia.[70] Some of the weapons remain in BiH and threaten not only US and SFOR peacekeepers, but also the process of reform.

Encouragingly, after nearly seven years of peace implementation in the Balkans, small arms and light weapons proliferation appears to have gained the spotlight in the regional and the international arena. On 8 May 2002, the South Eastern European Clearinghouse for the Control of Small Arms and Light Weapons (SEESAC), was established in Belgrade. Supported by UNDP and the EU's Stability Pact for Southeast Europe, it works with governments and regional and international institutions to formulate and develop projects which will tackle the Balkans' small arms problem. Region-wide weapons-reduction projects are being heralded as one of the West's priorities for the Balkans' shift from peace-keeping to nation-building and the control of organised crime.

In the larger region around Bosnia, national and local authorities, working with various international actors such as UNDP, NATO and aid organisations, have implemented some impressive small arms collection programmes. In Albania 188,000 weapons have been collected; Croatia has yielded 40,000; and in 2001 in the Federal Republic of Yugoslavia, 50,000 small arms were destroyed.[71] It is important to note, however, that these figures are merely the tip of the iceberg in many respects. In Albania, for instance, approximately 600,000 small arms were looted in the chaotic spring of 1997 and only a third are now accounted for. In Kosovo in 1999 and more recently Macedonia, instability meant that huge numbers of arms were trafficked into the area. Clearly then, as the example of US re-armament in Yugoslavia in the 1950s points out, successful disarmament will not be measured in months or years but rather in generations.

X Conclusion: A Sympathetic Critique and a Call for a Comprehensive Approach

COMPLAINTS are frequently made that international programmes in BiH are poorly coordinated and working at cross-purposes with each other. The disarmament/armament programmes described above are examples. An even greater problem is the lack of cooperation between the entities. With the exception of the police, which have introduced some effective inter-entity procedures, and the new State Border Service, the failure to establish common security institutions has resulted in competing agencies, often working against each other. These parallel agencies and structures are a waste of financial resources and can give rise to impotence in the face of domestic and international security challenges. Despite many years of international coaxing, the two entities remain two solitudes. The overall difficulties of coordination between entities and within the international community are succinctly summarised by the UN SRSG, Jacques Paul Klein:[72]

> In Bosnia and Herzegovina, despite the best efforts of committed personnel, we have not achieved the same sense of purpose, efficiency and utilisation of resources. Bosnia is the only state in the world where there is one country, two entities, three constituent peoples, four religions, and five international organisations running it.

The multiplicity of international actors with similar mandates and projects operating in the same areas has created recurring problems through the years. Ambassador Robert Barry, former head of the OSCE mission in BiH, recognises what he calls "turf wars" between the major organisations that have periodically strained relations among actors in the field offices. Ambassador Klein agrees: "on the ground, there are often five sets of field officers, all with an identifiable niche, but rarely with a combined strategic vision, and all of them seeking to meet with the same local officials. The result is a bonanza for manipulation by hard-line nationalists and obstructionists." This duplication and parallel chains of command has had a noticeable toll on the efficiency and effectiveness of the international efforts at a time of diminishing resources. International leaders have to constantly reinforce coordination in the field and, beyond that, a unity of purpose and vision. A grand vision for nation-building has to complement the coordination of scattered projects at the operational level.

Peace-building in the security sector, it is gradually being realised, must be a holistic undertaking, covering the entire array of security actors. The present survey of international activities shows that, while the initiatives cover many components of the security sector, support for reform across the security sector is far from uniform. Indeed, several components have been neglected, leaving a vacuum in the security infrastructure and the potential for overall failure at robust nation-building. For example, the police capacity-building efforts have far outstripped the pace of judicial reform, leaving holes in the law enforcement system. Without a comprehensive approach to SSR, the practices of these neglected agencies may slow down the entire process of reform and render other efforts completely ineffective.

In BiH, the primary focus of international efforts was on military and police forces, while largely neglecting other security institutions, especially intelligence agencies. This was in part due to the fact that training and deploying police officers is easier and quicker than training judges or prosecutors, who require longer and more extensive education before starting work. The training of intelligence officers is an even more difficult and sensitive task. Hence, the reform of the intelligence agencies was until 2002 utterly neglected, leaving a large lacuna in the SSR process and threatening reforms in other areas.

Not only must international SSR efforts encompass the entire range of government security agencies, they must also work to support the range of national actors, especially civil society. NGOs, think tanks and universities play an important role in monitoring security agencies and in developing security policy. Democracy, in the final analysis, is only as strong as the citizenry is knowledgeable and participating through civil society. As the prominent jurist Robert H Jackson once declared, "[i]t is not the function of our government to keep the citizens from falling into error; it is the function of the citizen to keep the government from falling into error."[73] Only by strengthening the involvement of civil organisations in the SSR process can the international community hope to make it sustainable over the long term. The foundation for permanent change must be a society of committed individuals who demand the highest standards of professional competence and behaviour.

Thus, again, a comprehensive vision and approach to SSR is vital. In retrospect, the Dayton agreement was not as comprehensive as was first thought. While it provided a basis for some programmes and innovations, the need for strategic planning remained great. In the negotiations at Dayton the focus was on the traditional agencies (military and police) rather than the broader spectrum. Over time, however, a wider scope of reform has been sought. The SSR concept, now gaining popularity, is a useful tool to move this great experiment forward.

To the credit of the international community, the unfolding SSR programme in BiH was more ambitious than any that had been undertaken up to that time. There have been lessons learned, including the need for comprehensiveness. With this Bosnia experiment in mind, in 1999 the UN decided to accept even more wide-ranging responsibilities in Kosovo and East Timor. In these two locations, one close by and the other on the other side of the world, the UN actually took on the mantle of government. The transitional administrations established in these locations have exercised both legislative and executive authority. UN responsibilities included overseeing health and education, banking and finance, post and telecommunications, and law and order. In both UN missions, early attention was paid at the strategic planning level to develop the legal/judicial infrastructure. The missions also paid careful attention to the effects of elections on the process of government, again learning from the Bosnian process, where many thought elections were held too soon (thus legitimizing extreme nationalists). In all these cases, the goal is to create a smooth transition to self-government, creating capacity not dependency and preparing the ground for a sustainable peace.

BiH has been relatively peaceful since the signing of the Dayton agreement, despite several shocks (such as the war in Kosovo) that might easily have unleashed widespread violence had the international community not been so intimately involved in SSR. The relative peace in BiH demonstrates that the peace-building efforts in the volatile and emotionally-charged security sector have gone a long way to establishing a foundation for stability. The structures of the state and society are being developed to such an extent, and generally seem to carry the support of enough citizens, that despite ongoing hatreds and inequalities, peace is expected to hold. The investment in peace, both locally and internationally, is now deemed too great to permit an easy relapse into war. With experience being gained each year and the hope for an ever expanding and deepening reform agenda, there are indications that this great experiment in nation-building might very well succeed.

Notes

1 A longer version of this paper is being co-published by Saferworld (UK) and the Bonn International Center for Conversion (Germany) as a report in the Small Arms and Security in South Eastern Europe series. It will be available online from BICC at <www.bicc.de/info/public.html>. The authors would like to thank Major David Last for suggestions that helped improve the quality of this paper. Dr Dorn would also like to thank the Department of Foreign Affairs and International Trade Canada for a Human Security Fellowship in 2001/02 that made possible the research for this paper.

2 Canada, Department of Foreign Affairs and International Trade, *Practical Disarmament, Demobilisation and Reintegration Measures for Peace-building*, (Ottawa: April 1997). Also Edward J. Laurance and Sarah Meek, *The New Field of Micro-Disarmament: Addressing the Proliferation and Buildup of Small Arms and Light Weapons, Brief 7* (Bonn International Center for Conversion, September 1996).

3 NATO, *NATO's Role in Bringing Peace to the Former Yugoslavia*, NATO Basic Fact Sheet, No. 4, March 1997.

4 NATO, *Press Briefing*, Transcript, COMARRC, Lt Gen Sir Michael Walker, Sarajevo, BiH, 20 April 1996.

5 "Two Bosniak Volunteers Die In Chechnya," *Oslobodjenje*, Issue 2.74 (24 April 2000), obtained from balkans-news@networkbosnia.org

6 *Jutarnji List*, 21 April 1999, http://www.monitor.hr/jutarnji/1999/04/21/index.html, accessed 14 May 2002.

7 "Volunteers Go With RS Mercenaries," *Dnevni Avaz*, 10 March 1998, translated by Tuzla Night Owl, http://teletubbie.het.net.je/~sjaak/domovina/domovina/tno/9803/11/i.html, accessed 9 September 2002.

8 Jon Swaine, "War Hungry Serbs Join Mobutu's Army," *The Sunday Times*, 9 March 1996, p. 12.

9 Jeremy King, *Building Peace in Bosnia: Lessons Learned in Disarmament, Demobilisation, Reintegration & Civilian Police Capacity-building*, Department of Foreign Affairs and International Trade, Canada, April 2000, http://www.dfait-maeci.gc.ca/arms/Building_Peacelong.pdf, accessed 13 May 2002.

10 International Development Association, http://www.worldbank.org/ida/idao.html, accessed 13 May 2002.

11 World Bank, *World Bank Helps Reintegrate Ex-Soldiers in Bosnia and Herzegovina*, Press release, http://www.worldbank.org.ba/news/2000/pr-jun00-03.htm.

12 Mijo Anic (Federation Defence Minister), quoted in "Criteria for Discharging FBIH Army Members," *Oslobodjenje*, 19 February 2002.

13 "SRSG Klein Calls for Reduced Military Expenditures in BiH," UNMIBH Official Web-site, 28 January 2002, www.unmibh.org/stories/.

14 "NATO SG Robertson Requests Reduction of Military Expenses," *Oslobodjenje* 2002.

15 Jacques Paul Klein, *Talking Points*, prepared by UNMIBH Civil Affairs Policy and Planning Unit, February 2002.

16 David Lightburn, "Armed Forces in Bosnia-Herzegovina," *NATO Review*, December 2000.

17 Ibid.

18 Military Professional Resources Incorporated, Homepage, http://www.mpri.com/channels/int_overview.html, accessed 13 May 2002.

19 NATO nations contributing to SFOR: Belgium, Canada, Czech Republic, Denmark, France, Germany, Greece, Hungary, Italy, Netherlands, Norway, Poland, Spain, Turkey, United Kingdom, United States. Non-NATO nations contributing to SFOR:

Albania, Argentina, Austria Bulgaria, Estonia, Ireland, Finland, Latvia, Lithuania, Slovakia, Morocco, Romania, Russia, Slovenia, Sweden. Nations contributing individuals by special arrangement with the United Kingdom: Australia, New Zealand. For a summation of SFOR organisation see http://www.nato.int/sfor/organisation/sfororg.htm.

20 Lightburn, op. cit.

21 ONASA News Service, *NATO Secretary General Calls on Integration of BiH Armed Forces*, ONASA News Service, 13 July 2001.

22 *Oslobodjenje*, issue of 17 April 2002.

23 Organisation for Security and Co-operation in Europe, *OSCE Regional Stabilisation Briefing Presentation*, presented in Sarajevo, August 2000.

24 Office of the High Representative, *Brief on the OHR Military Cell*, http://www.ohr.int/ohr-dept/mltry-cell/, accessed 13 May 2002.

25 Central Europe Online, "Bosnia Inaugurates First Military Contingent to Serve With UN," *Bosnia Today*, Central Europe Online, http://www.centraleurope.com/bosniatoday/, accessed 13 May 2002.

26 General Hilliard, Multi-national Division South-West Head Quarters, Banja Luka, briefing, November 2000.

27 Jaque Grinberg (Head of Civil Affairs, UNMIBH), "The Future Mission of SFOR," paper delivered to the NATO Policy Coordination Group, Brussels, 27 July 2001.

28 Jacques Paul Klein, "SRSG Klein Calls for Reduced Military Expenditures in BiH," 28 January 2002, found at www.unmibh.org/stories.

29 Brig Gen Carsten Svensson (Senior Military Advisor to the Special Representative to the Secretary-General, UNMIBH), interview, September 2001.

30 Ibid.

31 Laina Reynolds, "Public Security and Post-Settlement Peace-building," *UN & Conflict Monitor*, Issue 3, Centre for Conflict Resolution, Bradford University, Spring 1999. http://www.brad.ac.uk/acad/confres/monitor/mntr3_comment.html, accessed 13 May 2002.

32 International Crisis Group, *Is Dayton Failing?: Bosnia Four Years After The Peace Agreement*, ICG Balkans Report No. 80, Sarajevo, 28 October 1999, p. 44.

33 Michael Dziedzic and Andrew Bair, "Bosnia and the International Police Task Force," in *Policing the New World Disorder: Peace Operations and Public Security*, eds. Robert B. Oakley, Michael J. Dziedzic and Eliot M. Goldburg (Washington: Institute for National Strategic Studies, National Defence University, 1998), pp. 285 and 290–291.

34 Charles T. Call, "Institutional Learning Within the U.S. International Criminal Training Assistance Programme (ICITAP)," in Oakley, Dziedzic and Eliot, 1998, p. 315.

35 Dziedzic and Bair, op. cit.

36 Associated Press Newswires, "Bosnian Police Head Off for First Mission Abroad," Dow-Jones Interactive Database, 4 April 2000.

37 United Nations, *Report of the Secretary-General, on the United Nations Mission in Bosnia-Herzegovina*, UN Doc. S/1999/1260 of 17 December 1999, para. 11.

38 Jeremy King, UNMIBH Mission Brief, prepared by Jeremy King, Office of the SRSG, April 2002.

39 Ibid.

40 United Nations Mission in Bosnia and Herzegovina, *An UNMIBH Bulletin on the State Border Service Activities*, Borderline, UNMIBH Public Affairs, 1/1 (June 2000).

41 United Kingdom and Northern Ireland, Embassy Press Release, Sarajevo, September 2001.

42 Rade Duric (Business Manager, USAID Customs Training Team), interview, Sarajevo, July 1998.

43 European Union, "Bosnia and Herzegovina, the EU Contribution: Milestones in the Relations between the EU and Bosnia and Herzegovina," http://europa.eu.int/comm/external_relations/see/bosnie_herze/index.htm, accessed 13 May 2002.

44 United Nations Mission in Bosnia and Herzegovina, *Human Rights Office Monthly Report*, January 2002, UNMIBH, Sarajevo. Also, United Nations Mission in Bosnia and Herzegovina, "Interview with Head of CAFAO Mission in BiH," *UNMIBH News Summary*, 10 April 2002.

45 Howard Stallcup (IPTF State Border Service Team Manager), interview at UNMIBH Headquarters, Sarajevo, August 2000.

46 SBS Training Centre, Suhodol, BiH, http://www.unmibh.org/, accessed 13 May 2002.

47 See particularly the paper in this volume by Tufik Burnazovic, "Post-Dayton Bosnia: Achievements and Failures, 1996–2002."

48 Dziedzic and Bair, op. cit.

49 Office of the High Representative, "High Representative Issues Decisions Strengthening Judicial Reform Across BiH," *Press Release*, 24 May 2002.

50 Council of Europe, *Themis Plan, Project 4 (Prisons) Bosnia and Herzegovina, Report of a Council of Europe Co-operation Visit to Prisons and Other Institutions in Republika Srpska*, Council of Europe, 1998.

51 UNMIBH, *Human Rights Office Monthly Report*, January 2002, UNMIBH, Sarajevo.

52 Office of the High Representative, *Judicial Reform Programme*, OHR Website, http://www.ohr.int/ohr-dept/hr-rol/thedept/jud-reform/default.asp?content_id=5227, accessed 12 September 2002.

53 Norwegian Institute of International Affairs, *Security Sector Reform as a Development Issue*, submitted by Norway and produced by NUPI Working Group on Security Sector Reform, OECD Development Assistance Committee Task Force on Conflict, Peace and Development Co-operation, Paris, 2–3 June 1999, p. 15. The NUPI Homepage is http://www.nupi.no/.

54 Ena Latin, "Sarajevo Trial May Lift Lid on Assassinations," Institute for War and Peace Reporting (IWPR) *Balkan Crisis Report*, No. 338 (25 May 2002).

55 Alexandar S. Dragicevic, "Bosnian Croat intelligence officers targeted international officials, NATO says," *Associated Press Newswires*, Dow Jones Interactive Publications Library, 17 December 1999.

56 Latin, op. cit.

57 Herbert Wulf, *Security-Sector Reform in Developing Countries: An Analysis of the International Debate and Potentials for Implementing Reforms with Recommendations for Technical Co-operation*, Deutsche Gesellschaft für Technische Zusammenarbeit (GTZ) GmbH, October 2000, http://www.bicc.de/general/gtz_studien/securitysector.html, accessed 27 May 2002.

58 International Crisis Group, "Courting Disaster: The Misrule of Law in Bosnia & Herzegovina," *Balkans Report*, No. 127, Sarajevo, 25 March 2002, http://www.intl-crisis-group.org/projects/showreport.cfm?reportid=592, accessed 24 July 2002.

59 Office of the High Representative, 1999. OHR Website, http://www.ohr.int/.

60 Organisation for Security and Co-operation in Europe, Democratisation Office, *Concept for 1999*, http://oscebih.org/democratisation/homedem.asp, accessed 13 May 2002.

61 Noteworthy studies include those by Laurance and Meek (op. cit.) and by Walter Dorn, "Small Arms, Human Security and Development," *Development Express*, No. 5 (1999–2000), Canadian International Development Agency (CIDA), Ottawa, 2000, http://www.rmc.ca/academic/gradrech/dorn7_e.html, accessed 13 May 2002.

62 Jane Sharp, "Update on the Dayton Arms Control Arrangements," *Bulletin of Arms Control*, No. 25 (London: Centre for Defence Studies, March 1997), 8.

63 ONASA News Service, "Amnesty for Illegal weapons takes effect: SFOR," *Onasa*, 3 March 1998.

64 Captain Douglas A. Harding (Liaison Officer, MND-North), from the SFOR Coalition Press Information Center, Tito Barracks, Sarajevo, 22 April 1998.

65 Unclassified data received from SFOR HQ; ref. "Harvest total results 1998–2002," 2 July 2002. During the 1999 Harvest, the following were turned in: 7,500 weapons, over two million rounds of ammunition, 25,000 hand grenades, 8,000 mines, 3,000 kg of explosives and 22,500 other items (mortar rounds, light anti-tank ammunition and rifle grenades). During the first five months of 2000, the amnesty amassed 3,075 firearms, 713,932 cartridges, 5,579 hand grenades, 1,254 mines, 3,947 kg of explosives and 8,627 pieces of other ammunition. De-mining efforts have also made sizeable gains since 1995. The 40–50 injuries a month in 1995 were reduced to 2–5 injuries a month in 2000. See "Bosnia: NATO-led force sees success in Bosnia arms removal," *Reuters English News Service*, 18 January 2000. Also "Czech Battalion Collects Arms, Ammunition In Bosnia," *BBC News Wire Service*, 8 June 2000.

66 Military Professional Resources Incorporated, *Military Stabilisation Programme I, Draft Manifest*, obtained from AES Cargo, Sarajevo, BiH, July 1997.

67 Mats Berdal, "Disarmament and Demobilisation after Civil Wars," *Adelphi Paper*, 303 (Oxford: University Press, 1996), p. 30.

68 United Nations Mission in Bosnia and Herzegovina, Civil Affairs Policy and Planning Unit, Internal Note to File, 23 May 2002.

69 Terry Smith, ICITAP Police Trainer, Sarajevo, BiH, electronic correspondence, 12 April 2000.

70 Milso Vasic, "The Yugoslav Army and the Post-Yugoslav Armies," in *Yugoslavia and After: A Study in Fragmentation, Despair and Rebirth*, eds. D.A. Dyker and I. Vejvoda (London: Addison Wesley Longman Limited, 1996), p. 120.

71 Gordana Kukic, "Centre to Curb Balkan Small Arms Opens in Belgrade," *Associated Press Wire Service*, 8 May 2002.

72 Jacques Paul Klein, "Sharing Political Space in Peacemaking: The Case of Bosnia-Herzegovina," International Peace Academy Seminar, Vienna, 7 July 2000, http://www.unmibh.org/news/srsgspe/2000/07jul00.asp, accessed 13 May 2002.

73 *The Columbia World of Quotations*, 1996, http://www.bartleby.com/66/74/30374.html, accessed 9 September 2002.

TUFIK BURNAZOVIĆ

Legal Reform in Post-Dayton Bosnia: Achievements and Failures, 1996–2002

Introduction

THE DISINTEGRATION of Yugoslavia at the end of 1991[1] led to tragic, political, economic and social developments that altered almost all aspects of life in Bosnia and Herzegovina. These events can be described in three stages.

The first stage began with the outbreak of war in April 1992 and ended with the Washington Agreement[2] in March 1994 marking the cessation of hostilities between Croat armed forces and Bosniacs, the formation of the Bosniac-Croat Federation, and the consolidation of the Serb Republic.

The next stage included the period up to the conclusion of the Dayton General Framework for Peace in Bosnia and Herzegovina initialed in Dayton on November 21, 1995 and signed in Paris on December 14, 1995 – hereafter referred to as the Dayton Accords.

The third stage covers the period from the signing of the Dayton Accords onwards. The Dayton Accords establish a framework for rebuilding a multicultural, multiethnic, pluralistic society in Bosnia and Herzegovina, in its political, economic, social, legal, cultural and environmental aspects.

After a full decade of mounting internal tensions that started just after Tito's death in 1980, the disintegration of the Socialist Federal

DR TUFIK BURNAZOVIĆ is Director of the Centre for International Relations and Strategic Studies. Faculty of Political Science of Sarajevo University. Permanent Visiting Professor of Maryland University, European Program.

Republic of Yugoslavia accelerated with the determination of Slovenia and Croatia[3] to seek independence. Both republics declared independence in 1991 and were subsequently recognized by the international community. Discussions on the sovereignty of Bosnia and Herzegovina among its three national groups (Bosniacs, Bosnian Serbs and Bosnian Croats) represented by their national parties - the Party for Democratic Action (SDA), the Serbian Democratic Party (SDS), and the Croat Democratic Community (HDZ) – began immediately after the election in Bosnia and Herzegovina which took place on November 18, 1990. Bosniacs and Bosnian Croats were strongly in favor of independence for the republic; the Bosnian Serbs were opposed.

In a letter dated 20 December 1991 sent to the President of the Council of the European Communities (EC), the Minister of Foreign Affairs of the Socialist Republic of Bosnia and Herzegovina asked the Member States of the EC to recognize the Republic.

The Arbitration Commission (Badinter Commission) proceeded to consider this application in accordance, first, with the Declaration on Yugoslavia and the Guidelines on the Recognition of New States in the Soviet Union adopted by the EC Council on December 16, 1991 and, second, with the rules of procedure adopted by that Commission on 22 December.

The Badinter Commission[4] indicated that the Socialist Republic of Bosnia and Herzegovina satisfied the necessary conditions for being recognized as an independent state by the EC, provided that the desire for independence was confirmed by popular referendum. This referendum took place on February 29 and March 1, 1992. More than 64 percent of the eligible population voted; of these almost all (99.7 percent) voted for independence. The other third of the eligible voters, largely comprised of Bosnian Serbs, decided to boycott the referendum as a protest against independence.

Bosnia and Herzegovina was recognized as an independent state by the EC member-states on April 6, 1992, and by the United States on April 7, and became a United Nations member by Security Council Resolution 755 on May 22, 1992. The new state and its territorial integrity were immediately challenged by the Yugoslav Peoples' Army (Jugoslovenska Narodna Armija-JNA) and local Serb rebels and militias. By the end of 1992 almost two-thirds of Bosnia and Herzegovina's territory was occupied by those forces. In the spring of 1993 conflict broke out between the Bosnian Croats and Bosniacs. Almost a year later a partial political settlement was established between these two parties. A ceasefire reached at the end of February was followed by the US-brokered Washington Agreement of March 1994[5] which established a Federation between the Bosniacs and the Bosnian Croats.

The next stage of the war was concerned with the regaining by the Federation forces of the occupied territory of Bosnia and Herzegovina, and with continuous negotiations under international community sponsorship between the three parties in Bosnia and neighbouring countries. This phase lasted until the summer of 1995 when the Bosnian Army together with Croatian Army begun to recapture territory around Banja Luka, while negotiations under the Contact Group (consisting of the US, Russia, UK, Germany, France and Italy) proceeded in Geneva. In early September 1995 the parties accepted the principle that the Republika Srpska[6] would control 49 percent of Bosnia's territory, while the Federation would control 51 percent.

The last step was the negotiations in Dayton, lasting from November 1 to November 21, 1995 when the Dayton General Framework was initialed. The Accords were signed in Paris on December 14,1995. With that act, an uneasy peace was concluded in Bosnia and Herzegovina.

Bosnia and Herzegovina
Six Years after Dayton

Since Dayton, Bosnia and Herzegovina has experienced recovery and reform in many fields: military, political, economic and social. The military aims of the Dayton Accords have been achieved in the sense, first, that the armed forces of the parties to the conflict have been separated and there has been some progress in arms control. Second, these forces have been provided with the numbers and types of weapons agreed to in the Dayton Accords and other documents relevant to regional stabilization through the OSCE. The forces are in the process of being transformed and reduced to an eventual combined level of 15,000 solders by the end of 2002.[7] Success in this task is a pre-condition for applying for membership in NATO's Partnership for Peace. The other pre-condition as stated by NATO Secretary-General Lord Robertson[8] is that those three separated armed forces have to be united under single command. Failing this, it will not be possible to move in the direction of military integration into Europe.

The smooth implementation of the military part of the Dayton Accords owes a lot to the actions of SFOR and the OSCE. The latter organization is also authorized to deal with matters concerning the implementation of Annex 1A (Agreement on the Military Aspects of the Peace Settlement) and Annex 1B (Agreement on Regional Stabilization). Some countries such as Turkey and the US have also provided military training and education for officers of the military forces of the Federation of Bosnia and Herzegovina in their respective military academies.

On the economic side it is fair to say that six years after the war, the international community's financial aid and investment in BiH has done much to enhance the country's internal security and rebuild its infrastructure. Military units of SFOR have made a contribution here as well. For example, Turkish units have helped the local authorities in Zenica region where they are located to improve old or war-damaged infrastructure.

In the political sphere, freedom of movement for Bosnia's citizens has become more of a reality, although many problems still exist. Moreover the country has held openly contested state-level, entity-level, cantonal and municipal elections in 1996, 1998, and in April 2000, and combined elections at the cantonal, entity and state levels on November 11, 2000 run by the OSCE. In October 2002 new elections on all levels, including for the presidency of Bosnia and Herzegovina, took place organized by the local authorities.

According to the International Crisis Group (ICG), despite five years and five billion US dollars of international investment in Bosnia, the November 2000 elections demonstrated once again that international engagement has failed to provide a sustainable basis for a functioning state capable of surviving international withdrawal. The election highlighted once again the near complete failure – in the face of determined nationalist extremism – of an international approach that places emphasis on hopes that moderate, co-operative Bosnian partners will come to power through election.[9] One does not have to agree completely with such a bleak evaluation, because those nationalistic parties (particularly the HDZ and the SDS) now are more ready to show some interest in cooperating with the international community. The statements of some politicians from Republika Srpska that they will include in its government representatives of non-Serbs nationalities have some meaning.[10]

An Agreement on Implementation of the June 2000 Resolution of the Constitutional Court of Bosnia and Herzegovina concerning the full constitutional rights of all citizens – Bosniacs, Croats and Serbs – throughout the territory of the state, was adopted in the presence of the High Representative Wolfgang Petritsch, on March 27, 2002, in

Sarajevo. This Agreement is expected by the public to move social and political change in the right direction, especially concerning the return of refugees and displaced people to their homes.[11]

Although the Sarajevo Agreement still falls short of international and local expectations, it includes provisions concerning the formation in both entities of legislative bodies to deal with constitutional disputes in case any of the parties consider that their national interests are not respected. Nobody in the country believes that the High Representative would hesitate to act if any of the relevant entity authorities is not prepared to exercise all its ability and political will to implement the Agreement. This Agreement is in some ways a first real reconstruction of the Dayton Accords, which incorporated a provision to harmonize the entities' constitutions three months after its signing in Paris. As it happens, this will be realized almost six years later, and more than two years after the Constitutional Court's Resolution. (It is expected that the High Representative will use his power to implement it if the locals do not.)

With regard to security, stronger state institutions ensure the safe and free movement of goods, services, people and capital, safe settlement of refugees, and their social well being, including employment, health, and education – as set out in Annex 7 of the Dayton Accords.

In that respect the OHR's decision to create a Central Registry of passports in the Ministry of Civil Affairs and Communications (MCAC) represents the first critical step in establishing a secure regime for the control and issuance of international travel documents. The OHR has been instrumental in assisting MCAC in the design, specification and source selection for the manufacture of a single passport for all citizens of Bosnia and Herzegovina, in accordance with the New York Declaration agreed by the Presidency in September 1999. In addition, a legal working group of representatives from various ministries in BiH, assisted by the OHR, was established in September 2000 to finalize draft laws on identification cards, an individual citizen number, and residency. It has recently its work, and it is expected that the new personal identification for all citizens of the country will be in their possession very soon. This joint MCAC-entity Ministry of Interior working group, again with OHR assistance, is currently drafting state-level laws on data protection and mandatory data exchange as a part of an intensive effort to create appropriate protections for the first post-war citizen register.[12]

Six years after Dayton, has enough been done to implement the Accords? This question occasions much debate.

In general, the international community's efforts in Bosnia have had mixed results.[13] On the one hand, the international military presence has deterred a resumption of ethnic violence. On the other hand, the international civilian presence, led by the OHR, has condemned the nationalist parties for ignoring and obstructing the Dayton Accords: in the last four years the OHR has increased its intervention in the decision-making process at the state, entity, cantonal and municipal levels to remove obstacles the nationalists have put in the way.[14]

Dayton was a territorial and political compromise that ended the war in Bosnia. It did not, however, require the dismantling of the wartime regimes: armies, administrative structures, police and other security services remained in place. Some critics justifiably argue that an agreement of this sort, after almost six years of only modest success in implementation, needs to be replaced entirely.[15] Everyone has to keep in mind that treaties signed in similar circumstances have usually been a compromise. Those who count on a quick end to the international military presence in Bosnia are in fact proposing the partition of the country. But even very nationalist politicians now accept that Bosnia and Herzegovina is a state in real terms (leaving aside their desire for its dissolution and for union with their respective Croat or Serb nations), but a weak state with few institutions.

The Dayton Accords do not constitute a perfect legal document. They have their weaknesses, due to the circumstances in which they were created. But they can be changed. Changes may occur in many ways. The right way would be to let them be fully implemented and then amend them through legislative bodies. But that requires political will on the part of the authorized representatives, which has been until now a very weak point. The Dayton Accords provide the international community as well as Bosnian institutions with considerable authority to interpret their provisions (Art. 3, para 5 of Annex 4 – Constitution of Bosnia and Herzegovina) and move the country in the right direction. Over time strong state institutions may emerge.

In December 1997 at a meeting of the Peace Implementation Council (PIC) held in Bonn, Germany, the powers of the High Representative were greatly increased, including the right to make binding decisions. Recently the OHR has exercised these its prerogatives and has adopted decisions of crucial importance for Bosnia and Herzegovina: the formation of the State Court of Bosnia and Herzegovina, the Law on Creation of State Border Police, the Law on Formation of the Central Bank of Bosnia and Herzegovina, the Decision of the Constitutional Court of Bosnia and Herzegovina referred to above, the Arbitration

Award for Brcko, The Law on Foreign Direct Investments of Bosnia and Herzegovina (both entities have had their own laws on foreign direct investments) and some others. Those laws, regulations and decisions, plus the Dayton Accords and the Constitution of Bosnia and Herzegovina are the foundations of stability and security for the state and its citizens. With them now in place, attention can turn to the problem of refugees and displaced people. Other priorities will be further improvements in state institutions, improving the free market economy and stabilizing the rule of law. [16]

The Legal System:
Its Impact on Transition
in Bosnia and Herzegovina

AS mentioned above, the legal system and the rule of law and order is of substantial importance for any country and its citizens. It is even more important for a small, newly independent poor country in transition, such as Bosnia and Herzegovina. In addition the country went through a war in which about 250,000 citizens were killed, many more wounded, with two million refugees and displaced people and with 90 percent devastation of property. With that in mind, adoption of a new market legal order is the key to fast reconstruction and development. To that end modern economic laws concerning stable currency, attraction of foreign direct investment, modern tax law, customs regulations, and equal rights throughout the territory of the state for all is people, are basic requisites. What follows is an analysis of some of the most relevant laws, regulations, decisions and agreements in this area.

a) The Role of the Constitution of Bosnia
and Herzegovina in the Economy

Bosnia and Herzegovina is a small undeveloped state with a very complex institutional structure. In its present internationally recognized borders, it consists of two entities, the Federation of Bosnia and Herzegovina and Republika Srpska.

According to Art.1, para 3 of the Constitution[17] there shall be freedom of movement throughout Bosnia and Herzegovina. Bosnia and Herzegovina and the entities shall not impede full freedom of movement of persons, goods, services, and capital throughout Bosnia and Herzegovina.

Article III of the Constitution specifies the responsibilities and relations between the institutions of Bosnia and Herzegovina and the entities. Responsibilities of the institutions of Bosnia and Herzegovina are:

- Foreign policy,

- Foreign trade policy,

- Customs policy,

- Monetary policy,

- Finances of the institutions and for the international obligations of Bosnia and Herzegovina

- Immigration, refugee, and asylum policy and regulation,

- International and inter-entity criminal law enforcement, including relations with Interpol,

- Establishment and operation of common and international communications facilities

- Regulation of inter-entity transportation

- Air traffic control.

Other responsibilities come under the authority of the entities, unless the entities themselves agree to transfer some of them to the state of Bosnia and Herzegovina, as per Article III, para 5.

In Article VII the Constitution defines the status of the Central Bank of Bosnia and Herzegovina. It is stated that "There shall be a Central Bank of Bosnia and Herzegovina, which shall be the sole authority for issuing currency and for monetary policy throughout Bosnia and Herzegovina. The central Bank's responsibilities will be determined by the Parliamentary Assembly. For the next six years after entry into force of this Constitution[18] however, it may not extend credit by creating money, operating in this respect as a Currency Board; thereafter, the Parliamentary Assembly may give it that authority."

With such constitutional responsibilities the state through its legislative institutions or, more often, by the decisions of the High Representative, has proceeded with creating an environment for the emerging market economy. Legislative activity in 1997 was concentrated on bringing in laws aimed at accelerating reconstruction in Bosnia and Herzegovina.

b) The Law on Formation of the Central Bank of Bosnia and Herzegovina

The Law on the Central Bank came into force at the end of 1997. Its basic provisions are that the Bank's role is:

- To define, accept and control the monetary policy of Bosnia and Herzegovina through issuance of the domestic currency (convertible mark) with an exchange ratio of 1 to 1 to the German mark, and under full cover in free convertible currencies,

- To keep and govern the country's official monetary reserves on a secure and profitable base.

- To support or to establish and maintain corresponding payment accounts,

- To coordinate the activity of agencies which are entitled to issue bank licenses and to supervise banks in the entities in accordance with the decisions of the Board of Governors

- To receive deposits of Bosnia and Herzegovina and commercial banks in order to fulfill the requirements for fixed reserves,

- To place in or withdraw from circulation domestic currency.

With the German mark now gone, it is not quite clear why the convertible mark has not been withdrawn and replaced by the euro. Although there is a rule in the EU that only member states are entitled to it, some other states have discussed adopting the euro unilaterally. In fact Montenegro has now in circulation both the euro and its own national currency the dinar.

In its responsibilities the Central Bank is fully independent of the Federation and Republika Srpska, and from any other public agencies or institutions – all with the aim of being able to fulfill all its tasks – unless it is otherwise provided in the law. It represents Bosnia and Herzegovina at all inter-governmental meetings and organizations in matters of monetary policy and its other areas of responsibility.

The Central Bank is authorized to provide banking services for the benefit of foreign governments, foreign central banks and monetary authorities, and on behalf of international organizations in which it or the government of BiH is participating. It may participate in international organizations which deal with the stability of financial and economic systems through monetary cooperation. On behalf of

Bosnia and Herzegovina the Central Bank may undertake the responsibility and execute transactions in connection with the participation of Bosnia and Herzegovina in international organizations.[19]

The most important provision concerning the responsibilities of the Central Bank is that it is solely responsible for preserving the strict exchange ratio between the convertible mark and the euro, fixed at exactly two marks for one euro. This, along with some other elements of monetary, financial and economic policy, may be considered essential to the economic security of Bosnia and Herzegovina. In the long run, a stable currency may provide incentives attracting foreign investors.

c) The Law on Foreign Trade Policy [20]

This law states that in the course of international trade the movement of goods and services, people and capital is free. Free movement of goods and services does not preclude prohibition or restrictions concerning import, export or transit where justified by the relevant provisions of this law. But such prohibitions or restrictions shall not constitute arbitrary discrimination or any other effect or burden of equivalent value for international trade.

This law assumes under the notion of "foreign trade policy" the state's principles for the application of all unilateral measures to do with the international flow of goods and services and for the negotiation and conclusion of all agreements with third countries, and regional or international organizations in the field of international trade. By unilateral measures of international trade is understood all protective measures such as subsidies or antidumping provisions. But some attention may be paid to the protection of important national industries such as the production of cars.[21]

The law specifies that under the notion "third countries" is understood every agreement or instrument in connection with international trade, whether other countries, the European Union or membership in customs unions, or other trade bodies, including the World Trade Organization (WTO).

The other provisions of this law, including the export and import regime, are based on the national treatment principle, as is clearly stated in paragraph 4, of Article 6: "All imported goods shall be subject to the same tax and other rules and conditions, as is done with identical or similar locally produced goods."[22] National treatment is defined in Article 24, which states that the person (individual or legal entity) may extend its services under the same terms and conditions as they are defined for the citizens of Bosnia and Herzegovina.

Other principles which are in full compliance with the rules and regulations of the European Union and the WTO include those concerning intellectual property for trade, protective measures, and measures dealing with dumping and subsidies.

d) The Law on Customs Policy [23]

This law is another example of laws prepared with the help of the international community presence in Bosnia and Herzegovina and thus compatible with regulations in developed countries.

It clearly states that the customs territory includes all of Bosnia and Herzegovina, its territorial waters, interior navigable waterways and air corridors. Thus BiH is a single customs territory. This is important because there are still frequent misinterpretations of the respective customs responsibilities of the state of Bosnia and Herzegovina and the two entities.

As a Law on Border Police was introduced through a decision of OHR as of January 14, 2000, there is now hope that the Customs Policy Law will be implemented. Until the beginning of 2002, three quarters of the national frontier was managed by the state border police, with the rest to be covered by the end of 2002. Prior to that, the import and export of goods of all kinds was under the control of local authorities. The heavy smuggling of arms, drugs, people without documents, and corruption[24] remain characteristic of the country's border management, and it will take some time until matters improve.

e) The Law on Border Police [25]

This law states that the border police are the responsibility of Bosnia and Herzegovina. Their duties involve both the protection of the state's borders and the security of its air corridors. It is the responsibility of the presidency of Bosnia and Herzegovina to define the basic principles of its establishment, functioning and responsibility.

The border police are responsible, inter alia, for control of traffic at the borders, and at check-points in a zone up to 10 km from the international border of BiH, except where the distance from the entity line of limitation is shorter than 10 km, in which case the responsibility of the border police runs to half the distance from the international border to the entity line of limitation. This responsibility includes the review of documents at border check-points, control of border crossings, and prevention of unauthorized entry into the territory of Bosnia and Herzegovina.

The importance of this law is closely connected to the overall security matters with which Bosnia and Herzegovina is concerned. The everyday practice of drugs smuggling in and out of the country, the proliferation of arms, the smuggling of individuals coming from mainly Asian countries on their way to West Europe, the import of low-quality goods without paying the customs and other relevant duties are a heavy burden which can be overcome only by strict application of the Law on Border Police.

Unlawful relations between people living in the border areas of BiH, on the one hand, and the FRY and Croatia on the other, make it very difficult for the state to manage its responsibilities. Two things have to be very carefully monitored: first, to establish as many check- points as necessary at all border crossings; and second, to make a good selection of professional officers from all three peoples of Bosnia and Herzegovina. Only by doing those things and providing updated equipment, buildings, salaries for the police themselves will it be possible to expect positive results. And only then will the customs policy law have real meaning for the country's management of relations with its foreign partners.

f) The Law on Foreign Direct Investment Policy [26]

This law was promulgated in 1998 by the then High Representative, Carlos Westendorp, as the Parliamentary Assembly of Bosnia and Herzegovina had not yet adopted it. The law regulates the policy and principles governing the presence of foreign investors in the economy of Bosnia and Herzegovina.[27]

The law states that by "foreign investor" is meant an individual or company who has no permanent residence in Bosnia and Herzegovina and whose headquarters are not in Bosnia and Herzegovina, or a legal entity established in accordance with foreign laws which has its registered office, central management office or main place of business activity in some other country.

By "foreign direct investment" or "foreign investment" is understood: the acquisition or expansion of any business venture or any other activity which alone or with some others simultaneously or sequentially provides the opportunity to one or more foreign investors to gain control over a company. Such investments may include real estate or any other unmovable property, intellectual property rights, securities, leasing, contractual rights including concession rights, equipment, machinery, spare parts, and raw materials. "Foreign control" under this law means any investment above 10 percent of the capital and/or of the voting rights, by foreign investors or any local legal entity under foreign control.

"Resident of Bosnia and Herzegovina" means a person domiciled or resident in Bosnia and Herzegovina, whether employed or self-employed, or a company which has its centre of economic interest in Bosnia and Herzegovina, or any legal entity constituted according to the laws and regulations of Bosnia and Herzegovina or its entities, which has a registered location, headquarters or main place of business activity in Bosnia and Herzegovina.

The national treatment principle[28] is included in this law with the provision that unless otherwise defined by this law , a foreign investor has the right to invest dividends accrued from those investments in any or every sector of the economy, in the same way and on the same terms and conditions as residents of Bosnia and Herzegovina and in accordance with laws and regulations of the state and the entities. In Article 8 the law provides that foreign investors have the same rights and obligations as residents of Bosnia and Herzegovina. Neither the country nor the entities shall apply any kind of discrimination towards foreign investors, based on their citizenship, domicile or residence, religion, or country of origin.

Taxation of foreign investors and their direct foreign investments will be executed in accordance with laws of the entities. There are big differences in those laws. Through the intervention of the OHR that situation has been changing so that the whole of Bosnia will have united and harmonized laws on taxation. The entities may from time to time review their laws on taxation in order to better attract foreign investors.

The principles of taxation are based on non-discrimination against any foreign investors. This is a very important provision because of the possibility that some foreign investors – from neighbouring states, for instance – may be given privileged treatment by entities at the expense of some others. Such a practice would endanger legal security, which is based on equality and on national treatment of investors and investments.

As an internationally recognized standard, this law provides that foreign investments are exempted from any custom duties, unless otherwise provided in the relevant law on customs policy of Bosnia and Herzegovina.

A very important provision in this law allows foreign investors the same ownership rights in real estate as is provided for residents of Bosnia and Herzegovina. Investors from the former Yugoslavia have the same ownership rights regarding real estate and other unmovable property as the residents of Bosnia and Herzegovina, provided that the residents of Bosnia and Herzegovina have the same rights in those countries.

The equal treatment of foreign investors is also implied in the right to employ foreign manpower, unless otherwise provided in the specific law of Bosnia and Herzegovina. This provision is a guideline for the establishment of an employment market.[29] Consideration for the security of foreign direct investors and their investments is found in the provision that foreign investments shall not be nationalized, expropriated, requisitioned[30] or exposed to any other measures with similar consequences, except in the public interest and in accordance with the laws and regulations and with appropriate compensation. That compensation shall be deemed appropriate if it is adequate, prompt and effective. This principle should be defined in accordance with established international standards.

The law leaves it to the concerned parties to find a solution in case of a dispute in connection with foreign investments. They may choose either a domestic court or arbitration, or they may choose some other domestic means of settlement, or they can submit the case to foreign conciliation or arbitration proceedings. Thus, foreign investors may choose foreign arbitration, including the International Chamber of Commerce in Paris, or the Court of Arbitration mechanisms of the Center for Settlement of Investment Disputes in New York, under the *Convention pour le règlement des differends relatifs aux investissements entre états et ressortissants d'autres états*, known as the Washington Convention of 1965.[31]

Decision on Constitutional Rights of the People of Bosnia and Herzegovina[32]

AT THE END of July 2000 the Constitutional Court of Bosnia and Herzegovina adopted a very important decision by a majority vote of two Bosniac judges and three foreign judges. It requires the two entities, the Federation of Bosnia and Herzegovina and Republika Srpska, to amend their constitutions in order to ensure the equality of the three "constituent peoples" throughout the country.

This decision offers a real chance to push the Dayton Peace Accords to their limits and to allow BiH to be a functional multinational state. It can be implemented in one of two ways: to recognize the right of the Croats as a national group to have their own state-entity or to make both existing entities truly and effectively multinational. The second direction is the only one which is in the spirit of Dayton.

Opponents of effective Bosnian statehood quickly denounced this ruling, as they feared it would mean the disappearance of the entities from the political scene (especially worrying to the parties in Republika Srpska). Having succeeded in postponing implementation of the decision of the Constitutional Court for almost two years, these circles are now trying to persuade the new High Representative Lord Ashdown to retreat from his predecessor's position on the matter.

Those who support the integrity of the Bosnian state, on the other hand, consider the Constitutional Court ruling to be a political and con-stitutional watershed, and have forced the local representatives to agree upon it, or if necessary, expect the international institutions to implement it by imposing far-reaching reforms to make Dayton more workable.

From the beginning of 2001 the Council of Europe – of which Bosnia and Herzegovina became a full member on April 24, 2002 – High Representative Petritsch, and western embassies in Sarajevo, pressed the entities to draft the constitutional changes necessary to imple-ment the Court's decision. Amendments could be created through the establishment of multinational constitutional commissions attached to the entity legislatures, the engagement of political parties in draft-ing proposals of their own, consultations with foreign experts, public consultations, intra-party dealings and at the end intensive negotia-tions in the OHR.

Unfortunately no moves towards realization of the Court's decision have been made so far, although the political parties of both entities struck a political deal in Sarajevo on March 27, 2002, agreeing on a set of precepts and principles to be embodied in both entities' constitu-tional amendments. But even though this agreement was signed by leading political parties of the Federation and accepted by prominent parties of the RS, it has not been adopted in either of the entity parlia-ments. That is why the High Representative imposed the Sarajevo agreement, insisting that it be implemented in both letter and spirit.

This agreement, based on the Court ruling, says that all three con-stituent peoples and the other citizens of Bosnia and Herzegovina have full and equal rights on all territory of the country. That means the right to live where they lived before they were expelled or displaced, to enjoy full free movement, rights to employment without any restriction, the right to education, to their language, and to health.

In case these rights are not provided in the constitutions of the entities and other legal documents, and especially if the provisions are not implemented, the Peace Implementation Council must take action. With the support of the High Representative, these actions could be undertaken:

- Economic sanctions should be imposed by the international donors on any party that refuses or fails to implement the Court's decision. It is expected that the World Bank Group and International Monetary Fund and other relevant international financial institutions would cease to approve credits and loans, or even withdraw those already approved;

- SFOR's forces should buttress security for returnees, especially in the areas of RS and western Herzegovina under the control of hard-line nationalists, with ostentatious patrols if necessary;

- The international community should adopt a very strict stance on violence against "minority" returnees, holding the relevant authorities of the entities responsible for any improper behavior.

Amendments are needed to the entity constitutions concerning fair representation of all three national groups – Bosniacs, Bosnian Serbs and Bosnian Croats – in legislative, executive, judicial and other institutions, and in public utilities and associations, without any discrimination with respect to race, sex, religion or colour. The amendments should have the following characteristics:

- Appropriate reflection of the pre-war (1991) census in the representation of the peoples of Bosnia and Herzegovina in institutions at the state, entities, cantonal and municipal level. At this moment in both entities the constitutions do not comply with that requirement;

- The Republika Srpska constitution's definition of the implementation of Dayton Annex 7 limits and reduces – to the issuance of only a few thousand administrative decisions – the obligations of the authorities under the Accords to support refugee return.

- According to the Sarajevo Agreement, in both entities there should be a legislative house/council of the constituent peoples, and in both entities the vice-presidents should be from the nations not holding the presidency;

- The requirement that no one constituent people hold more than two of the six top entity positions is not the best solution but it should be upheld in both entities as a consequence of the political compromise. The presidents of the entities and the prime ministers should not be from the same people;

- The number of deputies in the Federation's House of Representatives and the House of Peoples should be reduced ;

- The other peoples must be appropriately represented in the RS Council of Peoples and the Federation House of Peoples as the Sarajevo Agreement prescribes;

- The Sarajevo Agreement requires that cantonal, district and municipal courts should have balanced national representation based on the 1991 census. This means that changes should be made to the Constitution of RS;

- Concerning the entity constitutional courts, the Sarajevo Agreement stipulates that at least two judges come from each constituent people (another one from the "others"). This reasonable requirement should be specifically defined in both entities' constitutions;

- The benches of the entity supreme courts should be constituted on the basis of parity, with a smaller number of seats reserved for the "others";

- Constituent peoples and "others" must be adequately represented in other public institutions, including the administrations at the entity, canton and municipal levels. This should remain the case at least until Dayton Annex 7 is fully implemented.

The Sarajevo Agreement of March 27, 2002 is specific on so called "vital interests." It provides that: "vital interests" must be defined in the same way at both the entity and state levels. "Vital interest," according to the Agreement, means: adequate representation in legislative, executive and juridical institutions; identity of each nation; organization of governmental bodies; equal rights of the constituent peoples in the process of decision-making; equal rights to education, religion, language, culture, tradition, territorial organization, the system of public media and any other matter to be determined by 2/3 of the constituent peoples in the House of Peoples or Council of Peoples.

Regarding the reform of the entities, the Sarajevo Agreement envisages that:

- Both the House and Council of Peoples should have the right to consider whether legislation is of a generally discriminatory character;

- For the next three years these bodies should have the right to review all existing legislation and to suggest revision or nullification of any that is contrary to the principles of the Agreement.

- Integration of entity public sectors and of police forces under entity ministries, as well as in the cantons and municipalities, should begin forthwith, with staffing proportions based on the 1991 census.

The Constitutional Court of Bosnia and Herzegovina ruled that in the Constitution of Republika Srpska the section defining that "this is the Entity of the Serbian nation" is annulled, as is the section in the Constitution of the Federation defining that "this Entity is the Entity of the Bosniacs and Croats." By this Decision the Bosniacs and Croats are defined as equally constituent peoples of Republika Srpska with the Serbs themselves. Similarly, in the Federation the constitutional peoples are Bosniacs and Croats, but also Serbs. The Decision should have a important and long-lasting effects on the full implementation of human rights for all citizens throughout Bosnia and Herzegovina.

Implementation of this Decision is the most important task facing domestic institutions and the international community. With its implementation the problem of refugees and displaced people will be less difficult to resolve, as they will have to be accorded the same rights as regular citizens of the entities. Property rights, social rights, the right of safe return to their homes, the right to work, to have access to schools, health treatment and the like – all will follow from the implementation of this Decision. All shall have the right to use the language they speak and its alphabet, and equal treatment before the courts and governmental institutions. Without equal rights before judicial institutions, and equal treatment by the police, human rights conventions cannot be implemented as expected.

The Decision will also have an impact in many other areas, including the reform of the military forces, language policy, education curricula, the issue of dual citizenship as between the entities, and even the names of the entities – "Republika Srpska," for example, implies the claim that it is exclusively the entity of the Serb people. With the implementation of this Decision the security of the state of Bosnia and Herzegovina and of its people should be enhanced, not only internally but with respect to its immediate neighbours. Regional security as defined by the Pact for Stability in South Eastern Europe[33] will also be affected.

The Law Establishing the Court of Bosnia and Herzegovina.

THE SECOND most important legal document promulgated recently by the authority of the High Representative is his decision on the Law to establish the Court of Bosnia and Herzegovina. The High Representative exercised the rights delegated to him by Annex X, Article V of the Dayton Accords, according to which he has the authority to interpret the agreement, and especially to facilitate, as he judges necessary, the resolution of any difficulties arising in connection with civilian implementation. Additional powers were granted to him in the Conclusion of the Bonn PIC held on 9 and 10 December, 1997, as well as in the Declaration of the Madrid PIC on 15 and 16 December, 1998. The Declaration stated (Paragraph 3, Annex II) that the establishment of judicial institutions at the level of the state is a necessity.

Article 1 of the law establishing the Supreme Court declares that in order to ensure effective realization of the state's competence and to ensure respect for human rights and the rule of law throughout the whole territory, it establishes the Court of Bosnia and Herzegovina.

The Court's competence includes that it is the final authority in connection with implementation of state laws and of international treaties. It may delegate implementation of the state laws to lower courts at the entity level. It can also decide issues of competence between courts of the Federation and of Republika Srpska and the courts of the entities and of the district of Brcko.

As the highest judicial institution, the Court of Bosnia and Herzegovina has the final word in criminal, administrative and appellate cases. Although it has no specified competence in civil and commercial matters, it is understood that such disputes may be included at the appellate stage, unless clarifying amendments to the contrary are added to this law.

The criminal law system in Bosnia stands on the verge of a major overhaul. After four years of designing a variety of substantive and procedural criminal laws it is currently expected that the High Representative will take a final decisive step on behalf of the entire country. The domestic politicians took a piecemeal and incremental approach to criminal law reform, which was finally abandoned in 2000. From then on the focus has been more on creating both substantive and procedural criminal law at the state level. At the end of 2001 the OHR drafted such laws modeled on German and Swedish legislation, which were presented to the relevant ministries of the entities, as well as to the state-level Ministry of Civil Affairs and Communications.

The current legislation gives too many opportunities for delays in judicial proceedings. Most importantly, in the existing legislation there is no definition of many crimes, including for example corruption and other economic crimes. The new proposed legislation will give more power to the prosecutors, rather than to the investigative judges who are now doing the job of prosecutors. In this regard it is proposed that prosecutors should run investigations of crimes punishable by up to five years' imprisonment, but that more serious crimes should remain within the purview of investigative judges.[34]

The provision that investigative judges should deal with the more serious cases is explained by the fact that prosecutors are less trained than investigative judges in the handling of more complex cases. The relevance of this argument is limited by the fact that the new laws and new procedures for dealing with complex economic crimes, organized crime and corruption will in any case require extensive retraining of the whole judiciary.

Important among these changes in the criminal law is the provision for the seizure and confiscation of the proceeds of crime. Individuals suspected of legitimizing illegal profits will have to prove that their investments, bank deposits or newly acquired real estate come from legally-made profits. This amounts to a radical change since, "as matters stand, ill-gotten gains are never confiscated because the law is so weak."[35] The new draft requires the start of trial within 120 days of an indictment, as well as obliging an appellate court to make a final decision on a appeal or to order a reinvestigation of the evidence if it is inadequate for the purposes of reaching a final verdict.

The role of expert witnesses will also be changed. Current practice exaggerates the impact of their testimony and is subject to abuse. According to the new provisions, the parties to a case will be able to appoint their own experts, while the court may itself engage them.

Another important new provision concerns witness protection. This is to be defined in another part of the package, but it is very worthwhile mentioning it as it is vital for the criminal law. Protection of witnesses is basic to prosecuting and punishing crimes, especially war crimes. At the moment this provision exists only in the Federation. The OHR's criminal law reforms include the extension of witness protection throughout Bosnia and Herzegovina. According to the proposed legislation, protection would include new homes, new jobs, and new identities for witnesses at risk, as well as agreements for the participation of neighboring states in the program. This reform seems very ambitious, as it presumes levels of inter-entity and inter-state cooperation that have yet to be found in the region.

International and inter-entity legal liaison is another issue that will have to be considered by the High Representative. The economic crimes which threaten the process of reform in BiH require an inter-entity agreement on judicial cooperation, continuous exchanges of data and information, and joint investigations – none of which exists at the present. As money-laundering and organized crime are transnational businesses, it can be expected that other countries will want to sign agreements, exchange confidential data and cooperate on prevention. It is expected that the international community will persuade the relevant authorities in BiH to create state-level enforcement mechanisms. If those local institutions prove incompetent in combating economic crimes, other countries may opt for quarantine measures such as visa regimes.

Conclusion

THROUGH THE AUTHORITY of the High Representative a number of appropriate laws and regulations governing the economy and social life of Bosnia and Herzegovina have been adopted, with provisions compatible with those of western Europe and other developed countries.

The most important of these is the decision on the constitutional rights of all peoples throughout the territory of Bosnia and Herzegovina adopted by the Constitutional Court and subsequently supported by the Sarajevo Agreement of March 27, 2002 concerning its implementation. The second is the decision of the High Representative to promulgate the Law establishing the Court of

Bosnia and Herzegovina. Another law of some significance is the Law on Establishment of the Border Police.

The new laws governing the economy, such as the Law on Foreign Direct Investment, on Foreign Trade, and Customs Policy comply with modern international standards and are in conformity with similar laws and regulations in the developed world. Looking at this legislation, it could be concluded that a positive attitude to the market economy has been established. But how and when implementation will proceed is another matter, and on this depends the stability and internal security of the country.

The Bosnian legal system belongs to the Central European legal tradition. But over the last 150 years the Bosnian legal system evolved out of the old Ottoman Sharia law to Austrian civil law, and then after 1918 it switched to the Kingdom of Yugoslavia's legal system based on the French Civil Code. After 1945 Bosnia, as part of communist Yugoslavia, implemented a legal system influenced at first by the Soviet communist legal system. After 1950 the Yugoslav legal system became *sui generis*, as it implemented various self-management principles in various sectors, but mainly in the economy. The foundation of that system was deep involvement of the ruling communist party in all aspects of political and social life.

With the dissolution of Yugoslavia the communist legal order did not disappear. It is still in use in many sectors, except those which are under the influence of the international community, notably through the activity and capacity of the OHR. As Bosnia and Herzegovina is a small, poor country in transition, the influence of the legal systems of other countries is noticeable. Some of the important legal decisions imposed by the High Representative embody the substance and the legal techniques of the Anglo-American tradition.

In what direction will the legal system of Bosnia and Herzegovina develop in the future? I would not be very surprised if the Anglo-Saxon legal approach made itself more deeply felt, since that system is increasingly integral to many international or regional treaties, conventions and agreements. Whatever we may say about globalization, it will not leave the legal system untouched.

Notes

1 Lenard J. Cohen, *Broken Bonds* (Boulder, San Francisco, Oxford: 1995), Laura Silber and Allan Little, *The Death of Yugoslavia* (London: 1996), Misha Glenny, *The Fall of Yugoslavia* (London: 1996), Robert D. Kaplan, *Balkan Ghosts* (New York: 1996), Warren Zimmerman, *Origins of a Catastrophe* (New York: 1999), John R. Lampe, *Yugoslavia as History* (Cambridge: 2000), Dusan Bilandzic i dr. *Rat u Hrvatskoj i Bosni i Hercegovini, 1991–1995* (Zagreb-Sarajevo: 1999), Alvin and Heidi Toffler, *War and Anti-War* (London: 1995), D.A. Dyker and I.Vejvoda, *Yugoslavia and After* (London and New York: 1999).

2 Kasim Trnka, *Ustavno pravo*, Sarajevo, 2000, pp. 118–119, Zlatko Salcic, *Zakoni Bosne i Hercegovine* (Stockholm: 1999), pp. 18–34.

3 See *Opinion No.7. On International Recognition of the Republic of Slovenia by the European Community and its Member States*, as was signed by R. Badinter in Paris on January 11, 1992 and *Opinion 5. On the Recognition of the Republic of Croatia*, B. G. Ramcharan, *The International Conference on the Former Yugoslavia*, Vol. 2 (The Hague, London, Boston: 1997), pp. 1275–1280 and 1268–1269.

4 B. G. Ramcharan, *The International Conference on the Former Yugoslavia*, Vol.2, pp.1265–1268. In that Opinion the Arbitration Commission delivered the following:

> By an instrument adopted separately by the Presidency and the Government of Bosnia and Herzegovina on December 20, 1991 and published in the Official Journal of the Republic of BiH on 23 December 1991, these authorities accepted all the commitments indicated in the Declaration and Guidelines of 16 December 1991. In that instrument the authorities in question emphasized that Bosnia and Herzegovina accepted the draft Convention produced by the Hague Conference on November 4, 1991 notably that the Constitution of SRBiH guarantees respect for human rights , and the authorities of Bosnia and Herzegovina have sent the Commission assurances that the new Constitution now being framed would provide full guarantees for individual human rights and freedoms., etc., Omer Ibrahimagic, *Dejton=Bosna u Evropi – pravna sustina Dejtona*, Sarajevo, 2001, p. 25.

5 The Washington Agreement was signed by representatives from the Republic of Croatia and the Republic of Bosnia and Herzegovina in the presence of the US President. The Parliamentary Assembly of BiH and the Constitutional Assembly of the Federation of Bosnia and Herzegovina adopted it on March 30, 1994. See Trnka, *Ustavno pravo*, p. 119.

6 Richard Holbrooke, *To End a War* (New York: 1998), Carl Bildt, *Peace Journey* (London, 1998).

7 The budget for military use is recommended by the International Monetary Fund not to exceed 294.million Convertible Marks for the two components of the Federation's military. The proposal of the Ministry of Defense of the Federation was about 700 million KM. Ten thousand soldiers of the armed forces of the Federation left the army with financial support for each of 10.000 KM (equal to 5.000 euros)

8 See *Oslobodjenje* (Sarajevo), 22 December 2000.

9 ICG. *Balkan Report No. 104: Bosnia's November Elections: Dayton Stumbles*, (Sarajevo, Brussels: 18 December 2000), p. III.

10 Dr. Mladen Ivanic (Party of Democratic Progress) nominated as the only candidate for the Prime Minister of Republika Srpska on TV Republika Srpska, on December 24, 2000, Prof. Dr. Tufik Burnazović.

11 See Draft Agreement published in daily *Oslobodjenje* (Sarajevo), March 28, 2002.

12 *Report by the High Representative for the Implementation of the Peace Agreement* to the Secretary-General of the United Nations, Sarajevo, October 17, 2000, p. 6.

13 Western, *Bosnia's Next Five Years: Dayton and Beyond*, United States Institute of Peace, Special Report, Washington, DC, November 3, 2000, p. 2.

14 From the middle of April to the beginning of October of 2000 the OHR dismissed twenty-one public officials for serious and persistent obstruction of the Dayton Accords. Nineteen cases out of those twenty-one were dismissed by the joint decision of the OHR and the OSCE Head of Mission. See *Report by the High Representative for Implementation of the Peace* to the Secretary – General of the United Nations, Office of High Represntative, p. 5.

15 Western, *Bosnia's Next Five Years: Dayton and Beyond*, p. 3.

16 Samuel P. Huntington, "Robust Nationalism," *The National Interest*, Number 58 (Winter 1999/2000), 31.

17 Annex 4 of *General Framework for Peace in Bosnia and Herzegovina*, initialed in Dayton on November 21, 1995, and signed in Paris on December 14, 1995.

18 Art. XII of the Constitution states that the Constitution shall enter into force upon the signature (in Paris on December 14, 1995) of the General Framework Agreement as a constitution amending and superseding the Constitution of the Republic of Bosnia and Herzegovina.

19 See Art. 2–4 of the *Law on Central Bank*- Sl. g. br. 1/97 (Off. g.) BiH. br. 1/97 od 29 oktobra 1997 godine.

20 Sl. g. BiH br. 17/98.

21 Ugo Schtolsch, director of Volkswagen, *Oslobodjenje* (Sarajevo), April 12, 2002.

22 *Law on Foreign Trade Policy*,-Sl. g. BiH, br. 1/97.

23 *Law on Customs Policy*,- Sl. g. BiH, br. 1/97.

24 Robin Theobald, "So, What Really is the Problem about Corruption?" in *Third World Quarterly*, 20/3 (June 1999), 491–503.

25 Sl. g. BiH, br. 2/2000, od 26 Januara 2000.

26 Sl. g. BiH br. 4/98, od 20 Marta 1998.

27 The *Law on Foreign investments* of FBiH was adopted on December 2, 2001, and published in the *Official Gazette*, of FBiH, Sl. n. FBiH br. 61/2001. The principles and provisions of this act comply with the *Law on Foreign Direct Investments*. The *Law on Foreign Investments* of Republika Srpska was adopted in 1997, which means the state law does not follow its principles and provisions.

28 Art. 3 of the Law.

29 Art. 14 of the Law.

33 Art. 16 of the Law.

31 Aleksandar Goldstajn, Sinisa Triva, *Medjunarodna trgovacka arbitraza*, Zagreb, 1987, pp. 365–405, Tufik Burnazović, *Strana ulaganja*, Sarajevo, 1996, pp.136–137. Tufik Burnazović i dr. *Svjetska banka i medjunarodni monetarni fond*, Sarajevo, Tuzla, Gracanica, 1999, pp. 229–235.

32 *Ustavni sud Bosne i Hercegovine*, Djelomicna odluka br. U/98III, Sl. g. BiH, br. 23/2000, od 14 septembra 2000.

33 SIPRI Yearbook 2000, *Armaments, Disarmament and International Security* (Oxford: 2000), pp. 220–226.

34 Apparently the proportion of cases punishable by sentences of up to five years represents 80% of all criminal cases – see: International Crisis Group, *Courting Disaster: The Misrule of Law in Bosnia and Herzegovina*, Sarajevo, March 25, 2002, p. 27.

35 Ibid., p. 28.

II

The International Presence

JOHN BLAXLAND

Contrast to Bosnia: Coalition Operations with the Australian-led International Force East Timor (INTERFET)

The skillful leader subdues his enemies without fighting.

Sun Tsu

S EVERAL RECENT international military operations have been criticized, but one success story stands in contrast – the Australian-led mission to East Timor. Australia has a history of seeking to "punch above its weight" with stealth, and battle cunning, backed up with, but not driven by, kinetic capabilities. Australia's disciplined, restrained and self-deprecating approach helped bind together a 22-nation coalition of the willing, demonstrating the application of a manoeuvrist philosophy adapted for the mass-media information era. The successful result in East Timor, coming after a decade of mixed results in the Balkans and elsewhere, suggests that this innovative method is valid for the military challenges of today and beyond. However, the similarities and differences with peace support operations in Bosnia, suggest broad lessons need to be applied carefully.

Lieutenant Colonel JOHN BLAXLAND is a serving Australian Army Officer posted as Australia's first Visiting Defence Fellow at Queen's University and War Studies PhD candidate at the Royal Military College, Kingston. He was the Intelligence Officer and principal staff officer responsible for Information Operations in Headquarters 3rd Brigade, 1998–99. He was born in Chile, is a graduate of the Royal Thai Army Command and Staff College and the Royal Military College, Duntroon.

Contrast to Bosnia: Coalition Operations with the Australian-led International Force East Timor

ONE OF THE MOST REMARKABLE of the post-Cold War conflicts occurred in 1999 in the Indonesian-controlled territory of East Timor, shortly after the situation in the Balkans reached a crescendo with the bombing campaign in Kosovo. The reader may wonder why East Timor merits consideration in a volume on Bosnia. Given the difficulties experienced in other post-Cold War peace support operations, including in Bosnia, the success in East Timor provides a potentially fruitful case-study, particularly as it happened when many of the difficult lessons faced by the international community in the Balkans were finally being absorbed. Consequently, it serves as an interesting contrast, a decade after the end of the Cold War, showing how some of the lessons learnt could be applied. Like the countries of NATO with regards to Bosnia in the early 1990s, Australia had not considered deploying forces to East Timor until events left it with little option.

Believing it could win, Indonesia agreed to let the United Nations supervise a ballot on the future of East Timor, a former Portuguese colony it had forcibly annexed in 1975. On 30 August 1999 the East Timorese voted overwhelmingly in favour of separation from Indonesia. Indonesian-sponsored militia forces raised to help ensure an outcome favourable to Indonesia were let loose in early September in an attempt to frustrate the independence process.[1] This situation triggered an Australian-led evacuation operation from 6 to 14 September. Known as Operation *Spitfire*, it used mostly Royal Australian Air Force (RAAF) C-130 Hercules aircraft to evacuate hundreds fleeing the terror, including unarmed UN staff and associated East Timorese. Indonesia appears not to have appreciated just how transparent the events would appear before the world and by 12 September, facing intense international diplomatic and economic pressure, agreed to accept a UN-mandated international force to restore order.

The Australian-led International Force East Timor (INTERFET) under Major General Peter Cosgrove, operating with a unified command and robust mandate, arrived on 20 September. The Force swiftly restored order in what has been described as a "by the book" or model operation authorised under Chapter VII of the UN Charter, that has set the benchmark for peace enforcement operations.[2] Since the handover to the United Nations in February 2000, several publications have been released providing detailed descriptions of the conduct of Operation *Stabilise* in East Timor.[3] The Australian Deployable Joint Force Headquarters or DJFHQ (doubling as Headquarters 1st Division) was renamed and expanded to form Headquarters INTER-FET, commanding a force of over 11,000 troops from twenty-two countries, including key regional Asian neighbours that added to the credibility of the force.

The initial deployment into Dili by sea and air consisted primarily of an Australian combined-arms, light-infantry brigade with naval and air supporting elements, special forces, and smaller attached British and New Zealand contingents. Initially troops had the responsibility of providing a secure environment in Dili in accordance with UN Security Council Resolution 1264. This task involved disarming the militia while avoiding inadvertent confrontation with Indonesian troops still in East Timor – many only grudgingly accepting the force's international mandate. Within three weeks, Dili was secure and a light-infantry brigade had deployed to secure the border with Indonesian West Timor, effectively opening the way for the restoration of basic services, provision of humanitarian assistance and preparations for full independence.

The contribution of 5,500 personnel to the East Timor operation at its peak was the largest single deployment by Australian forces since the end of World War II. While the Vietnam War involved a larger overall commitment of Australian forces, that deployment was much more gradual. Australia, like other countries, including Canada, has willingly contributed joint-force composite battalion groups since the late 1980s for a series of international missions, including those to Namibia, Cambodia, Somalia and Rwanda. Australian troops had acquitted themselves well and many lessons had been learnt, but the scale and scope of the East Timor mission was beyond anything previously entertained by Australian planners.

For a medium-sized power, Australia features prominently on the world map, but as in the case of Canada, the size of its land mass belies its limited economic and military power and influence.[4] The Australian Defence Force has long taken pride in being a relatively high-technology force in a low-technology neighbourhood. In addition, the small population base has long driven Australian defence planners' thinking towards fighting smarter – "punching above our weight." During World War II, Australia contributed to Allied efforts to outsmart enemies with such "soft" capabilities as psychological operations, intelligence operations, deception and electronic warfare.[5] During the Vietnam War, Australian commanders were always conscious of the need to conserve limited manpower, and fight as efficiently and effectively as possible by applying its more stealthy and less firepower-intensive tactics – away from the more heavy-handed US forces.[6]

Australia's experience in fighting in the nearby South-West Pacific in World War II and thereafter in such places as Malaya, Borneo and Vietnam intensified concerns about the effects of military actions on relations with neighbours. Consequently, Australian diplomats, politicians and commanders have often weighed the long-term political ramifications of military action against short-term expediency. While prepared to apply kinetic force – or firepower – when necessary, and structuring its defence force accordingly to include tanks, warships and fighter-bombers, Australia has always looked for ways to achieve its military objectives with minimal collateral damage. It has sought to keep its own casualties to a minimum and to contain the negative effects of forceful action on the nation's long-term strategic interests, including its relations with its neighbours.

Advances in information technology have been touted as triggering the most recent Revolution in Military Affairs,[7] and the term Information Operations has sprung into use along with it in the late 1990s, in recognition of the wider use of information in peacekeeping and crisis management.[8] Information Operations have also been referred to in Australia as "shaping and influencing."[9] By the late 1990s, many in the Australian Army had already learnt to think about military operations in ways appropriate for the Information Era. To most, that understanding is encapsulated in a manoeuvre warfare mindset – avoiding hard spots and going for the soft spots, or "gaps," to achieve a mission – where speedy and informed decision making is considered critical to maximise fighting power and minimise casualties.[10]

As the East Timor crisis unfolded, the international media had an important role to play in East Timor and helped to extend the political fallout during the crisis. Australian government policy had long placed high priority on good relations with Indonesia and therefore wished to avoid a confrontation that would harm that relationship. However, widespread revulsion at what was being reported from East Timor compelled the Australian government to act, mustering international support to pressure Indonesia to stop the carnage and wanton destruction, and let an international force assume responsibility in East Timor. At the same time, the Australian Defence Force appreciated that the situation could become more problematic if the force were to sustain significant casualties. Limited military logistics raised concerns about the prospects of sustaining the mission, should the situation in East Timor descend into a protracted conflict.[11]

The Australian government's policy of engagement with Indonesia was being de-railed, but the crisis brought together the ministers from the Department of Defence, the Department of Foreign Affairs and Trade, and the Attorney-General's Department, as well as the Prime Minister, John Howard, in the National Security Committee of Cabinet. They met regularly at the peak of the crisis and consulted with senior officials, including the Australian Chief of the Defence Force, Admiral Chris Barrie. The personal involvement of the Prime Minister in the crisis meant that the Department of the Prime Minister and Cabinet had *de facto* leadership, but how to divide responsibilities remained undetermined.[12] In effect they were validating Clausewitz's key dictum that military operations are "an extension of politics by other means."

At the highest levels, for instance, the Prime Minister and Foreign Minister of Australia engaged potential mission partners at the Asia-Pacific Economic Cooperation (APEC) Forum, fortuitously being held in New Zealand at the peak of the crisis. In the meantime, the Vice Chief of the Defence Force, Air Marshall Doug Riding, visited several South-East Asian countries, seeking contributions from long-time regional partners. The personal nature of the Vice Chief's negotiations helped shape the operation as he overcame many of the misunderstandings in South-East Asia that were arising as INTERFET was being assembled. Clearly the task of forming a coalition force at short notice presented Australian officials with enormous challenges that required cooperation and a degree of mutual understanding – itself something of a challenge given the different departmental cultures of Defence and Foreign Affairs. The cultural difference in Australia between Foreign Affairs and Defence was negligible when compared with the cultural differences between INTERFET, the militia groups and their Indonesian military backers in East Timor.

The commander directed a four-phase campaign in East Timor with specific but limited objectives. The first phase was the negotiation with the Indonesian force commander, Major General Kiki Shyanakri, to establish safe conditions for lodgment. The second phase involved the rapid lodgment of the necessary combat forces. The third phase concerned the establishment of a secure environment in Dili and then throughout East Timor. The final phase involved the transition of INTERFET to a UN peace enforcement operation. The security of INTERFET troops was the highest priority for each phase. Major General Cosgrove also committed the force to facilitate humanitarian aid to relieve the suffering of thousands of displaced East Timorese as quickly as possible.[13]

When INTERFET troops deployed to East Timor on 20 September 1999, they encountered minimal armed resistance, but they had to be prepared to fight in order to uphold their mandate under UN Security Council Resolution 1264. The maintenance of a high level of preparedness proved a potent deterrent to aggression, particularly in the first few hoursdays when the still heavily outnumbered INTERFET troops were most vulnerable. Furthermore, the collapse of the militia forces had as much to do with the knowledge that they faced a sharp and determined response as it did with the purported withdrawal of Indonesian military support and patronage.[14] As Major General Cosgrove noted, a less robust "force optimised for peacekeeping would have in my view invited more adventurous behaviour by our adversaries."[15]

The naval and air components were also prepared for other contingencies should the situation have deteriorated. The maritime forces deployed with INTERFET were assigned the "mission to act as an air-defence screen and to provide back-up if the lodgment did not go according to plan or was opposed."[16] The presence of the US Navy's Aegis cruiser USS *Mobile Bay*, the Royal Navy's destroyer HMS *Glasgow* and the Royal Australian Navy's FFG-7 frigates provided air-warfare sensors and weapons that gave reassurance to the land forces. Naval-force protection also helped sustain the troops ashore since it enabled merchant shipping to deliver 90 per cent of the cargo landed. The presence and contribution of the Royal Australian Navy helped shape the operational climate, bolster INTERFET's confidence and ability, and influence outcomes positively, especially in the first critical days of the operation.

Also crucial for the lodgment and sustainment of the force was air support, particularly with regard to surveillance, and the provision of airfield services in Dili and at East Timor's second airport, Baucau. A recent media report also suggests that Australian F/A-18 fighters were on readiness patrol and F-111 strike aircraft were on standby in northern Australia.[17] The Chief of the Defence Force was taking every precaution for the safety of INTERFET personnel and assets; a soft-spoken man, he was keen to ensure that his troops had a "big stick" should that have been required. Fortunately, in the end the land forces did not have to call on air or naval gunfire support.[18]

The land component operations in the first few days revolved around three elements. The first was the establishment of an INTERFET Response Force presence in the countryside, conducting reconnaissance, maintaining an Immediate Reaction Force and acting as pathfinders for follow-on forces. This force was a unique international group based around an Australian special forces squadron and including British and New Zealand components. The second element involved the 3rd Brigade's security operations using two Australian infantry battalions, a British Gurkha company, aviation and armour, as well as other components of the 3rd Brigade in support.[19] Colonel Bob Breen has described the third element as "human and technical intelligence collection, and psychological operations."[20]

This third element played a pivotal role in discretely and efficiently vectoring INTERFET's limited resources onto fleeting and difficult-to-locate militia concentrations.[21] Based on threat assessments and the intent to prevent an escalation of tensions, INTERFET did not deploy tanks, field artillery or anti-aircraft artillery. The armoured vehicles that did deploy had no adequate protection against a variety of threats, including heavy machine-guns, anti-armour weapons and mines. Armed with this intelligence, focused troops could then weed out the militia forces with precision and throw off balance those contemplating a strike against INTERFET. As Bob Breen has written, having established situational awareness in the first few days of the operation, INTERFET effectively exploited the decision cycle of the militia groups and their controllers to achieve superiority; conducting 24-hour and air-mobile operations, and dominating Dili. INTERFET then continued to intervene and to apprehend suspected militiamen; it also responded to threats to peace and security in the Dili area and beyond. This vigorous prosecution of operations prompted the remaining militiamen to leave East Timor while their controllers closed down their communications networks and withdrew.[22]

Before those militia networks closed down, several other incidents occurred that demonstrate the importance of Information Operations as they permeated through various levels of INTERFET's chain of command. In the first few days of the operation, Indonesian troops continued to gather in East Timor's capital, Dili, from outlying areas while the militia groups continued sporadic activity around Dili. Sensing that a deterioration in the security situation was possible, the brigade commander sought to pre-empt any increase in hostile actions by applying disciplined and restrained combat power for a psychological effect. He directed that all available rotary-wing and fixed-wing aircraft should deploy above the city. The brigade commander's plan was to demonstrate air superiority, mobility, observation and (even though only installed for self-protection) some aerial firepower. Aircraft were directed to fly low and hard across the city, appearing fearsome and making a great deal of noise to intimidate anyone likely to oppose INTERFET.[23] In the meantime, infantry troops and armoured vehicles conducted a "hammer and anvil" – style sweep through the city. Admittedly, as Bob Breen pointed out, this was an exhilarating but highly disciplined experience for those involved.[24] Some people had worried that the presence of armour might escalate conflict, but the adversary saw armour and would not engage. One commentator observed: "We saw people scared of armour. We often talk about the psychological effects of armour. We saw it in East Timor."[25]

These efforts paid off handsomely. The energy generated from the initial shock of the rapid deployment enabled the brigade commander to grasp the initiative at a critical juncture. After the initial deployment, the intent of the adversary became unclear. The brigade commander retained the initiative before the initial shock effect could wear off by adopting a suite of measures such as a series of night-time cordon-and-search actions and sustained overflights of the Dili area using helicopters equipped with forward-looking infra-red (FLIR) equipment. This operation served to deter anyone trying to undermine the INTERFET mission. It also demonstrated the brigade commander's keen sense of timing and measured use of force to unbalance the adversary.

Similar restraint and keen understanding of the mission's intent was being demonstrated at the grassroots level as well. One 22-year-old Australian platoon commander and his troops handled a potentially inflammatory situation involving an entire battalion of approximately 500 East Timorese territorial soldiers. These troops, travelling in about sixty trucks loaded with loot, barrelled into Dili, where Australian infantrymen had established a vehicle checkpoint. The territorial commander refused to show his identification and demanded passage as his troops began taking aim at the Australians. Good judgment and quick thinking were required to defuse a potentially disastrous escalation of tensions. The platoon commander checked with higher headquarters, which authorised him to allow the territorial troops to proceed westwards out of Dili to the border. The Australian troops' discipline had held, despite provocation, and an exchange of fire was averted.

The Australian platoon commander demonstrated that he had a sharp appreciation of his higher commander's intent, and although his rules of engagement authorised the use of lethal force against such provocation, he realised that the best approach was to seek to defuse the situation. Major General Cosgrove observed that "the decisions of junior leaders and the actions of their small teams can influence the course of international affairs."[26] This was never more obvious than during the tense days after INTERFET's arrival and before the withdrawal of Indonesian troops from East Timor. There were several other similar displays of stealth, discipline, cunning and a clear appreciation of the strategic consequences of tactical actions in the early days of the operation. These consequences included several clashes between militia groups and INTERFET's Response Force and between militia and INTERFET light-infantry troops near the border with West Timor and to the east of Dili.[27]

One of the key groups that INTERFET sought to influence, or control, was the armed faction of the Timorese pro-independence national liberation front, FRETILIN. The faction was known as the "Forças Armadas da Libertação Nacional de Timor Leste," or FALINTIL. INTERFET developed a "Three Ps" policy encouraging the "Progressive Laying Down of Arms," facilitating "Progressive Introduction" back into the civil structures, and encouraging "Progressive Reconciliation." Recognising that they had to avoid giving the Indonesians and their militia a pretext to justify excluding an international force, FALINTIL exercised considerable discipline in the days before INTERFET's arrival when the militia groups had run amok. Response Force personnel carefully administered arrangements in order to convince FALINTIL to defer aspirations of playing a stronger role in security issues, effectively preventing it from adding to INTERFET's challenges. This approach also made it easier eventually to give FALINTIL a positive liaison role alongside peacekeeping troops assisting in border management, particularly once INTERFET had accomplished the initial tasks of providing a secure environment.

In the days and weeks that followed the initial deployment, INTERFET numbers increased and a secure environment was established in Dili as militia groups and Indonesian troops withdrew to Indonesia. This withdrawal and force increase allowed Commander INTERFET to deploy the Brigade by sea, road and air to the border area adjacent to Indonesian West Timor. Evans' force included the two infantry battalions and integral 3rd Brigade units as well as a company of British Gurkhas and the 1st Battalion of the Royal New Zealand Infantry Regiment (1RNZIR). The lead element of 1RNZIR arrived shortly after the main force had landed in Dili. The remainder of 1RNZIR, as well as a company of Canadian "Vandoos" (R22eR) and a platoon of Irish Rangers, joined the lead New Zealander element in October. Other national contingents deployed to the more benign sectors in central and eastern East Timor. By mid-October the manoeuvre phase of the operation had wound down, with forces allocated distinct areas of operation in which to establish security and facilitate humanitarian aid.

A major factor in promoting peace operations has been the force of public opinion. Because the maintenance of the collective will of INTERFET's member states was the operation's centre of gravity in East Timor, public relations was one of the most significant aspects of the operation to be managed as INTERFET evolved. The legitimacy of INTERFET as a peace enforcement mission was dependent on achieving a high degree of international consensus, and Commander INTERFET fully recognised this fact. Legitimacy was demonstrated by the strong regional core membership in a truly cooperative international force.[28] As Alan Ryan has observed, "Those members of the Association of South-East Asian Nations (ASEAN) that were involved in INTERFET were particularly concerned that their participation not damage their relationship with Indonesia, ASEAN's largest member."[29] Moreover, the Commander appreciated that international satellite broadcast television and the internet had increased his ability to influence the perceptions of key individuals and groups.[30] Consequently it was incumbent on him and his staff to ensure that a carefully managed and scrupulously honest media-awareness program was maintained to foster ongoing cooperation. Commander INTERFET's media conference in Darwin prior to the commencement of the operation demonstrated his understanding of this issue. He knew that he was going "live" to Jakarta and Dili and those first impressions would be lasting. He also knew that his words and manner could either intensify or ease tensions.[31]

Consistent with this appreciation of the media's role, and to the chagrin of the infantry troops deploying to Dili on the first day of Operation *Stabilise*, 20 September, two C-130 aircraft loads of journalists were flown into Dili. The Australian Defence Force's Media Support Unit assigned to assist journalists accompanied them. The arrival of the journalists was scheduled at late notice, reflecting the ad-hoc initial efforts at the strategic level to conduct the campaign with an Information Operations mindset. Still, despite the initial resentment over the risks had the situation deteriorated, and the additional burden of protecting accredited journalists, many soon came to appreciate that the "double edged sword" of media attention was working in favour of INTERFET. Media attention reinforced the mandate's legitimacy and further discredited the militias and their Indonesian sponsors. In the first few days before Headquarters INTERFET was fully established, and while 3rd Brigade was busy establishing a secure environment in Dili, the Brigade Commander's immediate action on the discovery of militia and Indonesian military burning or looting was to cue the media.[32]

Critical to the plan for cueing the media was a confidence in the troops' discipline, high level of training, and understanding of the laws of armed conflict. The Australian Chief of the Defence Force, commenting on the degree of competency displayed by Australia's Army, Navy and Air Force during Operation *Stabilise*, observed that: "we don't regard this as a one off – it is built into the system."[33] It was the calibre of the troops that gave the commander the confidence to bring in the media on that first day. Australian troops have rules of engagement and orders for opening fire drilled into them, producing disciplined and alert soldiers. This kind of training proved instrumental in ensuring that the "strategic corporal"[34] worked towards the common goal of INTERFET. Such discipline, combined with a clear and moral mandate, gave commanders confidence not to fear the media presence, but to work with it, wielding the double-edged sword advantageously.

In addition to media and legal concerns, a concerted psychological-operations effort was undertaken by INTERFET. Conscious of the damaging effect of the backlash that misinformation could generate, the Psychological Operations Platoon was tasked with generating material that was scrupulously honest. The Platoon Commander worked closely with the INTERFET Information Operations Cell as well as with the subordinate elements. This material included leaflets and loud-speaker broadcasts that were used in the early stages of the operation. In such a low-technology environment, leaflets and broadcasts were essential and effective tools for disseminating messages to a range of audiences. Then, as the force was established, radio messages for a repaired radio station and a weekly newspaper were produced and well received by the locals and supporting aid organisations. The newspaper was the main source of news for many people in the first few months since no other news media outlet had been left undamaged throughout East Timor as the Indonesians and the militias departed. The radio program, which took longer to reach a wide audience, included what came to be known as the "INTERFET Hour." An appeal in Australia led many to donate spare radios for the people of East Timor. Over 300 radios, many of them large enough for use in a community hall, along with thousands of batteries, were shipped to East Timor and distributed.

In a low-technology environment such as the one in East Timor in late 1999, counterintelligence operations primarily meant field intelligence work – teams of humans collecting information, asking questions. These teams played an important role complementing the other available information collection capabilities to enhance situational awareness. They also helped provide feedback on how successful the Information Operations efforts were being in influencing specific audience groups. Infantry battalion commanders who had, at first, expressed reluctance to include such elements as part of their units changed their tune within the first few days of the operation, even requesting additional support.

Today electronic warfare is widely considered to be a conventional component of any military force, and once it became clear that an operation was to be launched, resources were allocated and information became available. Once deployed, the coordination elements were retained in Dili but the Signals Squadron teams were deployed out with elements of the 3rd Brigade.[35] At battalion level, the lack of regularly working together on exercises meant that the Light Electronic Warfare Teams and the command elements were not conversant with battalion procedures, suggesting that more integrated training was required.[36]

Despite the concerted application of the various aspects of Information Operations, INTERFET would not have achieved its mission without the support of the contributing coalition countries. Consequently, a concerted effort was made by INTERFET and the higher Australian defence machinery to "shape and influence" in order to quickly muster the necessary international support, particularly from key allies and regional partners.[37] These troops came with their own professional skills and heritage, complementing the force with their unique strengths that contributed to the successful outcome of the mission. Many nations also provided military airlift assets – critical for the lodgement phase of the operation. It was no mean feat to enlist and then maintain the support from so many diverse countries with different cultures, languages and religions. Shaping perceptions and influencing opinions was an important part of the equation. This achievement alone is a mark of the success of the INTERFET operation in countering external pressures aimed at undermining the INTERFET coalition.

Arguably one of the most important aspects of US support for INTERFET was the critical moral, political and financial pressure applied at the APEC Forum in New Zealand in early September that helped persuade Indonesia to accede to the international intervention.[38] The United States went on to provide civil affairs, intelligence and communications support to INTERFET, as well as unique heavy-lift and combat-support capabilities – capabilities in short supply in the Australian Defence Force. The offshore presence of major components from a US Navy-Marine Amphibious Ready Group, with about 2,500 Marines, was an additional important demonstration of US interest and resolve as well as of alliance solidarity. Their pressure also shaped perceptions and helped influence the opinions of key stakeholders, convincing wavering minds in the militia and among Indonesian local commanders not to confront INTERFET directly, particularly in the vulnerable first few days of the deployment.

INTERFET had been created partly to help the United Nations Assistance Mission East Timor (UNAMET), which had supervised the fateful ballot on 30 August 1999. Once INTERFET had completed its essential tasks, particularly establishing a secure environment, the Australian government – keen to minimise costs and restore relations with Indonesia – was eager to shift responsibility for East Timor back to the United Nations. The United Nations resolved to establish a Transitional Authority for East Timor (UNTAET) to supervise the transition to full independence. While the fate of UNTAET is not the topic of this paper, it is encouraging to note that, despite the usual challenges associated with UN mandates, UNTAET has successfully managed to assist the East Timorese progress towards independence by providing a relatively peaceful environment. As commander of INTERFET, Major General Cosgrove understood that his mission was finite in scope and time. Once his mission was successfully completed, he set about ensuring that the United Nations was best placed to take over as soon as possible, and INTERFET handed over to UNTAET on 23 February 2000.

INTERFET's Broader Application

ALTHOUGH the threat environment in East Timor did not feature adversaries as heavily armed and equipped as those in Bosnia and other recent international military operations, the evidence suggests that the INTERFET mission could have been less successful and far more turbulent in character. Instrumental in its success and the avoidance of significant clashes was the clear understanding demonstrated by the troops of the higher commander's intent for the mission. Showing restraint throughout the operation, the INTERFET troops and their commanders appreciated the need to limit the collateral political effects that an escalation of violence would have generated, particularly with the rapid dissemination of news made possible by the ever-present mass media.

The adaptation of established practices and procedures to meet emergent circumstances resulted in a classic example of manoeuvre tailored for the information era, and featuring applied and controlled Information Operations. The manoeuvrist approach that was prevalent in East Timor would assist in the development of Australian Defence Force doctrine for Information Operations. Focused Information Operations efforts, incorporating fused and timely intelligence, allowed for careful and efficient vectoring of combat forces to hot spots in the early days that effectively unhinged the adversary in Dili, along the border with Indonesian West Timor, and throughout the remainder of East Timor. The coordinated application of stealthy and highly mobile Response Force assets – along with the light infantry, armour and air elements – quickly put the adversary off balance and gave INTERFET the clear psychological advantage. This was the case even while INTERFET was still outnumbered by the militia and Indonesian troops, which – at the lower levels and among territorial units at least – were prepared only grudgingly to accept INTERFET's mandate.

Operation *Stabilise* also demonstrates the significance of a shift from reliance on kinetic (or blast) effects to an emphasis on perception management as a key tool to accomplish a mission. With this approach, carefully crafted and timed actions, demonstrations and announcements were targeted at specific audiences as part of the efforts aimed at "shaping and influencing" – , that is, pressuring them to bend to the will of INTERFET. Such actions were only credible because they were backed up by highly trained, mobile and well-equipped forces on the ground that were in turn supported by the maritime forces and air elements. Overall, the mission succeeded because tactics and television coverage carried the day.[39]

Perception management did not replace the potent threat represented by the promise of force; and it is not the intention of this paper to denigrate the place of blast effects. Kinetic or blast effects are important and they remained important for INTERFET as well. The point is the degree to which we emphasise one over the other, not whether we emphasise one at the total expense of the other. They are not mutually exclusive. Yet commanders historically have paid little more than lip service to "shaping and influencing" the "battle-space" in non-kinetic ways. INTERFET demonstrated that this need not be the case.

The Australian commanders involved in launching Operation *Stabilise* demonstrated their understanding that an obsession with kinetic effects – blowing things up – can have long-term, detrimental effects on national and international interests. Adherents of a Clausewitzian approach would echo his call to "let us hear no more about generals who conquer without bloodshed." Yet, in conventional wars of the future, such concerns should perhaps be relegated to second place. As recent events have demonstrated, convention in armed conflict is becoming increasingly difficult to define. In multinational operations, however, where a fragile coalition plays a pivotal role, relegating such concerns can have long-term, drastic and damaging ramifications. Furthermore, in the case of Operation *Stabilise*, the effective display of military prowess in a measured, constrained and focused way laid the solid foundations for the nation building that is still occurring in East Timor today. The disciplined and careful application of force limited the collateral political damage to Australia's relations with regional neighbours, and particularly helped contain any political damage in relations with Indonesia. For instance, had less-disciplined troops not understood the intent of the mission in the tense first few days, unintended confrontations could have resulted in a far more difficult situation, further damaging Australia's relations with Indonesia and threatening to unravel the coalition that was so critical to INTERFET's legitimacy.

In the wake of the attacks of September 2001 and the US-led war on terrorism, strategists are re-examining old notions of warfare. The traditional focus on conventional high-intensity operations is in the process of shifting to address asymmetric threats and to influence the course of non-state-based conflicts. This new thinking stresses the use of public diplomacy, public affairs, and psychological warfare to achieve objectives while containing the "collateral damage."[40] The East Timor operation joins a long list of low-intensity military operations that have increasingly become the focus of military forces worldwide, but its innovative handling of information sets it apart from many previous military coalitions. Military theorists have argued and experience has shown that in contemporary land operations there may be no fronts, since fighting may occur almost anywhere in the theatre as the modal size of operational units becomes quite small – even well below the size of the typical 700-man battalion. In this context, information, in all its dimensions, can greatly enhance the capabilities of small units.[41] The emergent nature of conflict, as reflected in recent events, has echoes in the East Timor operation.

East Timor is predominantly rural, and in September 1999, it was a largely desolate and devastated land. Yet despite the predominantly rural setting, Operation *Stabilise* featured operations in urban areas. INTERFET troops exercised remarkable restraint, resulting in very few casualties and a speedy elimination of the threat from armed militia members wherever INTERFET troops deployed. Given the likelihood that future operations will include urban areas – where combat has historically been very costly in terms of casualties – the East Timor example merits attention. The troops' self-discipline, restraint under provocation, and focus on the higher commander's intent proved a noteworthy feature. Arguably, the approach taken by the Commander of INTERFET demonstrates a less manpower-intensive and a more media-savvy alternative to high-casualty urban operations that is more suitable for a country such as Australia, which has a challenging strategic environment and which, like Canada, is constrained by limited resources.[42]

The most obvious reason for examining the East Timor operation is that it contrasts markedly with widely criticised recent operations elsewhere, including Somalia, Haiti, Bosnia and Kosovo.[43] First, the East Timor crisis presented a more compelling challenge to Australia, the main force contributor, than had previous international missions in Africa, Asia and Europe. It also provided an opportunity for atonement over a sense among Australians of past neglect.[44] Australia's commitment of troops to East Timor helped ensure crucial popular support in Australia and elsewhere for the commitment of military forces. This sense of compulsion was arguably less evident for the Balkans.

The move to commit Australian troops was critical to enlist the support of ASEAN and other partners. Without Australia taking the lead, the others would not have participated. In turn, the wide support for Australia's lead role generated greater home-based enthusiasm for the operation. The spirit in which the troops approached their task to give the East Timorese "a fair go" reinforced this popular support.[45] Of equal if not greater significance to the outcome of Operation *Stabilise* was the robust wording of the mandate, explicitly authorising the use of lethal force, the specific and achievable tasks assigned, and the focused approach taken in executing them, where the end state was always in mind.

Studies also point to the strong and unified command-and-control arrangements as being pivotal in such operations. As Alan Ryan has observed,

> The Australian role as the dominant lead-nation flew in the face of the experience of most peace operations. UN and multilateral peacekeeping missions generally follow a more bureaucratic and collegiate model of command, where national representation often has priority over operational effectiveness. This mode of command has proven to be the 'Achilles heel' of high-intensity coalition peace operations time and again.[46]

In contrast, strong central command in East Timor allowed effective and comprehensive responses to issues as they arose, and in a timely manner that was suitable for the media and appropriate for specific audiences.

The INTERFET operation also has broader significance as an operation not led by the United States or the European Union, demonstrating how a small to medium-sized power like Australia or Canada can play a leading role among forces from many contributing nations.[47]

East Timor and Bosnia share a few common circumstances. Like Bosnia, the East Timor situation was tragic, involving many deaths. Bosnia, like Timor is also a clear example of a failed state that called for external intervention. Timor also faces transition challenges now that the United Nations has handed over to the Timorese. Although Bosnia has been an independent state since 1992 it, too, is undergoing a difficult transition, under international governance, toward political and economic viability.[48]

Apart from these commonalities, there are several unique circumstances that pertain to East Timor. First of all, East Timor experienced a confluence of fortunate circumstances that are not found in Bosnia or Kosovo. East Timor also has benefited from the rhetoric of reconciliation and from a higher quality of domestic political leadership; but Timor's land mass and population are small, presenting peacekeepers with a more manageable challenge than their contemporaries in Bosnia. Timor is also very poor with little prospect of independent wealth until at least 2005 when the Timor Sea oil and gas fields are expected to become productive.[49]

PERHAPS THIS OPERATION also serves to demonstrate what some have already argued: that Sun Tzu's notion of victory with minimal violence may displace Clausewitz's emphasis on the deadly clash of armies amid fog and friction.[50] Regardless, Operation *Stabilise* was no fool's errand. It was an operation launched with a sense of regret over the events of early September, but also with measured determination. This combination ensured that INTERFET was an unqualified military success, and those nations that contributed to it can be justifiably proud of their enduring legacy. Moreover, students of military operations can refer to it as a "by the book" example of applied military force for limited strategic aims in a coalition environment – an appropriate way to use military forces as an extension of national and international policy. Operation *Stabilise* also demonstrates the measured application of force with a manoeuvrist approach mind-set in what is arguably the most likely form of military conflict in the current era – asymmetric, low-intensity and urban operations.

This paper is written as my personal opinion. It is not an official account of events or government policy. The views expressed do not necessarily represent the views of the Australian Army, or the Australian Department of Defence.

Notes

1 See for instance: James Dunn, *Crimes Against Humanity in East Timor, January to October 1999: Their Nature and Causes*, 14 February 2001 (http://www.etan.org/news/2001a/dunn1.htm, downloaded 8 July 2001); Don Greenlees and Robert Garran, *Deliverance: The Inside Story of East Timor's Fight for Freedom* (Sydney: Allen and Unwin, 2002); Ian Martin, *Self-Determination in East Timor: The United Nations, the Ballot, and International Intervention* (Boulder: Lynne Rienner Publishers, 2001); *Guns and Ballot Boxes: East Timor's Vote for Independence*, ed. Damien Kingsbury (Clayton: Monash Asia Institute, 2000); H. MacDonald et al., *Masters of Terror: Indonesia's Military and Violence in East Timor in 1999*, Canberra Papers on Defence and Strategy, No. 145, Strategic and Defence Studies Centre, Canberra, 2002; John Martinkus, *A Dirty Little War* (Sydney: Random House, 2001).

2 See Ian Bostock, "By the Book: East Timor – An Operational Evaluation," *Jane's Defence Weekly*, 3 May 2000.

3 See, for instance, Bob Breen, *East Timor, Mission Accomplished* (Sydney: Allen & Unwin, 2001); Alan Ryan, *Primary Responsibilities and Primary Risks – Australian Defence Force Participation in the International Force East Timor*, Study Paper No. 304, Land Warfare Studies Centre, Canberra, November 2000; David Horner, "Testing the Australian Defence Force," in *Making the Australian Defence Force*, in the series *The Australian Centenary History of Defence* (Oxford: Oxford University Press, 2001); and Jeffrey Grey, *The Australian Army*, in the series *The Australian Centenary History of Defence* (Oxford: Oxford University Press, 2001). For a detailed description of the foreign policy background to the events, see *East Timor in Transition 1998–2000: An Australian Policy Challenge* (Canberra: Australian Department of Foreign Affairs and Trade, 2000). The economic and national interest dimensions are also explored in Nicholas J. Wheeler and Tim Dunne, "East Timor and the new humanitarian interventionism," *International Affairs*, 77/4 (2001), 805–827.

4 With a GDP of US$ 416.4 billion, Australia is ranked as only the fourteenth largest economy in the world. See *The World in 2000*, Economist Intelligence Unit, London.

5 See, for instance, Judy Thomson, *Winning With Intelligence* (Sydney: Australian Military History Publications, 2000).

6 Australia committed an infantry battalion to fight alongside the 173rd US Airborne Brigade in Bien Hoa in South Vietnam in 1965. The experience disturbed Australian commanders, who were concerned to reduce casualties and more effectively implement the Australian tactics of stealthy jungle patrols and ambushing. By 1966 Australia had increased its deployed force to an independent combined-arms infantry brigade in addition to its air and naval contributions. See, for instance, Bob Breen, *First to Fight: Australian Diggers, N.Z. Kiwis and U.S. Paratroopers in Vietnam, 1965–1966* (Sydney: Allen & Unwin, 1988); and Ian McNeill, *To Long Tan: The Australian Army and the Vietnam War 1950–1966* (Sydney: Allen & Unwin, 1993).

7 See, for instance, Alvin and Heidi Toffler's seminal work *War and Anti-War: Making Sense of Today's Global Chaos* (New York: Warner Books, 1993).

8 The Australian Defence Force has sought to define Information Operations into three components: offence, defence and support. Offensive Information Operations is defined as including: Electronic Attack (EW), Psychological Operations, Deception, Computer Network Attack, and Destruction. Defensive Information Operations includes: Information Assurance, Counter-intelligence, Counter Deception, Physical Security, Operational Security, Electronic Protection (EW), and

Counter PSYOPS. Support Information Operations includes: Intelligence; Electronic Support (EW); Public Information; Civil Affairs; Information Management; Command, Control, Communications and Intelligence (C3I) Systems Infrastructure; and Situational Awareness.

9 Email correspondence with author from Lieutenant Colonel Mark Smethurst, 26 July 2001.

10 Popular books read and absorbed by junior Australian Army officers in the mid-1990s included William Lindt's *Maneuver Warfare Handbook*; and Robert Leonhard, *The Art of Maneuver: Maneuver-Warfare Theory and AirLand Battle* (Novato, CA: Presidio Press, 1991).

11 Email correspondence from Lieutenant Colonel Mark Smethurst with author, 27 July 2001.

12 Ryan, *Primary Responsibilities and Primary Risks*, p. 39; and Horner, *Making The Australian Defence Force*, p. 1417.

13 Breen, *Mission Accomplished*, pp. 23–24.

14 Ryan, *Primary Responsibilities and Primary Risks*, p. 17.

15 Major General P. J. Cosgrove, "Peace-Making Subcontracted: The UN in East Timor," *The ANZAC Lecture*, Georgetown University, Washington, DC, 4 April 2000.

16 Breen, *Mission Accomplished*, p. 29.

17 Hamish MacDonald, "East Timor – Revealed: When Australia was forced onto a war footing," *Sydney Morning Herald*, 22 June 2001.

18 Horner, *Making the Australian Defence Force*, p. 38.

19 Breen, *Mission Accomplished*, p. 38.

20 Ibid., pp. 53–54.

21 For a discussion of how these elements were employed in 3 Brigade during Operation *Stabilise* see John Blaxland, "On Operations in East Timor: The Experiences of the Intelligence Officer, 3rd Brigade," *Australian Army Journal*, 2000.

22 Breen, *Mission Accomplished*, pp. 53–54.

23 Some have argued that this was courting a similar disaster to that which occurred to US forces in Mogadishu in 1993. What marks this incident as different is that, although it entailed risks, it had not been done before in Dili; it did not involve the firing of weapons from aircraft; it took place in an environment with no heavy weapons in use by militia groups; it was for a short duration only; and arguably, its positive effect justified the limited risk. Arguably, the sweep was deliberately timed to test the waters – to see what the reaction might be – but not to allow sufficient time to organise any form of coordinated reaction. Correspondence with author from Lieutenant Colonel Marcus Fielding and Major Chris Field, 30 July 2001.

24 Breen, *Mission Accomplished*, p. 55.

25 Major Chris Websdane, Officer Commanding, C Squadron, 2nd Cavalry Regiment, discussion with author, 2000.

26 Peter Cosgrove, "The night our boys stared down the barrel," *Age*, 21 June 2000, cited in Ryan, *Primary Risks and Primary Responsibilities*, p. 72.

27 See Breen, *Mission Accomplished*, pp. 56–57 (Com incident), 63 (on the border), 77–78 (Motaain) and 87 (October incidents).

28 Ryan, *Primary Risks and Primary Responsibilities*, pp. 55 and 66.

29 Ibid., pp. 41.

30 Andrew Garfield, "Information Operations as an Integrating Strategy," in Alan D. Campen and Douglas H. Dearth, *Cyberwar 3.0: Human Factors in Information Operations and Future Conflict* (Faifax, VA: AFCEA, 2001), p. 269; and correspondence with Lieutenant Colonel Chris Shine, 27 July 2001.

31 Breen, *Mission Accomplished*, p. 25.

32 Email correspondence with author from Lieutenant Colonel Marcus Fielding (the S3 of Headquarters 3rd Brigade during Operation *Stabilise*), 22 July 2001.

33 Interview with Admiral Chris Barrie, AO, RAN, Australian Defence headquarters, Canberra, 31 July 2000, cited in Ryan, *Primary Responsibilities and Primary Risks*, p. 2.

34 General C.C. Krulak, "The Strategic Corporal: Leadership in the Three Block War," *Marines Magazine*, January 1999.

35 Blaxland, "On Operations in East Timor," p. 9.

36 Field, correspondence with author, 30 July 2001.

37 Ground-forces capabilities were enhanced by contributions from Canada, New Zealand, Italy, Ireland, the Philippines, the Republic of Korea, Thailand, and the United Kingdom.

38 *East Timor in Transition*, p. 137.

39 Fielding, correspondence with author, 22 July 2001.

40 Richard Holbrooke, "Get the Message Out," *Washington Post*, 28 October 2001, p. B07.

41 John Arquilla and David Ronfeldt, "A New Epoch – and Spectrum – of Conflict," *In Athena's Camp: Preparing for Conflict in the Information Age*, eds. John Arquilla and David Ronfeldt (Washington, DC: RAND Corporation, National Defense Research Institute, 1997), chap. 1, p. 2.

42 See Brigadier M.A. Swan, Director General Future Land Warfare – Army, *Land Warfare Conference 2000*, Melbourne, 2000, pp. 2–8.

43 In Somalia, arguably only UNOSOM II "failed," UNOSOM I (Humanitarian) and UNITAF having been relatively successful, but the overall outcome of the combined missions was not successful. The initial deployment to Haiti proceeded well, but today Haiti's problems reflect fundamental flaws in the original mission objectives. In the Balkans, UNPROFOR was a failure and even IFOR/SFOR have met with what at best is described as limited success. The Kosovo air campaign could also be described as less than successful and KFOR faces vast challenges. See Gary T. Dempsey with Roger W. Fontaine, *Fool's Errands – America's Recent Encounters with Nation Building* (Washington, DC: Cato Institute, 2001).

44 At great personal expense, many East Timorese had assisted Australian Commandos to fight Japanese troops in East Timor from 1942 to 1943. Many Australians have long felt obligated to them for that assistance and have been ashamed over Australia's unilateral recognition of Indonesia's 1975 annexation of East Timor.

45 Breen, op. cit., p. ix.

46 Alan Ryan, *Primary Responsibilities and Primary Risks*, LWSC Study Paper 304, p. 83 *From Desert Storm to East Timor: Australia, the Pacific and 'New Age' Coalition Operations*, Paper No. 302, Land Warfare Studies Centre, Canberra, January 2000.

47 Twenty-two nations contributed forces to INTERFET. INTERFET's peak strength was 11,500 personnel of whom 5,500 were Australians. Breen, op. cit., p. 5.

48 Presentation in Montreal by Dr Mark Baskin, Research Director, Pearson Peacekeeping Centre, 16 May 2002.

49 Ibid.

50 Arquilla and Ronfeldt, *In Athena's Camp*, p. 18.

CHARLES C. PENTLAND

Brussels, Bosnia and Beyond: The European Union's Search for a Role in South Eastern Europe

Introduction

FOR THE EUROPEAN UNION (EU) the violent disintegration of Yugoslavia presented a double challenge – in part strategic, in part existential. The strategic challenge was how to organize and lead an international response to a crisis in its own back yard. The existential challenge was that events in the Balkans, and the political culture from which they flowed, seemed the antithesis of everything the EU stood for, namely a prosperous, secure and integrated Europe. In the first half of the 1990s Brussels largely failed to meet the strategic challenge, particularly with respect to the war in Bosnia. Since the signing, at Dayton in late 1995, of the General Framework Agreement for Peace (GFAP) in Bosnia, which marked the nadir of Europe's influence in the region, it has, however, gradually begun to fashion a more coherent and effective response and to reassert the leadership it had so boldly and – as it turned out – prematurely, proclaimed a decade earlier.

This story can be told as a classic narrative of hubris, humiliation and hope of redemption. It shows the EC in 1991 asserting and being granted leadership in the Balkan crisis and then conducting a reactive policy in the absence of a coherent strategy and bereft of the tools

CHARLES C. PENTLAND is Professor of Political Studies and Director of the Centre for International Relations at Queen's University.

to impose it. It shows the EU drifting to the periphery of international action as the crisis intensifies in Bosnia, and remaining frustrated in the wings as the US belatedly but forcefully imposes its will and negotiates a peace at Dayton. It shows the EU assuming a modest, low-profile role in the first three years of the international protectorate for Bosnia but then, after the Kosovo campaign in 1999, re-emerging with a comprehensive vision for the Balkans and a renewed claim to leadership.

There is, however, a darker, more nuanced subtext to this tale, which speaks to the deeper existential challenge. Questions that were raised a decade ago about the EU's ability to manage conflict in its neighbourhood remain unanswered. Is the EU equipped, not just in the institutions, processes and instruments of its common foreign and security policy, but in its way of thinking, to deal with ethnic and sectarian conflict? Should it be aspiring to an increased presence in the "high politics" of security in the Balkans, or sticking to what it knows and does best – trade and aid? Will a regional policy based on international protectorates and political and economic conditionality serve to bring the Balkans to Brussels or, in perpetuating dependency, does it risk keeping Brussels in the Balkans for longer than is good for anyone? And in the mix of motives driving the EU and its member-states, what is the balance between making the Balkans safe for democracy, markets and human rights, and the new Europe's search for coherence, power and status in the post-Cold War world?

These questions are of interest not just to Europeans but to their friends and allies across the Atlantic. Canada's involvement in southeastern Europe – first as a peacekeeper in the wars of Yugoslavia's dissolution, subsequently as part of the post-Dayton international presence – is as long as that of the EU. It has shared many of Europe's assumptions and illusions about how to manage ethnic conflict, having its own aversion to the prospect of a world where ethnicity trumps civil nationalism. Like the EU, too, Canada has found itself struggling to define the right mix of hard and soft power to contribute to European security. Moreover, as the US draws down its presence in the Balkans to deploy elsewhere, Canada, like Europe, faces the demoralizing possibility of yet another long, Cyprus-like commitment in a seemingly intractable region. Finally, Canada has an interest in how the EU itself copes with southeastern Europe and what sort of regional and global power it shows itself to be in the process.

The European Union
and the Balkans after Dayton

AYTON was not only a negotiated settlement for Bosnia; it was an employment programme for multilateral organizations. To NATO went the all-important job of enforcement. To the OSCE went a variety of political and security-related tasks such as elections-monitoring. To the EU went the leading role in the economic reconstruction of Bosnia and in the gradual integration of the Balkans into the Brussels-centred European economic complex. In addition, in conjunction with the WEU it was to continue its search for a stable political, administrative, and policing framework for Mostar – a task made daily more difficult by rampant organized crime and deteriorating inter-communal relations in the city.

However marginal it had become by the end of the Bosnian war, the EU was bound to emerge as a central player in the regime imposed by the Dayton Agreement. The Agreement – the General Framework and its 11 Annexes containing the specifics – says little about the all-important task of economic reconstruction except for Annex 10 which refers to "civilian implementation" under the direction of a High Representative. It says nothing about the EU. Nevertheless it was clear from the outset that among all the actors in the international community the EU was uniquely placed by virtue of interest and capacity to take the lead in post-conflict peace-building for Bosnia. Some of the dynamics of 1991 reappeared: the US was once more reluctant to undertake a long-term engagement in a region it deemed to be of dubious strategic significance, while the Europeans were once more eager to prove themselves in their own back yard. In early 1996, however, the Americans were prepared to take on a robust enforcement role through NATO and IFOR – if only for a year initially – while the EU's efforts would be embedded in a multilateral, multi-institutional regime in which it would be the prime, but not the sole, player. That regime has now been in place for seven years, with little sign of winding up in the near future. Events in the wider Balkan region, however, particularly the Kosovo war in the spring of 1999, changed perceptions and policies in Brussels and Washington and marked a turning point for the Bosnian international protectorate. The discussion that follows looks first at EU policies and actions from the beginning of 1996 to mid-1999, and then at the more dramatic developments of the past three years.

From Dayton to "Allied Force"

IN THE THREE YEARS from the signing of the Dayton Agreement to NATO's intervention in Kosovo, the EU's presence in the emergent Bosnian protectorate and in the wider Balkans seemed, at least on the surface, a continuation of the marginality and subordination to which it had been reduced in the heat of the Bosnian war. In Bosnia, as the international presence struggled to establish its priorities, institutions and credibility, the EU's work in economic reconstruction got quietly under way, overshadowed and hampered by the political and security issues that dominated the early agenda. With respect to the other successor states of the former Yugoslavia – Slovenia aside – its leverage was limited and its policies tentative. By and large, the EU's role, as before Dayton, remained politically modest and mostly focused on Bosnia.

The Bosnian protectorate consists of a military and a civilian element. On the military side, EU member states have contributed forces to the Implementation Force (IFOR) and the Stabilization Force (SFOR) that succeeded it at the beginning of 1997. These forces operate, of course, under the NATO chain of command, although not without increasing coordination under the auspices of the emerging European Security and Defence Policy. The EU as such, however, is a major component of the civilian part of the Dayton regime for Bosnia, where it is charged with overseeing the task of economic reconstruction. In addition, most EU members are involved individually in these tasks. The civilian side is under the overall direction of the Office of the High Representative (OHR). The High Representative, who reports to the Peace Implementation Conference (PIC) and through it to the UNSC, has responsibility for the post-war peace-building activities of the international agencies that constitute the regime. Besides the EU, these include the UN Mission in Bosnia and Herzegovina (UNMIBH) whose mandate includes promotion of the rule of law and the reform and training of civilian policing under the IPTF, the UNHCR (refugee returns), the OSCE (human rights, media, elections), and financial institutions such as the World Bank Group, the IMF, the EIB and the EBRD. It has been understood from the start that the High Representative will be an EU national, as indeed all four have been.

From the outset the principal instruments of EU policy have been its traditional ones: access and aid. In this first period, however, the emphasis with respect to Bosnia was overwhelmingly on the latter. True, more than 80 percent of Bosnia's exports had duty-free access to EU markets, but this meant little in the almost total absence of a functioning economy. On the other hand, the EU quickly emerged as the largest single donor of humanitarian and economic development assistance to the devastated country. From 1996 through 1999 it provided almost 1.35 B euros in this form, including over 780 M euros through the PHARE and Obnova programmes, over 390 B euros through the ECHO humanitarian assistance programme, and smaller amounts to administer Mostar and to provide support for refugee returns, demining, media, democracy and human rights, and the balance of payments. Aid through PHARE was specifically directed to projects in support of the Dayton Agreement, such as institution-building or the development of "civil society," while Obnova had a broader mandate for reconstruction, including support of refugee returns.[1]

The extent and effectiveness of these programmes was hostage to the political and security context of those first three post-conflict years. In 1996, the first year of the Dayton regime, the secure environment on which all else would depend was not yet fully established, despite the presence of the 60,000-strong IFOR. Fragility and uncertainty led to an emphasis on emergency response, improvisation and to corresponding delays in more foundational work. Moreover, the priorities of the international presence were heavily influenced – some would say skewed – by the Americans' insistence on holding elections as early as possible to man the representative bodies set up by the GFAP at the national, entity and municipal levels. This insistence had less to do with the political state of play in Bosnia than with the American election year and the perceived need to show evidence of progress and hope of an early exit.[2]

The saga of successive elections and their sub-optimal results – voters' persistence in electing the usual nationalist and often anti-Dayton suspects – continued through 1997 and 1998. These patterns, particularly at the municipal level, drastically slowed the rate of refugee returns, which in turn limited what could be undertaken in respect of longer-term reconstruction and development. The existence, despite IFOR, of significant areas of non-compliance with Dayton – not to mention violence – in both the RS and the Croat areas of the Federation, also meant that economic and humanitarian progress was very unevenly distributed across the country and virtually nonexistent in many areas. Much of the "dull stuff"[3] that the EU was doing had the virtue of providing immediate, practical returns to ordinary Bosnians – public transport up and running, houses rebuilt, water and electricity restored, and so forth – but in the absence of a more coherent, long-term and higher-profile strategy, Brussels risked always being vulnerable to the sometimes-unintended local effects of others' policies.

Recognizing this, the EU began, in 1997 and 1998, to give more coherence and focus to its work in Bosnia. Taking its cues from the 1997 London meeting of the PIC, the Commission began to focus more closely on the crucial linkage between refugee returns (to which the bulk of its early spending had been directed) and economic reconstruction. Other areas given new priority were economic reform (privatization and freeing of markets), job-creation, rebuilding of technical and social infrastructure, institution-building and administrative reform. From 1998 on, the three principal foci of EU action became: first, institutions – the national-level administration, the customs service (corrupt and ineffective in controlling borders, especially between the RS and the FRY), broadcasting, the courts, and the Dayton institutions for human rights, the ombudsman and property claims; second, economic reform – modernizing the banking and financial systems, clearing obstacles to trade and investment, promoting privatization, developing local industries and small and medium-sized enterprises, and re-establishing agriculture; third, social cohesion and development – particularly in health and education.

In the first three years of the Dayton regime, therefore, the EU emerged as an omnipresent if low-profile player in the complex enterprise of rebuilding and reforming the Bosnian state, economy and society. In addition to its role as a provider of economic and technical assistance and as overall coordinator of the international reconstruction project, the EU retained its difficult governance of Mostar, until replaced in January 1997 by the OHR. Brussels also encouraged, and later took the lead in, the Royaumont Initiative, a multilateral effort to encourage and harness the efforts of NGOs, initially in Bosnia but eventually in the Balkan region as a whole. It was learning on the job, trying where possible to adapt development and peace-building lore from experience elsewhere, and engaged in constant self-assessment and adjustment to the shifting circumstances of those early years. The EU did appear, however, to be searching without much success for a more coherent strategy for

Bosnia and the region – one that would not only do its appointed task better but also move the EU into a more powerful and prominent position in the complex of overlapping and often competing agencies that made up the Bosnian protectorate.

One symbol and, in a sense, surrogate, for this more powerful European presence on the ground, was the OHR, particularly once the first High Representative, Carl Bildt, was succeeded in mid-1997 by Carlos Westendorp, who was able and willing to wield the increased powers granted the OHR by the Bonn PIC in December of that year. Over the next two years Westendorp took a series of decisive, if controversial, actions to sack duly-elected but anti-Dayton officials and to impose – in the absence of Bosnian government decisions – national institutions including a flag, currency and non-communal licence-plates. As noted earlier, the High Representative answered not to the EU but to the PIC and, ultimately, to the UN Security Council. Nevertheless, as an EU national he became identified as the bearer of Europe's colours while the EU itself worked less visibly and forcefully in the trenches of reconstruction.

If the EU's role in Bosnia during this initial phase was constrained by circumstances on the ground, by great-power politics and by turf-wars among the multilateral agencies in the protectorate, its role in the broader Balkan region was limited by the varying domestic conditions and international postures of the Yugoslav successor states, which made a coherent overall strategy difficult to envisage. Only in the case of Slovenia, whose secession had precipitated the crisis in 1991 and which had been rapidly approaching EU economic, social and political standards since then, did Brussels have a clear, workable policy – accession to membership. Slovenia signed a "Europe" Association Agreement on June 10, 1996. On the same day it applied for membership in the EU and, thanks to its zealous efforts at transition, found itself among the first six candidates for accession with which the EU opened formal negotiations in the fall of 1998. Over the next four years Slovenia proved an especially adept navigator of the 31 chapters into which the negotiations were structured, and was among the ten applicants accepted, in December 2002, for admission to the EU in 2004.

Rather against expectations, Macedonia (the FYROM) remained relatively quiescent, as it had during the Bosnian war under the watchful eye of UNPREDEP. In 1997 it, like the rest of the Balkans, fell under the new regional approach enunciated by the Council of

Ministers, which applied economic and political conditionality to the development of bilateral relations. This country-by-country approach was a logical response to the variety of national situations in the region. The EU's global judgement at this point was that, with the exception of Slovenia, none of the successor states was a credible candidate for accession to the EU in the near future.

In its relations with Croatia, the EU was resolute – despite some differences among member-states – in applying conditionality. Rhetoric aside, however, it was clear that Croatia was unlikely under President Tudjman, to undertake the kind of political and economic reforms needed to fulfill its announced aim of joining the EU and NATO. Indeed, Zagreb's open flouting of the Dayton agreement by supporting the secessionist Croat project in Herzegovina, and its continuing intransigence on the issue of Serb refugee returns to the Krajina and other regions from which they had been driven in 1995, kept tensions high in the relationship. The EU linked prospects for better trade access and aid for reconstruction, with progress on refugee returns, to no great effect. In April 1998, for example, the EU Foreign Ministers agreed to boycott a Croatian Refugee Return and Reconstruction Conference unless the Tudjman government could show that a credible and workable returns procedure was in place. Zagreb, however, continued to speak European but to act Balkan.

As a partner in dialogue, the Federal Republic of Yugoslavia – now a rump state consisting of Serbia and Montenegro – proved every bit as intransigent as Croatia. Here, too, the EU attempted to use its traditional tools of improved trade access and economic aid to encourage political and economic reform and to sustain the FRY's support of the Dayton Agreement. At the end of 1996 it made a *demarche* to Belgrade demanding respect for the recent Serbian election results and an end to the repression of demonstrations against the regime. In January 1997, the EU Council of Ministers endorsed the OSCE's Gonzalez Report of December 27, which had confirmed the opposition's electoral victory, and called for free media, free and fair elections, and respect for human rights in the FRY. At the end of January Brussels granted the FRY Autonomous Trade Preferences (ATP) for the balance of the year, to be reviewed if no progress had been made by then on implementing the Gonzalez Report. The preferences were duly withdrawn on December 29. This pattern continued into 1998 until overtaken by more ominous developments in Kosovo.

After "Allied Force":
Again the Hour of Europe?

NATO's action in Kosovo in the spring of 1999 had a dramatic effect on the Balkan region, transforming its political landscape and confronting the EU with new risks and opportunities. Along with political change in Croatia, gradual shifts in great-power involvement, and developments in the EU itself, the Kosovo intervention moved Brussels decisively toward a comprehensive strategy for the former Yugoslavia – and indeed beyond that to the whole of what came to be called "south eastern Europe" – in which it could again aspire to leadership of the international community's efforts. To some, it might have seemed that after a decade the clock was once more chiming the hour of Europe. This time around, would the EU be able to answer the bell?

The most significant effect of NATO's action was the destabilization of the regime in Belgrade, resulting eventually in its electoral defeat and the extradition of Slobodan Milosevic to the ICTFY in the Hague to face charges of war crimes and crimes against humanity. Political change in 2000 and 2001 at both the federal and Serbian levels of government meant an almost instant inflow of western humanitarian and economic assistance, and an equally swift transformation of the FRY from rogue state to the centrepiece of western-led strategies for the economic reconstruction and political rehabilitation of the region. In truth, the comprehensive regional approach that the EU had begun to fashion as early as 1998 made little sense without the participation of Serbia, the largest of the former Yugoslav republics, located astride the key east-west and north-south transport corridors.

After the fall of Milosevic, in fact, there was even some concern in Brussels that recognition of Serbia's centrality would combine with the latent pro-Serb tendencies of some EU members to produce a rush to Belgrade at the expense of other states in the region. In the end, the EU did provide significant amounts of aid while nonetheless continuing to adhere to the western policy of linkage to Serbia's cooperation with the Hague tribunal. Some American critics suggest, however, that the Europeans have been less than rigorous about maintaining that linkage.[4]

With respect to Montenegro, Serbia's junior partner in the FRY (and now – at least temporarily – in the newly-constituted state of Serbia and Montenegro), the growing secessionist movement in the late 1990s posed a dilemma for the international community. On the one hand, it was a useful diversion for, and source of pressure against, the Milosevic regime. On the other, the west (especially the EU) had set its face against the further dismantling of Balkan states, given the continuing fragility of territorial arrangements in Bosnia under Dayton, and the crises in Kosovo and Macedonia. Sensitive also to the need for a stable post-Milosevic FRY at the heart of its regional strategy, the EU assumed the role of mediator between Belgrade and Podgorica, managing with some difficulty to broker an agreement which changed the constitutional relationship between the two republics while leaving the door open for a possible referendum on Montenegrin secession in the near future.

Another direct consequence of NATO's action in Kosovo was the destabilization of the delicate ethnic balance in the FYROM, first by the influx of massive numbers of Kosovar Albanians and later through the radicalizing influence of the KLA on the Albanian minority in the west of the country. Alongside the US, the EU's response was to mediate between the two Macedonian communities in attempt to find a constitutional adjustment that would satisfy at least the moderates on both sides. Clearly convinced that this was just the sort of problem for which the CFSP was designed, the EU was noticeably assertive in pursuing the lead role through its twin foreign-policy heads – External Relations Commissioner Chris Patten and the CFSP High Representative Javier Solana. All the same, the Americans tend to claim at least equal credit for the agreement signed between Macedonia's Slavs and Albanians at Ohrid in August 2001.[5] As the need for a follow-on operation to replace NATO's Amber Fox security force for the peace-monitors in the FYROM became apparent, the EU offered its services in the form of a force under the new ESDP. For over a year its implementation was held hostage to the continuing dispute between Greece and Turkey over the EU's prospective use of NATO resources for its new rapid-reaction force, but is now set for the spring of 2003.

In working to seize the opportunities and manage the risks arising in the wake of the Kosovo operation, the EU not only resorted to its traditional tools of trade and aid, but sought an active and prominent place for itself in the international community's efforts to mediate the ensuing domestic conflicts on neighbouring countries. Its motives here appear mixed. In part they had to do with thwarting irredentist and secessionist movements in the region, drawing on a general presumption among EU members against ethnically-driven solutions and a specific concern about spillover into Bosnia. In part, too, they flow from a reflex to demonstrate that the CFSP can go beyond mere rhetoric to solve substantive if modest-scaled problems – the same reflex that had first drawn Brussels into the Yugoslav crisis in 1991.

Independently of events in Kosovo, political change also came to Croatia beginning with the death of President Franjo Tudjman in late 1999, followed by the defeat of his HDZ party and the election of a moderate president eager to take the country into NATO and the EU. The new leadership has been able to face down residual nationalist opposition in breaking Zagreb's ties with the extremist Croats in Herzegovina, and in beginning to permit the return of its Serb refugees. Both actions should have positive effects on Bosnia, both for refugee returns there and for national cohesion. The EU was quick to respond to these developments by acknowledging Croatia's "European vocation," offering aid and trade concessions that had been denied the previous regime, and bringing it into the new regional framework for south eastern Europe.[6]

The emergence of that regional framework in the last three years is the most important innovation in the EU's strategy for the successor states of the former Yugoslavia. Its two principal elements are the Stabilization and Association Agreements (SAA) and the Stability Pact for South Eastern Europe. Both elements represent a decisive shift to a comprehensive approach to the region – the SAA by offering parallel paths to eventual EU membership to all associated states, the Pact by creating a multilateral context for regional cooperation. In the first case, EU leadership is a given; in the second, it is there for the taking.

The SAAs are an adaptation of the Europe Agreements signed with the three Baltic states, the four Visegrad states of central Europe, Romania, Bulgaria and Slovenia in the mid-1990s. They contain provisions for trade liberalization, economic and technical assistance, and political dialogue. Most importantly, they hold out the promise of eventual membership in the EU once the state has transformed itself by meeting a demanding set of political and economic conditions. In an initial phase each country undertakes reforms to bring it to the point where the EU will offer it an SAA. Among the Balkan states only Macedonia (signed in April 2001) and Croatia (October 2001) have so far reached that point. Once an SAA has come into force it governs the next phase of transition in which the state gradually adopts the EU's legislative *acquis*, applies for membership and readies itself for accession. The assumption underlying the SAA strategy is that its incentives and disciplines will do for the Balkan states what they did for Spain and Portugal and appear to be doing for the states of central and eastern Europe – modernize and pacify.

The Stability Pact had its origins in discussions among the EU foreign ministers in 1998. It was given form and direction in early 1999 by the German presidency of the EU and signed at Cologne on June 10.[7] The parties – about thirty states (including those from the region) and a dozen international agencies – reaffirmed their commitment at a summit in Sarajevo on July 30. The Pact's aim is to "strengthen the countries of south eastern Europe in their efforts to foster peace, democracy, respect for human rights and economic prosperity in order to achieve stability in the whole region."[8] By September 1999 a complex structure had been put in place, involving three "Working Tables" – for democratization and human rights, for economic reconstruction and for security – plus a Regional Table to coordinate them under the chairmanship, initially, of Bodo Hombach (a close political associate of German Chancellor Schroeder). He has been succeeded by an Austrian, Erhard Busek.

In its brief life the Pact has been able to generate considerable financial support for both its Quick Start projects (designed to show immediate payoffs) and its longer-term programmes. A first regional donors' conference on March 2000 raised almost 2.4 B euros, while a second, in October 2001, raised another 3 B euros. Further funds are made available by governments, international agencies and other donors on an *ad hoc* basis. The three Working Tables have directed these resources to projects overseen by participating agencies. For example, Table 1 has task forces on human rights and minorities and on gender issues (OSCE), on good governance (Council of Europe) and on education and youth; Table 2's economic development goals were set out by the World Bank, with projects being overseen by the EIB (infrastructure) and the EBRD (private-sector development); and Table 3 has two sub-tables, one dealing with arms control, de-mining and disaster preparedness and prevention, the other with EU "third-pillar" issues such as corruption, policing, immigration and the rule of law.

The Pact naturally invites comparison with the Marshall Plan, particularly inasmuch as it controls financial resources which dwarf those available to the region, and which it offers on condition that the recipients take initiatives to reform and to integrate on a regional basis. The EU's members constitute half of the participant states and three-quarters of the donors; they are also represented through the EU Commission, the EIB and the EBRD. Brussels seeks to complement the

Pact with the SAA strategy and with a new, integrated aid programme, Community Assistance for Reconstruction, Democratization and Stabilization (CARDS), replacing the previous patchwork of different programmes for the region. All this looks like a well-designed comprehensive strategy for the region with a built-in EU claim to leadership.

Although barely three years old, the Pact has already been subject to criticism both from within the region and from without. While it is arguably too early to judge its results, skeptics have focused on issues of duplication, structural excess, procedural complexity and slowness to deliver results – qualities some argue are characteristic of anything having to do with the EU. A related criticism of both the Pact and the SAA, is that the region's problems are too urgent to allow for the deliberate, complex processes of conditionality to work their transformative magic on the states of south eastern Europe. The EU, it is argued, should be more open and less demanding, lest it frustrate the well-intentioned in those states and open the way to nationalist backlash.[9]

Where has the emergence of a comprehensive EU approach to the region since the Kosovo campaign left the international protectorate in Bosnia? On the one hand, the changes of regime in Croatia and the FRY remove – or at least greatly reduce – centrifugal forces at work on the territorial arrangements agreed at Dayton. Moreover, the regional cooperation and integration promised by the Stability Pact can go a long way to restoring the links – markets, infrastructure, even social and cultural ties – between Bosnia and its neighbours, from which it once benefited in the Yugoslav federation. On the other hand, the diversion of western attention to the returned prodigals in Zagreb and Belgrade, and the perception that the main regional security risks now centre on Kosovo, may mean fewer resources devoted to Bosnia's ongoing problems. Continuing cuts to SFOR are the most visible manifestation of this trend; these seem driven more by needs elsewhere (especially after September 11, 2001) than by strong evidence that security on the ground has become self-sustaining.

EU policy in Bosnia now sits at the intersection of the seven-year old multilateral structures and processes based on Dayton, and the broader regional approach just described. From 1999 on, the Stability and Association process and the Stability Pact provided the governing framework. In 2000, expressing the mix of frustration and optimism so often encountered in Bosnia's benefactors, Brussels published a Road Map setting out eighteen steps it considered vital that Bosnia take toward implementing the Dayton agenda of economic, administrative and political reform, before the EU would consider undertaking a feasibility study on initiating negotiations for an SAA. Many of these referred to reforms in public administration, property law and the like, on which there had been years of delay or backsliding by local leaders. In Chris Patten's words: "We wanted Bosnia to be absolutely clear about what they needed to do: and we are not about to change the goal posts. But I very much regret that so far too few goals have been scored."[10] A major theme in much EU comment on Bosnia has become that of "ownership." In the face of local intransigence or stalemate, High Representative Wolfgang Petritsch (1999–2002) had felt compelled (as has his successor, Lord Ashdown) to continue the practice of imposing necessary change by fiat in the name of the international community. This got things done, but at the price of Bosnians' sense of responsibility for their own future. As Patten said with respect to the prospect of an SAA: "Unless we insist on Bosnia keeping its side of the bargain, we risk creating a permanent international dependency which will never be able to dig itself out of its own difficulties."[11]

As elsewhere in the Balkans, the EU's main assistance programmes for Bosnia from 1991 to 2000 (PHARE and Obnova) have now been folded into the new CARDS programme. In 2001, its first year of operation, CARDS allocated 105 M euros to Bosnia, of which over one-third (37.3 M euros) went to support refugee returns. The next largest spending categories were institutional capacity-building (16.7) and infrastructure development (14.3).[12] Although the overall total is more than matched by member-states' bilateral aid, it is worth noting that the 2001 figure is less than half the annual figure for the years 1996 through 1998, and 20 percent less than that for 1999. The EU's own critical assessment of Bosnia's progress does not, therefore, seem to have prevented it from reducing its assistance for reconstruction and development, perhaps to the benefit of other states in the region. (Although not Kosovo, to which CARDS aid has also been cut.[13]) In that respect, however, it may simply be in line with the general tendency of the international community to de-emphasize Bosnia in favour of other areas perceived to be more pressing. On the other hand, an EU police-training training mission (EUPM) has this year taken over from the UN's police-training mission (IPTF) in Bosnia – in this case the reduced level of the operation actually reflects a degree of success on the part of the UN mission.

Changes in the international community's pattern of involvement in the Balkans, initiated by the Kosovo crisis, have accelerated in the past year. For a variety of reasons, both Russia and the United States have been reducing their presence in the region, including their respective military roles in Bosnia. On a regional basis, the EU has been organizing to take up the slack and assume leadership of the transition process. This makes sense as a division of labour. As Patten says, the Balkan states "identify the EU with security, with jobs, with a decent and rising standard of living, with the rule of law upheld by accountable, democratic, clean public institutions, a system in which rights of minorities are protected by law, not by carving out territory. They recognize the EU as probably the most successful conflict prevention and resolution mechanism in history. And they desperately want to be part of it. This gives the EU enormous leverage."[14] But if the EU, like the rest of the international community, redirects too much of its attention away from Bosnia to the broader region or beyond, it risks losing some of that leverage in a country where, by its own admission, too many of the big problems remain unresolved.

Conclusion

I T TOOK TEN YEARS, and the seismic jolt of Kosovo, for the EU to fashion a coherent, long-term leadership strategy for itself in Bosnia and south eastern Europe. After much trial and many errors its response to the strategic challenge of the Yugoslav wars of succession now seems in place. But what of the existential challenge?

First, Yugoslavia forced the EU, really for the first time, to confront the issue of ethnic and sectarian conflict. The crisis challenged the very foundations of the Brussels doctrine of "civilian power" – that the promise of economic rewards, including the possibility of association and even full membership, and/or the threat of economic sanctions, can pacify countries or regions torn by conflict, including conflict flowing from the demands of ethnic nationalism. It raised the possibility that some protagonists cannot be bought off or otherwise persuaded by such means. What made the Yugoslav case existentially unsettling for Brussels was thus the seeming irrationality of its ethnic wellsprings, which put in question the EC's liberal, rationalist premises. These held that ethnic nationalism was a relic, quaint and folkloric at best, politically and economically irrational at worst, whose demise was pre-ordained in the process of economic modernization and integration. But in this case it seemed as if the rational inducements of economic assistance and market access and the deterrent effects of sanctions had little impact on the course of the conflict, seriously altering neither the perceptions nor the priorities nor the conduct of the belligerents. As one observer has noted, "aggressive nationalism has so far been largely insensitive to economic incentives."[15]

Ten years' experience seems not to have altered much in the EU's governing doctrine with respect to ethnic nationalism. The consistent theme of its policies in Bosnia, Kosovo, Montenegro and Macedonia has been to reject proposals for ethnically-based "solutions" such as partition or secession. The underlying premises of the SAA programme and the Stability Pact, too, are consistent with the notion that economic incentives will indeed trump atavistic urges – this time around. The difference now, it is assumed, is that the peoples of the Balkans and their leaders have a decade's experience of the consequences of those urges, and that Europe's response is more resolute.

Second, in 1991 the EC saw the Yugoslav crisis as an opportunity to give its emergent CFSP a running start. In its eagerness to get beyond the limits of "civilian power" it forgot where its comparative advantage lay, and how fragile the bases still were for any venture into the realms of high politics. If its capacity to influence others had been demonstrated anywhere, it was in the realms of trade and aid. By contrast, what the proposed CFSP should do, and how it should do it, were still matters of fierce debate in the pre-Maastricht IGC, and its predecessor, EPC, was hardly an unblemished success. In retrospect, then, it was a mistake for the EC to assume the mantle of leadership thrust upon it by the US, since it did not yet have the capacity to act as a full-service great power.

Ten years later, what has changed? The EU has undoubtedly made progress in acquiring the diplomatic and military attributes of a true global actor. The treaties of Maastricht and Amsterdam, combined with a lot of real-world experience, have given more substance to the CFSP. And the British-French agreement at St Malo in December 1998, on the creation of an EU intervention force, promises the EU a military capacity it lacked in 1991. That said, there is an eerie familiarity about some trends. The US once more looks as if wishes to vacate the Balkans and turn leadership over to the EU, which once more seems eager to embrace it. To the extent that leadership means coordinating reconstruction and development and promoting integration, Brussels is better equipped to lead than it was ten years ago. But if it also requires the credible capacity to use force, it is not. The St Malo project remains a work in progress, with some doubts expressed that it will meet its 2003 deadline with the needed capacity truly in place. That force would not, of course, be able to do what NATO did in Serbia in 1999, or even in the Bosnian end-game. But it will have to be visibly available for more modest tasks, lest Europe once more find itself handing off leadership in a future Balkan crisis because it is "not ready."

Third, the civilian side of its Balkan policy raises questions about the EU's sense of itself as the arbiter of Europe's destiny. The Bosnian and Kosovo protectorates, the SAA process and the Stability Pact are premised on asymmetries of economic power and on the capacity – legitimized by the international community – of the strong to persuade the weak through rewards and punishment and where necessary, to intervene and manage their internal affairs directly. This is the Balkan variant of a policy the EU has fashioned over the past decade for central and eastern Europe: sustaining the virtuous circle of free markets, democracy, human rights and regional security by liberalizing access to its markets, acting as the principal external patron of a Marshall-type investment and trade-liberalization plan, and promising admission to full EU membership for qualified candidates sooner rather than later.

This policy embodies the forthright assertion that Brussels is the destiny of the Balkan states, a proposition now endorsed by all the region's governments. The problem for most of them, however, is how to get there from where they are. An end to either of the international protectorates is nowhere in sight. A culture of dependency has become entrenched, especially in Bosnia. The SAA process, on the other hand, seems to be progressing with some states, although again Bosnia is the laggard. Here, as in its relations with some central and eastern European states, Brussels is discovering the limits of what it sometimes assumes to be an irresistible power to attract: alienation in the face of western arrogance and self-righteousness is hardly new to the Balkans. The Stability Pact shows some of the same defects. In addition, the approach it represents cuts two ways. On the one hand, it usefully anchors Bosnia in a regional framework providing some insurance against abandonment. On the other, it may result in EU resources being spread thinner or diverted from Bosnia, as already seems to be happening.

Finally, the question of interests – national and other. In the early 1990s, a consensus on the need to act, and on the importance of a "European" solution to the conflict, could not conceal real differences of national interest among the member states – principally Germany on one side and France and Britain on the other. These differences surfaced in debates over the recognition of seceding Yugoslav republics, over the distribution of blame and, hence, of sanctions, among the parties to the conflict, and over the employment of various international institutions. The fate of the EC's early policy in the former Yugoslavia can thus be explained partly by its internal disarray, in which member states' conflicting views of the Balkan crisis were exacerbated by their disagreements over Maastricht and European security.

Much of that rivalry has now dissipated, partly because differences of interest are bound to loom larger in times of crisis than in postwar reconstruction. Member-states continue, of course, to pursue their own agendas in the region, but these now tend to be about contracts and trade rather than geopolitics. For the EU and the international community, however, interests are still at play in another sense, reminiscent of the early 1990s. Now, as then, it can sometimes seem as if the needs of the region and its peoples matter less than the EU's need to prove itself, or than the narrow agendas of the states, international organizations and NGOs involved in the protectorates and reconstruction programmes.[16] Institutional self-interest, it may be countered, is a more reliable foundation for international action than sentiment. The question, however, is whether, as the perceived risk of renewed violence recedes in Bosnia and elsewhere, and as immediate humanitarian concerns fade in the public mind, it will suffice to sustain the EU's renewed claim to leadership in south eastern Europe.

Notes

1 PHARE is an economic and technical assistance programme created by the European Community in 1989, originally for the post-communist countries of Central and Eastern Europe. In 1992 it began to be extended to the countries of the western Balkans. Obnova (Renewal) was a programme created by the EU in 1994 expressly for the countries of the former Yugoslavia.
2 John Graham, "Black Past, Grey Future? A Post-Dayton View of Bosnia and Herzegovina," *International Journal*, 53/2 (Spring 1998), 210.
3 Chris Patten, "EU Strategy in the Balkans," *Speech to the International Crisis Group*, Brussels, 10 July 2001, p. 4 (quoting Tim Judah).
4 Morton Abramovitz and Heather Hurlburt, "Can the EU Hack the Balkans?" *Foreign Affairs*, 81/5 (September–October 2002), 4–5.
5 Ibid., p. 6.
6 Having signed a Stabilization and Association Agreement with the EU in October 2001, the Croatian government is pressing to be admitted to the EU alongside Romania and Bulgaria in 2007.
7 For an account of the origins of the Stability Pact, see Likke Friis and Anna Murphy, "Turbo-Charged Myths: The EU and the Stability Pact for South Eastern Europe," *Journal of European Public Policy*, 7/5 (2000), 767–786.
8 *Stability Pact for South Eastern Europe*, Cologne, 10 June 1999, sec. III, para. 9

9   Benn Steil and Susan L. Woodward, "A European 'New Deal' for the Balkans,"
    Foreign Affairs, 78/6 (November–December 1999), 95–105.
10 Patten, *Speech to the ICG*, p. 8.
11 Ibid., p. 9.
12 European Union, *Bosnia-Herzegovina: The European Contribution*, at http://www.
    europa.eu.int/comm/external-relations/see/bosnie-herze/index.htm.
13 See Abramovitz and Hurlburt, p. 6.
14 Patten, *Speech to the ICG*, pp. 4–5.
15 Mihailo Crnobrnja, *The Yugoslav Drama* (Montreal: McGill-Queen's Press, 1994),
    p. 257.
16 David Chandler, *Faking Democracy After Dayton* (London: Pluto Press, 1999).

JÜRGEN DÖBERT

Germany's Approach to Peacekeeping and the Balkans Conflict: Political and Constitutional Context

Introduction

I N THE MID-1990s, shortly before Germany took part in the NATO mission in Bosnia, a soldier asked me: "Commander, when I joined the Bundeswehr I signed a contract to defend my country, Germany. Do you think that agreement permits me to take part in such a mission?" My answer was "yes," for reasons I shall set out in this paper.

At about the same time, at the Centre for Leadership Development and Civic Education of the Bundeswehr in Koblenz various questions were asked about the rationale for the German mission in Bosnia or in the Balkans. Some said about the conflicts there, "We don't know who is right or wrong." These questions were asked by asked by regulars, temporary career volunteers and conscripts alike.

Certainly, behind these questions there lay personal concerns for life, health and family. But there was, and still is, much more to it. The questions have their roots in German history – especially that of the Third Reich – and, after the World War II, in Germany's constitution, in the educational and ideological foundations of the Bundeswehr, and in German public opinion.

Commander JÜRGEN DÖBERT of the German Navy was Visiting Defence Fellow at the Centre for International Relations, Queen's University, Kingston, from 1999 to 2002.

Bismarck once said that without knowing history we won't understand the present and we can't live the future. German history, especially from 1933 to 1945, is well-known and need not be summarized here. But it must be kept in mind when looking at the creation of the Bundeswehr and the evolution of its role and missions in the context of the Federal Republic's constitution and domestic politics.

New Beginnings –
Politically, Constitutionally and Militarily

O N 23 May 1949, with the promulgation of the Basic Law, the Federal Republic of Germany came into being. At the end of the war it had seemed inconceivable that there would ever again be German forces on German soil, let alone in foreign locations such as the Balkans. Those convictions, however, began to change with the onset of the Cold War, even as the new Germany was taking shape.

In view of the steadily deepening rift between the Western allies and the Soviet Union, the fact that the Soviet Union had not downsized its armed forces as the Western allies had done, and with the memory of the Berlin blockade still fresh, the Basic Law renounced neither military sovereignty (for example Art. 87a) nor participation in systems of mutual collective security (Art. 24). But it would still take nearly seven years more to get West Germany back into the Western military community. One reason was the allies' aim to create a new Germany rooted less in the military ethic and more in democratic political culture. This tension became obvious during the long-lasting and vigorous discussions about the rearmament of Germany. Other reasons were suspicions, in France particularly, of a strengthened Germany, and the preference of some allies to neutralize it or at least to confine it militarily.

The interests of the Western states more or less coincided: France wanted effectively to tie down its traditional enemy, whilst the United States wanted the Federal Republic to be an equal member of the European community and of the defence system of the West. In spite of their different approaches to handling the new Germany, one lesson the allies had learnt from the Versailles Treaty was that freedom in Central Europe could not be firmly established by discriminating against and controlling Germany. Germany had to be integrated into

Western Europe and share responsibility for its fate. This lesson came to play an important role again later, at the time of Germany's reunification and its participation in peacekeeping and peace support missions in the Balkans.

The driving force behind the military integration of Germany into the Western defence community was the growing sense of threat emanating from the Soviet Union. After 1948 Hungary and Czechoslovakia definitely belonged to the Soviet sphere of influence. Civil war-torn Greece narrowly escaped falling victim to Soviet expansionism. In the autumn of 1949, the German Democratic Republic emerged from what had been the Soviet occupation zone.

After the communist attack on South Korea in the summer of 1950, the government of the Federal Republic of Germany sought admission to the defence community of the Western nations. The question of a German military contribution became a top priority. From the German standpoint what had to be achieved was not only security against the Eastern threat but also, through a German defence contribution, the full realization of national sovereignty. At the end of October 1954, the Federal Republic of Germany, along with Italy, acceded to the Western European Union (WEU), an extension of the Brussels Treaty. Under the Paris Agreements Germany was allowed to build up an army with a maximum strength of 500,000 and to integrate it into the North Atlantic Treaty Organization (NATO). On 6 May 1955 the Federal Republic was admitted to the Atlantic alliance. For Germany this meant a major step forward on the road to national sovereignty.

By August 1955, when the Bundestag adopted the Voluntary Military Service Act as a prerequisite for enlisting soldiers, the Federal Ministry of Defence – established in June of that year – had already received around 150,000 applications from volunteers who wished to join the new "Bundeswehr" (so named since 1 April 1956). But in spite of the huge numbers of volunteers it was obvious from the start that because of the tight labour market in the growing economy and because of negative historical associations, Germany's required contribution to the Western alliance could not be met with volunteers alone. Therefore the Bundestag voted in favour of introducing universal conscription.

When the first contingent of 10,000 conscripts reported for duty in army units on 1 April 1957, a conscript army came into being for the first time in a democratic Germany.

Lessons Learnt:
The Foundations of the Bundeswehr

IN 1950 in the monastery of Himmerod ten generals and five staff officers met, all from the former Wehrmacht. The memorandum from their meeting concluded that a completely new military had to be created without any ideological link to the Wehrmacht except the memory of the brave deeds of the resistance movement.

The roots of this new concept were in the liberal principles of the Prussian reforms initiated mainly by General Gerhard von Scharnhorst, chief of the Prussian General Staff, but also by Field Marshall August Count Neidhardt von Gneisenau and Major-General Carl von Clausewitz between 1807 and 1814.

The model of the soldier became known as the "citizen in arms": the soldier was a citizen and when circumstances made it necessary the citizen became a soldier. Gerhard von Scharnhorst provided a brief and apt description of the basic concept underlying the Prussian military reforms: "Its aim was to unite even more closely the army and the people. Every citizen after all is the born defender of his country. However only those who are free can defend freedom."[1] These liberal principles and ideas that have left their marks on German military history determine the self-image, leadership concept and training of the armed forces of the Federal Republic of Germany: external freedom cannot be preserved unless citizens share responsibility for it and unless close ties exist between the army and the people. The principles of freedom and human dignity, justice and democracy are determining factors also within the armed forces. Command authority and obedience are subject to law and to the individual's conscience.

Therefore, right from the start the model of the "citizen in uniform" (*Staatsbürger in Uniform*) was institutionalized and of course legally based. Section 6 of the military law, established in March 1956, says: "The soldier has the same civic rights as all other citizens. According to the necessities of military service his rights can only be restricted by law." This model sees the soldier as an independent personality retaining his civil rights and liberties, as a responsible and politically educated citizen, and as a soldier ready for action who understands military service as his contribution to national defence and to the preservation of liberty, peace and human rights, and who is willing to fight for these values.[2]

To develop such "citizen soldiers" a completely new intellectual approach was chosen – the "concept of leadership and civic education" (*Konzeption der Inneren Führung*). The concept, whose origins coincided with the re-establishment of the German armed forces, has two principal sources: the experience of German history between 1919 and 1945, and the Basic Law of 1949. Article 1, paragraph 1 of the Basic Law reflects this historical experience and gives primacy to human dignity: "The dignity of man is inviolable. To respect and protect it shall be the duty of all public authority." The concept of *innere Fuhrung* is intended to harmonize the principles of liberty held by the democratic state and governed by the rule of law with the principles of order and function, which the armed forces must observe if they are to fulfil their constitutional mandate.

The fundamentals of *innere Führung* combine the demands of the military mission and duty with the dignity and rights of the citizen. They aim to balance the tensions arising from the military duties of the soldier on one hand with the rights and liberties of the soldier as citizen on the other. In other words, *innere Führung* demands a balance between the functional effectiveness and individual rights of soldiers, between hierarchical order and participation, between discipline and free will, and between the leader's responsibility and delegation. As a fundamental principle of leadership and conduct, it pervades all aspects of military service.

Innere Führung is put into effect in training, leadership, care and welfare, political education, military law and military discipline. In this way, military personnel learn about the political and legal foundations of military service and are made to appreciate the purpose of the military mission. They are motivated to fulfil their duties conscientiously, to shoulder responsibility and to cooperate with others, for example within multinational operations. *Innere Führung* thus promotes the integration of the Bundeswehr and its military personnel into the state and into society and helps foster appreciation of the obligations of the German armed forces in the alliance and in collective security systems.

This concept has a static element, consisting of principles derived from the constitution and therefore only changeable through legislation, but its practical application requires a high degree of flexibility and dynamism in the face of changing challenges in the area of security and defence policy. These include UN and NATO missions abroad as in the Balkans, domestic challenges related to globalization, reduction in defence spending and the future of conscription, and issues within the armed forces including legitimacy, recruitment and reform.

Innere Führung provides an intellectual foundation on which the German armed forces can support themselves in difficult periods such as immediately after the Cold War and the emergence of international missions such as those in the Balkans, which introduced new tasks and intellectual requirements beyond the traditional military ones. Particularly with a view to the new tasks of conflict prevention and crisis management, Bundeswehr soldiers must more than ever be firm advocates of the values laid down in the German constitution. Acting as a mediator between parties who just a short time earlier were implacable enemies requires political discernment, diplomatic sensitivity and strength of character.[3]

In addition the concept helps soldiers to cope with the physical and psychological burdens of those missions. These derive from the duration of the tour of duty in countries and regions with different cultures and religions, from issues of multinationality and language among the troops, from different mentalities, from legal concerns, from having to act under the rules of an international organisation, and of course from direct confrontation with the conduct and the aftermath of war.

Another lesson learnt, especially from the experience of the Weimar Republic and the Third Reich, is reflected in the control mechanisms of the Bundeswehr and their partially restrictive consequences for peacekeeping missions. The Bundeswehr is bound to the primacy of politics, and the German constitution provides for political control of the armed forces by the elected Bundestag – the lower house of parliament. Democratically elected politicians lay down the rules governing security and defence policy and make decisions on the mission, employment, structure and equipment of the armed forces. Both the Federal Minister of Defence, as the peacetime commander-in-chief of the armed forces (Art 65 of the Basic Law), and the Federal Chancellor, who exercises the power of command over the armed forces in a state of defence (Art 115b of the Basic Law), are answerable to the Bundestag. Decisions on the deployment of the Bundeswehr in armed operations cannot be taken without the approval of the Bundestag. This principle was reaffirmed by the Federal Constitutional Court in its ruling of 12 July 1994 on the commitment of Bundeswehr forces to operations abroad.

Under the constitution two parliamentary organs exercise political control of the Bundeswehr: the Bundestag Committee on Defence (Art 45a) and the Parliamentary Commissioner for the Armed Forces (Art

45b). Because of its task of ensuring effective democratic political control of the individual soldier, his equipment and his deployment, the Committee on Defence is a parliamentary body of particular importance. This committee deliberates on all questions concerning defence policy – from soldiers' pay to the procurement of weapons to political decisions taken by NATO. Its parliamentary weight is also reflected in the fact that – unlike other Bundestag committees – it can set itself up any time as a committee of inquiry. It is thus at the same time an important and effective instrument for controlling the Federal government's defence and security policy.

In much the same way this is also true for the Budget Committee of the Bundestag. Art 87a of the Basic Law prescribes that the strength, organisation and armament of the armed forces be detailed in the budget. The Budget Committee has to review and authorize the Federal budget and hence also the defence budget. The Bundestag must then approve its decisions in plenary session.

The Parliamentary Commissioner for the Armed Forces, an office instituted by the Bundestag as early as 1957, monitors adherence to the principles of *innere Führung* and the observance of soldiers' rights. Since the peacekeeping missions in the Balkans this field has become a significant part of his work. The Commissioner is answerable solely to parliament and every soldier, regardless of his rank, is entitled to refer his case directly to the Commissioner, without fear of any subsequent disadvantage. Any superior who treats a soldier incorrectly because he has petitioned the Commissioner is in breach of the law.

Should information about undesirable developments in the armed forces come to the Commissioner's notice, he will inquire into the circumstances. He has a variety of options at his disposal. All Bundeswehr agencies and members are obliged to furnish him with information and to grant him access to files. He may visit any unit, agency and authority without previous notice, attend the hearings of disciplinary courts and ordinary courts of law, and request administrative assistance from courts and authorities. Important information on conditions in the Bundeswehr is contained in the Commissioner's annual report to parliament, which is available to the general public.[4]

Two other constitutional authorities merit at least a brief mention: the Joint Committee (Art. 53a of the Basic Law), through which parliamentary participation in defence planning is ensured; and the Petitions Committee. German citizens, even when serving in the military, are guaranteed the protection of their civil rights. Within the context of military service and its special requirements, however, these rights are governed by legally based duties. This basic tenet is manifested in Germany's principle of the "citizen in uniform." Observance of these rights and their legal limitations is watched over by the Bundestag. Whenever a soldier feels that his rights have been infringed upon, he may, in addition to the intra-service remedies available to him (such as report, remonstrance, complaint, disciplinary complaint, legal proceedings in an administrative court, and application to the Parliamentary Commissioner for the armed forces) take his case directly to parliament via the Petitions Committee without making use of official channels.[5]

End of the Cold War and German Reunification

THESE RELATIONSHIPS among state, military, society, constitution, and the individual as a soldier or a civilian, are the indispensable foundation of Germany's participation in peacekeeping missions. Let me turn now to this new task of the Bundeswehr as it has developed since the Cold War. This period has seen not only a dramatic increase in the number and extent of UN peace missions, but also a change in their character.

The task of traditional peacekeeping during the Cold War period was primarily to observe the parties to an international conflict, with their consent, to see that both kept to an armistice agreement. Since 1989 the majority of these operations – some with NATO and therefore Germany involved – have been aimed at settling domestic conflicts between political, ethnic and religious groups.[6] To the traditional task of peacekeeping have therefore been added the protection and support of the civil population, the restoration of law and order, the rebuilding of administrative and political infrastructure, and the preventive use of force both for humanitarian reasons and as a measure of deterrence. To take these extended tasks into account, the expression "peace support operations" has gained acceptance. This covers a range of activities including conflict prevention, peacemaking, peace enforcement and peace building[7]; as the conflict in the Balkans has illustrated, a combination of these activities, in parallel or in succession, may be employed as part of an overall strategy.

Until the wholesale change of the political world in 1989 and after, there was little discussion of foreign missions for the Bundeswehr.

Against the background of the East-West confrontation the only task of the Bundeswehr was the defence of West Germany. The Bundeswehr's mission consisted of suporting NATO and defending the eastern border of the Federal Republic of Germany against an immediate military threat from the Warsaw Pact forces.[8] The constitutional basis for this task was unambiguous. Article 87a, paragraph 1 says: the "federation shall establish armed forces for defence purposes"; paragraph 2 adds that "other than for defence purposes the armed forces may only be employed to an extent explicitly permitted by this Basic Law." At that time, the political and the constitutional restrictions corresponded with each other. Germany fulfilled its international obligations in other ways than by military missions: the Federal Republic supported its NATO allies and the UN through considerable financial and logistical contributions well as by providing military personnel and equipment for humanitarian activities.

These humanitarian activities – roughly 120 since 1960 – were not military deployments in the sense of Art 87a of the Basic Law. Examples are the auxiliary flights of the Bundeswehr to Angola (1960), Pakistan (1970), Uganda (1982), Ethiopia (1984), Sudan (1985/1989), Somalia (1992/1993), and Yugoslavia (1992–1996).[9] A lot of these were carried out on the basis of bilateral agreements with the UN or NATO or between Germany and the recipient of the aid.[10] Germany's deployment of medical soldiers to Cambodia (1993) under the auspices of the UN led to no constitutional problems since it was also a purely humanitarian activity.

Requests by NATO allies and the UN for soldiers of the Bundeswehr for military purposes were few, and were always rejected with reference to the constitution and – until 1989 – with reference to Germany's political and historical situation as a divided nation. Another explanation of the German attitude lay, of course, in the historical experience of the use of military power during the Third Reich.

With the reunification of Germany in 1990 and the rise of new domestic and international challenges, the parameters of German foreign policy fundamentally changed. The end of bipolar confrontation brought new freedom for states once trapped in the ideological cages of the Cold War; previously inconceivable forms of cooperation became possible, in Europe and elsewhere. Germany, the second most populous state in Europe after Russia, situated in the heart of Europe, a transit country for people, goods and traffic and an intersection of political, cultural and intellectual currents both between Scandinavia, Southern Europe and the Mediterranean, and between the Western and the new Central and Eastern European states, and one of the major exporting nations, stood to benefit from this new and promising situation.

Another positive development of that time was that national isolationism lost its significance. Against the background of a more and more interdependent world, and of its neighbours' suspicions about the power-political ambitions of a unified Germany, the changes of 1989/1990 not only confirmed Germany's earlier decision for multilateralism but also reinforced it. The same applies to the majority of the other European states which, like Germany, have learnt the lessons of the world wars and the East-West conflict, that only the multilateral integration of power and only the multilateral resolution of conflicts will lead to a durable stability among states.

The most obvious manifestation of these developments is globalization, transcending national borders in various ways. Nor is that all: for decades situated at the boundary between East and West, and therefore as a front-state directly exposed to the military threat of the Warsaw Pact, Germany now sees the security situation profoundly altered in its favour. There are no more risks of a large-scale military attack on Germany and Western Europe. Today Germany is surrounded by friendly or allied countries, and the eastward enlargement of the EU and NATO increases the comfort level of a country that rarely in its history could feel at home in its own neighbourhood.[11]

But in spite of a substantial gain in stability and security in various parts of Europe and recognizeable steps toward European integration following the end of the Cold War, the golden age anticipated in the Charter of Paris of November 1990 – the realisation of human rights, democracy and the market economy throughout Europe[12] – did not occur. The hope of a peace dividend from these changes is still not fulfilled. Instead, we have found ourselves confronted with more complex and less calculable military and non-military challenges both on the global stage and in Europe.

Conflict in the Balkans has shown clearly that ethnic, religious and economic antagonisms continue to exist in Europe accompanied by the rise of a massive human-rights violations, the suppression and extermination of minorities, ethnic cleansing and genocide. Many of these antagonisms, based on older historical identities of the 19th and early 20th century, could not come to the surface until the collapse of communist rule in Eastern and South Eastern Europe and with it the collapse of the last multinational states of Europe.[13]

These and other clashes since the early nineties have shown that the character of conflict has changed. As already mentioned, classic war between two states has become rare. The dominant form of conflict has become domestic. But this does not mean that its impact on global or regional stability is any less. The Balkans are a good example: consider the number of nations from Europe and beyond attempting to helping to resolve the conflict and stabilize the region.[14] The protagonists in these conflicts have also changed. Besides national governments, we now find non-governmental as well as transnational forces at work, perhaps supported by other governments or elements in them.

In addition to regional or "low intensity" conflicts, international terrorism as well as the proliferation of biological, chemical, radiological and nuclear weapons of mass destruction and their means of delivery assumed a new importance after the Cold War. Instability caused by the threat of proliferation will increase further through the growing connections between terrorists and their access to these weapons.[15]

Beyond this direct military context it is necessary to note some other developments causing conflicts which are closely linked to the North-South dimensions of world politics. These include underdevelopment, impoverishment, the population explosion, and the shortage of critical resources, especially water, leading to the likelihood of future waves of mass migration from the poor nations of the Southern Hemisphere to the rich and developed countries of the Northern Hemisphere and the Western world. Also to be noted are organized crime with its possible access to weapons of mass destruction in the future[16] and its connection to drug trafficking, which has reached strategic dimensions.[17] There is no doubt that these developments, by themselves or in connection with extreme ethnic, religious and economic antagonisms, are capable of destabilizing states and regions in Europe and elsewhere. Given these trends, there is likely to be steady demand for military missions by NATO, the UN or the EU.

Germany's Foreign and Security Policy

TO ADDRESS these complex challenges adequately, it is necessary to broaden the concepts of security and defence both geographically and substantively. At its core it consists of three aspects which are closely linked to each other and which are of particular consequence for the future of German security policy.[18]

1. Comprehensive Approach:

Modern security is more than deterrence and the defence of national borders. It cannot be confined to a certain region or a certain political dimension and cannot be assured by military means alone or even primarily. To cope with the plethora of new challenges the whole spectrum of policy – foreign, defence, economic, cultural, educational, development and ecological – must be considered[19] based on close cooperation and coordination of states as well as international organisations and national institutions.

Although efficient crisis management doesn't mean dominance by the military, well-trained and educated armed forces provide a range of options in all phases of a conflict, contributing to the credibility and effectiveness of security policy in total. For example, the ethnic cleansing and genocide initiated by Milosevic could only be stopped by NATO. And it remains the role of the military, as part of a multidimensional international strategy, to ensure a secure environment as in the cases of Bosnia-Herzegovina and Kosovo, as the basis for political reconstruction, economic recovery and the peaceful coexistence of the different ethnic communities.

2. Prevention and Effective Reaction

Prevention is the key to any successful foreign and security policy. In a world of globalization it is imperative to prevent conflicts from arising, or crises from building and spreading to jeopardize the security and stability of other areas.[20] In a world of growing interdependence and cross-border risks any investment one makes in the political and economic development of a country or region - in democracy, the rule of law, and the internal stability of states – is a preventive measure with respect to security for all concerned.

Removal of the structural reasons for conflicts and crises is not only a long-term issue. In the short term, military instruments must also be available for conflict prevention and crisis management. A good example of a preventive military mission is the deployment of peacekeeping forces in the Balkans, as in the case of UNPREDEP in Macedonia.

Closely linked to prevention is the after-care of a crisis. It is a similar process to crisis-prevention, calling for many of the same instruments. An example is the Stability Pact for South East Europe, initiated by the German government and the EU, an ambitious multilateral attempt at regional after-care on various levels and dimensions – all ultimately related to security and stability.[21]

3. Common Security

Modern security and defence policy has to take into account that there are no longer any self-sufficient islands – either national or regional – in today's world. Security has become indivisible. Less than ever can any nation provide for its own security by itself.

The complexity of the challenges, the indivisibility of security, the possibilities of cooperation through alliances, and the necessity of common answers to common risks all make security and stability a common task. Their critics notwithstanding, the combined missions of NATO, the UN, the EU and the OSCE in the Balkans are an example of the growing responsibility of international coalitions and institutions for the realization of common security. These intergovernmental organizations are more and more accompanied by non-governmental organizations in the service of crisis prevention.

But understanding security as a common task, given the difficult experience of recent peacekeeping and peace support missions in the Balkans, makes it necessary to remind ourselves that for this to work, a state must be willing to contribute to the support of allies and partners, and even to compromise its sovereignty.[22]

With these aspects of security in mind, what are the consequences, for Germany's foreign and security policy, of Germany's changed role after the Cold War, of the risks of international politics in the future, and of the new, broadened concept of security?

Given Germany's strategic position in Central Europe, and its economic power as the largest and industrial nation of Europe, its foreign and security policy is bound to have a major impact on its neighbours and beyond. Based on its interests, to be sure, but also on its constitution, Germany must accept responsibilities for the preservation and – if necessary – restoration of peace, international law, human rights and a fair economic order based on market principles, not only in Europe but also on the global stage. To these ends, the Federal Republic is a member of all major European and Euro-Atlantic organizations serving international cooperation and systems of collective security.

Therefore the framework within which German foreign and security policy is conducted continues to be determined by the close ties it has with partners in the EU, the Council of Europe, the Atlantic alliance, the OSCE and the UN.

The most important tenets of Germany's foreign and security policy are:[23]

- to safeguard the freedom, security and prosperity of the German citizens and the independence of our country;
- to cooperate cooperation peacefully with our neighbours in a spirit of partnership;
- to continue development of the North Atlantic alliance and deepen the transatlantic relationship, in which Europe must assume a greater share of the responsibility;[24]
- to strengthen supranational and international organizations and improve cooperation between them to enhance conflict prevention and crisis management in the Euro-Atlantic area.

German foreign and security policy thus puts a high premium on promoting integration and stability, on establishing a strong and lasting order of peace in the whole of Europe, civilising international relations and placing them on a legal foundation, and on the development of effective strategies of conflict prevention and peaceful conflict settlement. All these foreign and security interests are reflected in the the most recent mission statement of the Bundeswehr.[25] Outlined therein are the Bundeswehr's principal functions:

- Protecting Germany and its citizens against political blackmail and external threats,
- defending Germany and its allies,
- contributing to the preservation of peace and stability in Europe and in the Euro-Atlantic area,
- advancing world peace and international security in accordance with the UN Charter, and
- providing disaster relief and other forms of humanitarian assistance.

From the mission statement the following roles[26] can be deduced:

- performance of tasks related to sovereign rights,
- national defence including the fulfilment of national territorial tasks,
- collective defence,
- conflict prevention and crisis management, mainly confined to Europe and its periphery,
- partnership and cooperation through military tasks performed in support of political measures aimed at preventing crises and conflicts, assisting post-crisis and post-conflict rehabilitation (also

known as "peacebuilding") or promoting confidence building and stability, as well as

- carrying out rescue and evacuation operations on a national basis or in collaboration with allies and partners in Germany and else-where.

Peacekeeping and the Constitution

HAVING ESTABLISHED that the foreign and security policy of the new, post-Cold War Germany, and the military missions and tasks derived from it, give the Bundeswehr a new emphasis on peacekeeping and peace support missions through NATO, the UN, the OSCE and the EU, we must now ask how this new role is to be brought in line with the constitution.

To answer this question, vital for Germany in general and for the armed forces in particular, we have to go back to the Gulf War of 1991. This war undoubtedly had a great effect on public opinion and on the domestic, partisan discussion about the use of military force for political purposes.[27] German resistance to demands for an active military contribution to the Desert Storm coalition revealed a deep confusion in society about the legality and legitimacy of the use of force in defence of international law, rights, values and objectives other than the defence of one's own territory. The public displayed a widespread inability to recognize the nature of political reality and its inherent requirements.

Although the Federal Republic was the logistical turntable of this war, had contributed DM 17.2 billion, and had provided military assistance to the coalition, it earned harsh and widespread criticism, particularly in the United States which had been the main supporter of Germany's unification. The Federal Republic was branded as a "free rider," despite having spoken eloquently with its pocketbook.[28]

Combined with this emotional criticism was the demand – which continued after the war – that Germany should give up its reservations against international military missions, especially since it had regained complete sovereignty. Central to the domestic discussion caused by these demands was whether the Basic Law would allow for the deployment of the Bundeswehr for missions other than defence.

Two articles of the constitution played an important role. First, Article 87a states that the Bundeswehr should be used for defence only. But how broadly should the expression "defence" be understood? This article was the cornerstone of the Social Democratic Party's arguments against new German military commitments abroad, meaning missions under UN command and within the framework of the UN Charter but outside the area covered by the NATO treaty.[29] Second, Article 24, paragraph 2, grants Germany the right to join collective security systems and accept associated limitations upon its sovereign powers. This article shaped the argument of the ruling Christian Democratic and Liberal Democratic parties, which asserted that the UN, NATO and the WEU constituted such security systems. A minor role was played by Article 59, paragraph 2, which deals with the role of the Bundestag in treaties or related matters concerning Germany's foreign relations.

During these discussions, the government was under political pressure from events in Somalia and especially the Balkans. Based on resolutions of the Security Council, and in the case of the Balkans also of the NATO Council and the WEU Ministerial Council, the German government agreed to take part in the following three missions,[30] which later became subject to the decision of the Federal Constitutional Court on 12 July 1994:

- In Somalia (1993), where Germany deployed a supply and transportation unit with around 1700 soldiers equipped with light weapons and armoured vehicles. Its military task was restricted to logistical support and all measures were strictly tied to Chapter VI of the UN Charter. The German rules of engagement only allowed the use of weapons in case of self-defence, and the German armed forces were deployed in a secure environment.

- NATO/WEU naval operations in the Adriatic to monitor the UN weapons and trade embargoes on Yugoslavia and later on the Federal Republic of Yugoslavia (1992), where besides three German maritime patrol aircraft, two frigates took part. Given that at that time the constitutional issue was undecided, the German ships were allowed to participate in surveillance but not in coercive measures. In 1994, after the court's decision, the German navy was allowed active control of suspicious ships.

- AWACS monitoring of the no-fly zone over Bosnia-Herzegovina (1993). The problem was that the UN Security Council's authorization included the shooting down of enemy aircraft. This meant that a German AWACS operator could have led an allied fighter into combat with a Yugoslavian one. Nevertheless the German government, with the votes of the Christian Democratic ministers but not those of the Liberal Democrats, decided to leave the German soldiers on board the AWACS.

What is the essence of the decision by the Federal Constitutional Court?[31] The court decided that Art. 24, paragraph 2 of the Basic Law serves as authorisation for the deployment of armed forces abroad. Referring to Art. 87a, the court said clearly that this article does not preclude the deployment of German armed forces within a system of mutual and collective security. The court kept open the long-lasting debate on the definition of the word "defence" in Art. 87a, and argued that the only reason for establishing this article in the constitution was to limit strictly the use of the armed forces for domestic purposes.

Furthermore, by characterizing a mutual and collective security system as only "establishing a framework of rules for the preservation of peace" and "founding an organisation," and by waiving the traditional point about "taking assertive action against a hostile member within the ranks of the collectivity of states," the court made it possible for not only the UN but also NATO and the WEU to qualify as such a system. With this broad definition of a mutual and collective security system the court not only made it constitutionally possible to integrate NATO and the WEU into the UN for purposes of maintaining the peace, but also acknowledged the developing independent capability of these alliances in peace support and peace-keeping missions beyond their traditional collective-defence roles.

Related to the issue of NATO and the WEU was another problem: if the NATO treaty were to be modified in light of its new strategic concept of November 1991, or the WEU treaty in light of the Petersberg Declaration of June 1992 on crisis- management tasks, would they be seen as new international treaties regulating Germany's foreign relations?

Only the formal amendment of a treaty would require – in accordance with Article 59 paragraph 2 of the Basic Law – consent of the parliament. To resolve this uncertainty the court concluded there was general prior constitutive consent by the federal parliament in all cases involving activation of Germany's armed forces within a system of mutual and collective security. This consent could be deduced from the German constitutional tradition since 1918. It was expressed in the constitution of Weimar and became part of the Basic Law as a historically determined embedding of intensive parliamentarian control of the armed forces.

This consent is not deemed necessary in humanitarian missions abroad but is indispensable in case of armed operations. In the latter case it makes no difference if the armed operations take place in the framework of national or collective defence, or if the mission serves other purposes within a system of mutual and collective security.

To sum it up one can say that the court's decision allows the German armed forces to participate in all missions within a mutual and collective security system under the condition of a general prior constitutive consent of the federal parliament. The ruling ended the dispute on the legal aspects, but left questions of the legitimacy and political motives of Bundeswehr missions – for example those related to peacekeeping – to the political sphere. Here there developed a greater pragmatism and willingness to accept new responsibilities. Decreasing legal, societal and political constaints, and the changed threats and risks ranging from humanitarian catastrophes (e.g. Kosovo) to the terrorist attacks of 11 September 2001, have increased the government's freedom of action and the parliament's will to give consent to peacekeeping and peace support missions.

Peacekeeping and the Ongoing Political and Constitutional Discussion

THE DECISIONS of the Bundestag related to missions in the Balkans such as SFOR and KFOR, as well as those related to the campaign against terrorism, are all in line with the structure of the Bundeswehr, with Germany's foreign and security policy, with the German constitution and therefore with the lessons learnt from history. But this does not mean that the German public, politicians or even the Federal Constitutional Court consider all the issues settled. To illustrate the point, we may refer to an important recent decision of the court concerning the Bundeswehr.

Is NATO's New Strategic Concept Unconstitutional?

That decision is the judgement of the Federal Constitutional Court of 22 November 2001. It deals with the expansion of NATO's security tasks, under its new strategic concept, of crisis response operations. In the face of this expansion, the (communist) PDS parliamentary group in the Bundestag asked whether the Federal government, in approving the adoption of NATO's new strategic concept at the 1999 summit without initiating the consent procedure prescribed by the constitution, might have infringed Art. 59, paragraph 2, and thereby violated the rights of parliament. The PDS also argued that the new strategic concept deviated from the alliance's pure purpose of maintaining peace in accordance with the UN Charter. Thus Art. 24, paragraph 2, which allows participation only in alliances whose purpose is maintaining peace, might have been infringed too.

The court rejected the application of the PDS as unfounded and argued[32] that by approving NATO's new strategic concept the Federal government did not violate those two constitutional provisions, because the Washington Treaty signed at the summit did not amend the North Atlantic Treaty. The expansion of the alliance's security approach to embrace crisis response operations constitutes only a further development of the 1949 NATO treaty: the new strategic concept leaves the alliance's function of collective defence unaffected, and interprets the peace and security missions set forth in the preamble in the light of the new security situation. The alliance's main purpose continues to be defence against or deterrence of aggression by any state.

It is true that the possibility of crisis response operations out of the alliance's area, which constitutes an important expansion of NATO's tasks, is not implied in the treaty. Compared with the 1991 strategic concept the 1999 strategic concept represents a considerable change in this respect. The declarations of intent which prevailed in the 1991 concept, are replaced by serious, concrete plans, reflecting procedures developed in the context of crisis response operations conducted since 1994. But it cannot be inferred from this that an amendment of the NATO treaty has taken place. The North Atlantic Council explicitly declared that the purpose and nature of the alliance remained unchanged.

Moreover the mutual obligations that arise from the treaty are less demanding in the area of crisis response than in defence: the member states coordinate their measures on a case-by-case basis through consultations; an obligation to collective response is not established; and the primacy of politics and decision by consensus in the Council still apply. Since in this area the member states still must act on the basis of their respective constitutional laws, the Federal government needs the general prior constitutive consent of the Bundestag.

Negotiation and implementation of treaties is the task of the Federal government which, in the area of foreign policy, is granted considerable latitude for action.

Certainly, the field of foreign affairs is not beyond parliamentary control and is governed by the Basic Law. However, an obligation to seek the consent of parliament for informal developments of the Treaty would not only result in legal uncertainty, but would also reduce unreasonably the Federal government's capacity to act in the field of foreign and security policy.

Moreover the parliament is not defenceless against the risk of gradual alteration of the content of the Treaty through a series of legal actions falling short of the status of formal amendments. The parliament's general rights of control already oblige the government, pursuant to Article 43, paragraph 1 of the Basic Law, to account to the parliament for its activities in NATO organs. Furthermore, given the parliament's right to decide on the budget and to give prior approval for any deployment of German troops – even for crisis response – the government will as a precaution seek the political support of the Bundestag in matters of NATO's further development.

It can be concluded, then, that the Federal court's decision strengthened Germany's foreign and security policy without restricting the parliament's rights with respect to future participation in peacekeeping and peace support missions.

Peacekeeping and Germany's Limits

MUCH DISCUSSED both in the military and in the political class is the question of the Bundeswehr's capacity to bear burdens and to take stress. As mentioned above, the German armed forces are undergoing a fundamental reform even as they undertake their missions in the Balkans, Afghanistan and elsewhere. These reforms are indispensable in order to improve their capabilities for collective defence, as conflict prevention and crisis management through the UN, NATO, the EU (where Germany will provide 20 percent of the new rapid reaction force) and the OSCE. Their most urgent needs are in the areas of strategic transport, strategic and tactical reconnaissance, and high performance, compatible communication, command and control facilities. In addition the armed forces will have to be totally restructured toward a complement of 150,000 soldiers for readiness forces and 105,000 for the new Basic Military Organization.[33]

Such a fundamental renewal, involving modernization, rationalisation and a complete restructuring, requires a solid financial basis.

Here is the problem. Without sufficient funds, achieving objectives such as interoperability will be difficult, and Germany will not be able to fulfil peacekeeping or peace support missions in the future to the extent expected. Or it will fulfil them only with increasing risk to individual soldiers and possibly to the mission itself.

As the recent deployment to Afghanistan indicated, the participation of German armed forces in a considerable number of different missions is an enormous human, material, and logistical challenge. With respect to communications the situation is especially embarrassing: nearly all the technical systems needed for ISAF were in the Balkans, and a major logistical effort was needed to move them to Afghanistan.[34] The same was true for the new Dingo armoured vehicle, which provides soldiers on patrol with good protection against mines.

There are also visible difficulties with respect to personnel. As mentioned earlier, in missions abroad the Bundeswehr can only deploy regulars, temporary-career volunteers and conscripts as short-service volunteers, in all 208,000 troops. The 91,000 conscripts are not at the Ministry of Defence's disposal for those missions. There are roughly 7000 troops deployed with SFOR, KFOR and Task Force Amber Fox, 2700 more with Enduring Freedom and ISAF. If we add those posted to the NATO Standing Naval Forces in the eastern Mediterranean, and at NATO AWACS bases in the US, around 10,200 soldiers are involved in missions abroad at the moment.

Considering the cycle of preparation for, participation in, and evaluation after the mission, and the logistics and the 1000 troops responsible for the protection of American bases in Germany, roughly 55,000 soldiers are committed to international tasks. Given the strength of the contingents in the framework agreed to by the Bundestag, it is conceivable that a third of the available Bundeswehr troops will be involved in international missions.[35] It goes without saying that this is also a hindrance to the realization of the above-described reforms.

The Minister of Defence himself admitted that the Bundeswehr is exposed to enormous stress caused by the conflict between growing international demands for peacekeeping and peace support missions, and the need for fundamental renewal of the armed forces.[36] But the prospects of improving the budgetary situation in the medium term are not good. On the contrary, during a conference of the commanders of the German armed forces on 8 April, 2002, Chancellor Schröder supported the need for reforms, but said he did not want to talk about money. At the same conference the Defence Minister spoke of the solid financial situation of the Bundeswehr. Only the Chief of

Staff admitted that the armed forces find themselves in a growing discrepancy between tasks and financial means.[37] It goes without saying that this causes problems in the dialogue between the military leadership and the political leadership of the Ministry of Defence. At the same conference General Gliemeroth stated that he was concerned, first that Mr Schröder had nothing to say about Bundeswehr's financial problems except that the government must reduce spending and, second, that Mr Scharping considered the Bundeswehr's financial situation "not comfortable, but adequate." He asked the chief of staff to comment on how such different perceptions of reality could arise. The commander of the Command and Staff College in Hamburg concluded that, "we find ourselves between 'adequate' funds and financial disaster."[38]

A further consequence of this discrepancy between tasks and financial means and of the poor prospects of resolving it soon, is the decreasing attractiveness of military service. Recruitment of enough young people is indispensable for fulfilling the Bundeswehr's new tasks of crisis prevention and conflict management.

Summary and Conclusion

WILLY BRANDT, the former Chancellor of the Federal Republic of Germany, wrote in his memoires in the early nineties that after reunification it would not be enough for Germany to provide only verbal contributions to peacekeeping.[39] This proved a wise assessment. Germany's road to peacekeeping was long and rocky, full of ambivalence and uncertainty. The painful experience of the Third Reich demanded a new constitutional, political and military beginning centred on the fundamental values of our free democratic constitutional structure and based on human dignity and civil rights. In the military all these changes are reflected in the strict parliamentary control of the armed forces, in the model of the *Staatsbürger in Uniform* and the idea of *innere Führung*. This last concept underpins the legitimacy of the forces' missions, enhances the motivation and responsibility of soldiers, and ensures the full integration of the military into German society. The concept should also in future help soldiers to respond to changing demands and the armed forces to adjust to political, social and economic changes. It will help them cope with the combination of extensive reform, on the one hand, and growing burden of missions abroad, on the other. The soldier himself will be allowed to question the legality or legitimacy of peacekeeping missions in the same way as politicians and parliament must do.

Today, unlike ten years ago, there is a broad consensus on security and foreign policy among all parties in parliament that Germany, because of its geostrategic position, its political influence and its economic, cultural, and social capabilities, must take on international responsibilities in the face of new security risks and challenges. In this context peacekeeping and peace support missions for crisis prevention and conflict management will be the main tasks of the Federal armed forces.

The decision of the Federal Constitutional Court in 1994 laid the constitutional groundwork for participation in such missions. Like past missions in the past in the Balkans and those related to the campaign against terrorism, all future missions will be assessed according to the Constitutional Court's guidelines – and by the parliament. No distinction will be drawn between missions executed by the UN itself and those based on a UN mandate but carried out by regional organisations such as NATO or the EU.

It may be that the constraints of the constitution and their exploitation by political parties will lead to slower decisions about the deployment of forces. But these constraints are the consequence of our liberal, democratic constitutional order, including the principles of the rule of law and of the separation of powers, for which the Bundeswehr and society are equally responsible. They protect the rights of individual soldiers and the respect they have earned as a result of their peacekeeping missions.

In spite of the high motivation of German troops at home and abroad, an increase in the strength of the crisis reaction forces, and slowly rising investment in equipment for the Bundeswehr, the demands it faces will remain very high, close to the limits placed on it by the coincidence of reform and a growing number of foreign missions.

Finally, in the future we can expect questions to be raised related to conflict prevention and crisis management missions, in which the Federal Constitutional Court will again be involved. It is to be hoped, however, that important political questions like the future of conscription – which is very meaningful for future peacekeeping missions – will be resolved by the political parties in parliament as they should be, and not by the court.

Germany's journey to peacekeeping was driven by historic changes which found expression through judicial interpretation of the Basic Law. The road ran from strict refusal to use military force for political purposes and from pocket-book diplomacy, to responsible membership in the international community, contributing seriously through missions abroad, to peace and stability in Europe and elsewhere. Its service as lead nation of a sector within KFOR in Kosovo, and as the lead nation of Amber Fox in Macedonia responsible for NATO and non-NATO troops, shows that Germany's contribution is welcomed.

There is now no turning back for Germany's foreign and security policy. Germany will remain a reliable participant in peacekeeping and peace support missions helping, as Kofi Annan said in his February 2002 speech to the German parliament, "to create the prerequisites for a long-lasting peace."[40]

Notes

1 Hans-Christian Beck, "Scharnhorst-Wegbereiter für die Innere Führung," in *Gerhard von Scharnhorst*, ed. Bundesministerium der Verteidigung (Bonn: 1995), p. 48.

2 Karl Dieffenbach, "Die deutsche Militärreform, Staatsbürger in Uniform: Ausgangspunkt und Ziel der Inneren Führung," in *Streitkräfte in der Demokratie, 40 Jahre Beirat für Fragen der Inneren Führung*, ed. Bundesministerium der Verteidigung (Bonn: 1998), pp. 16–22; "Die Konzeption der Inneren Führung," in *Zentrum Innere Führung*, ed. Zentrum Innere Führung (Koblenz: 2001), p. 11; *The Bundeswehr – Advancing Steadily into the 21st Century, Cornerstones of a Fundamental Renewal* (Bonn: Federal Minister of Defence, 14 June 2000), para. 29.

3 "Die Konzeption der Inneren Führung," in *Zentrum Innere Führung*, pp. 6–9; *The Bundeswehr – Advancing Steadily into the 21st Century, Cornerstones of a Fundamental Renewal*, para. 30, 31.

4 Erlass: *Truppe und Wehrbeauftragter* – Neufassung –, Deutscher Bundestag – 14 Wahlperiode, Drucksache 14/8330, pp. 33–36.

5 Legal and administrative procedures protecting the rights of all forces personnel in *Federal Republic of Germany: Information exchange on the OSCE Code of Conduct on politico-military aspects of security* (Bonn: Federal Minister of Defence, 5 November 1999), pp. 11, 12.

6 Rudolf Scharping, Rede des Bundesministers der Verteidigung anläßlich des 12. Forums "Bundeswehr und Gesellschaft" der Welt am Sonntag am 02.10.2001 in Berlin, "Neue Bedingungen und Herausforderungen unserer Sicherheit," *Bundeswehr* online, 2 October 2001, available at http://www.bundeswehr.de/news/reden/reden/_minister/010210_wams_forum.html, p. 1.

7 Ortwin Buchbender, Hartmut Bühl, Harald Kujat, Karl H. Schreiner, Oliver Bruzek, *Wörterbuch zur Sicherheitspolitik mit Stichworten zur Bundeswehr*, 4. Aufl. (Hamburg, Berlin, Bonn: 2000), pp. 101, 112, 113, 284.

8 *White Paper 1985 – The Situation and the Development of the Federal Armed Forces* (Bonn: Federal Minister of Defence, 19 June 1985), para. 81–98.

9 *Bestandsaufnahme, Die Bundeswehr an der Schwelle zum 21. Jahrhundert* (Bonn: Federal Ministry of Defence, 3 May 1999), p. 25.

10 Wolfgang Fechner, "Hoffnung auf Frieden, Die Bundeswehr bei internationalen Friedensmissionen – Bewährungsprobe bestanden," *Der Mittler-Brief, Informationsdienst zur Sicherheitspolitik*, 13 (no. 4/4th quarter 1998), 1.

11 Jürgen Döbert, "German Security Policy and NATO's New Strategic Concept: Implications for the Alliance's North American Members," in *Over Here and Over*

There Canada-US Defence Cooperation in an Era of Interoperability, ed. David G. Haglund (Kingston: Queen's Quarterly, 2001), p. 192; *Erlaß: Verteidigungspolitische Richtlinien für den Geschäftsbereich des Bundesministers der Verteidigung* (Bonn: Federal Minister of Defence, 26 November 1992), para. 9.

12 Karl Kaiser, "Die ständige Mitgliedschaft im Sicherheitsrat-Ein berechtigtes Ziel der deutschen Außenpolitik," *Europa-Archiv*, 48 (19/1993), 542.

13 Bernd Weber, "Kriege-Konflikte-Krisen in dieser Welt," *IAP-Dienst Sicherheitspolitik* (Bonn: 2000), pp. 8, 9; Steven L. Burg & Paul S. Shoup, *The War in Bosnia-Herzegovina, Ethnic Conflict and International Intervention* (New York: 1999): 1; *Erlaß: Verteidigungspolitische Richtlinien für den Geschäftsbereich des Bundesministers der Verteidigung*, para. 20.

14 Rudolf Scharping, Rede des Bundesministers der Verteidigung anläßlich des 12. Forums "Bundeswehr und Gesellschaft" der *Welt am Sonntag*, am 02.10.2001 in Berlin, p. 1.

15 "Warnung vor 'neuem' Terrorismus," *IAP-Dienst Sicherheitspolitik*, no. 6 (June 1999), p. 12.

16 Gerhard Hubatschek, "Veränderter Auftrag und veränderte Auftrags-bedingungen," *IAP-Dienst Sicherheitspolitik, Sonderheft Zukunft Bundeswehr* (February 2000), p. 21.

17 Jörk-Eckart Reschke, "Sicherheitspolitik in neuen Dimensionen," *Der Mittler-Brief, Informationsdienst zur Sicherheitspolitik*, 14 (no. 1/1st quarter 1999), 2.

18 Rudolf Scharping, "Erweiterte Sicherheit angesichts aktueller Risiken – Mit kühlem Kopf," *Y. Magazin der Bundeswehr*, Oktober 2001, p. 18; Thomas Kossendey, "Verteidigung morgen – eine gesamtgesellschaftliche Aufgabe," *Europäische Sicherheit*, 50 (November 2001), 15.

19 Dietmar Buse, "Das gesamte Spektrum," *aktuell, Zeitung für die Bundeswehr*, no. 42, (22 October 2001), p. 1.

20 *Erlaß: Verteidigungspolitische Richtlinien für den Geschäftsbereic desBundesministers der Verteidigung*, para. 23; Harald Kujat, *Rede des Generalinspekteurs der Bundeswehr anlässlich der 39. Kommandeurtagung der Bundeswehr* am 9. April 2002 in Hannover, *Bundeswehr* online, 9 April 2002, available at http://www.bundeswehr.de/news/reden/ reden_inspekteure/020409_ kujat_kdr-tagung.html, p. 2.

21 Rudolf Scharping, *Statement of the German Minister of Defence at the Friedrich Ebert Stiftung Conference in Berlin* on 19 October 2001, "Security Policy and Global Stability," *Bundeswehr* online, available at http://www.bundeswehr.de/news/reden/reden/_minister/011019 _ebert_stiftung.html, p.2.

22 Rudolf Scharping, "Erweiterte Sicherheit angesichts aktueller Risiken – Mit kühlem Kopf," p.18; Rudolf Scharping, *Rede des Bundesministers der Verteidigung auf der 8. Internationalen Konferenz* "Estonia and the European Union" am 2. November 2001 in Tallinn, "Welches Europa wollen wir?," *Bundeswehr* online, 2 November 2001, available at http://www. bundeswehr.de/news/reden/ reden/_minister/011102_tallinn_d.html, p. 2.

23 Joschka Fischer, "Multilateralismus als Aufgabe deutscher Außenpolitik," Rede des Bundesministers des Auswärtigen Politik anläßlich der ersten Konferenz der Leiterinnen und Leiter deutscher Auslandsvertretungen," *Europäische Sicherheit*, 49 (November 2000), 7–9; Peter Goebel, "German Security Policy," *Strategic Forum*, no. 164 (June 1999), 2; *Bestandsaufnahme, Die Bundeswehr an der Schwelle zum 21. Jahrhundert*, p. 158.

24 Jürgen Döbert, "German Security Policy and NATO's New Strategic Concept: Implications for the Alliance's North American Members," p. 193.

25 *Erlaß: Verteidigungspolitische Richtlinien für den Geschäftsbereich des Bundesministers der Verteidigung*, para. 44; *The Bundeswehr – Advancing Steadily into the 21st Century, Cornerstones of a Fundamental Renewal*, para. 15.

26 *Erlaß: Verteidigungspolitische Richtlinien für den Geschäftsbereich des Bundesministers der Verteidigung,* para. 37, 38, 48; *The Bundeswehr – Advancing Steadily into the 21st Century, Cornerstones of a Fundamental Renewal,* para. 17–24; Rüdiger Moniac, "Bundeswehr ganz neu: Kein Stein mehr auf dem anderen," *loyal,* September 2000, p. 5.

27 Rupert Scholz, "Deutsche UNO-Soldaten im Spannungsfeld von Politik und Grundgesetz," in *Die Blauhelme, Im Einsatz für den Frieden,* ed. Ernst Koch, Frankfurt am Main, Bonn 1991, p. 205.

28 Wolf-Reinhardt Vogt, "Peacekeeping: Germany's Balance Between Domestic Limitations, National Interests and International Demands in Peacekeeping at a Crossroads," in *Peacekeeping at a Crossroads,* ed. S. Neil MacFarlane, Hans-Georg Ehrhardt (The Canadian Peacekeeping Press 1997), pp. 73, 81.

29 Stefan Lang, *Internationale Einsätze der Bundeswehr unter rechtlichen, politischen und militärischen Aspekten,* Dissertation, Seehausen am Staffelsee 1997, p. 11.

30 Wolfgang Fechner, "Hoffnung auf Frieden, Die Bundeswehr bei internationalen Friedensmissionen – Bewährungsprobe bestanden," pp. 2–4.

31 BVerfG, 2 BvE 3/92, 5/93, 7/93, 8/93 of July 12, 1994 in BVerfGE 90, pp. 286, 287.

Basic principles of the decision:

The authorization in Art 24 paragraph 2 Basic Law not only allows the Federation to participate in a system of mutual and collective security and to consent to the requisite restrictions of sovereignty. It also forms the constitutional basis for undertaking tasks which are typical of participation in such a system, and thus for using the Bundeswehr within the framework and by the rules of that system.

Art 87a Basic Law does not preclude the application of Art 24 paragraph 2 Basic Law as a constitutional basis for the activation of armed forces within a system of mutual and collective security.

3.a) The Basic Law requires that the Federal government, to activate the armed forces, request the general prior constitutive consent of the Bundestag.

b) It is the business of the legislature to specify, beyond the minimal requirements mentioned in this decision and within the limits of the rule of law (*Parlamentsvorbehalt*), in what respect the nature and extent of activation of the armed forces requires a consent of parliament.

4. For the preservation of peace, the Federal Republic of Germany may under Art. 24 paragraph 2 Basic Law assent to a limitation of its sovereignty by accepting decisions of international organizations as binding even without having transferred sovereignty to those organizations in the sense of Art. 24 paragraph 1 Basic Law.

5.a) A system of mutual and collective security in the sense of Art. 24 paragraph 2 Basic Law is characterized by the establishment of a framework of rules for the preservation of peace and of an organization that results, for each member, in an obligation, under public international law, mutually requiring the preservation of peace and granting security. It is of no significance whether such a system exclusively or primarily guarantees peace among the member states or ensures collective support in the case of third party attacks.

b) Furthermore, pacts of collective self-defence can be systems of mutual and collective security in the sense of Art. 24 paragraph 2 Basic Law if and insofar as they are strictly bound to the preservation of peace.

6. If the legislature consents to participation in a system of mutual and collective security, such consent also extends to the participation of forces in integrated units of the system or to the participation of soldiers in military actions of the system and under its command, if such participation can be seen as part of the consent to those foundational documents (*Gründungsvertrag, Satzung*)

which required approval. Consent to the limitation of sovereignty also includes the participation of German soldiers in military action on the basis of cooperation in security systems and within their framework, if Germany has been integrated into these systems with parliamentary approval.

7.a) Acts concerning foreign affairs and not included in Art. 59 paragraph 2 sentence 1 Basic Law are generally matters for the government. Art. 59 paragraph 2 sentence 1 Basic Law cannot be construed in such a way that all acts of the Federal government regulating Germany's foreign relations in the field of public international law or concerning topics of federal legislative power require the form of a treaty approved by parliament. An analogous or extensive interpretation of this provision is not warranted (Following BVerfGE 68 pp. 1, 84, 85).

b) The decision further concerns the power of the legislature to consent, under Art. 59 paragraph 2 sentence 1 Basic Law, to participation in such a system and thus also to using the Bundeswehr for actions within the framework and the rules of that system.

32 BVerfG, 2 BvE 6/99 of 22 November 2001, para. 1–35, *Bundesverfassungsgericht* online, available at http://www.bverfg.de/ – search for Entscheidungen; Wolfgang Janisch, "Fortentwickelt, Bundesverfassungsgericht: Strategisches Konzept der NATO von 1999 kein Fall für den Bundestag," *aktuell, Zeitung für die Bundeswehr*, no. 47, (26 November 2001), p. 1; "Karlsruhe stärkt Außen- und Sicherheitspolitik der Regierung," *IAP-Dienst Sicherheitspolitik*, no. 1 (January 2002), p. 3.

33 *The Bundeswehr – Advancing Steadily into the 21st Century, Cornerstones of a Fundamental Renewal*, para. 4–27, 48, 58; Alexander Siedschlag, "Deutsche Truppe für 'Enduring Freedom' – Neubeginn oder Kontinuität?," *Y. Magazin der Bundeswehr*, December 2001, p. 14

34 "Auslandseinsätze: Die Bundeswehr stößt an ihre Grenzen," *IAP-Diens t Sicherheitspolitik*, no. 1 (January 2002), p. 2; Harald Kujat, Rede des Generalinspekteurs der Bundeswehr anlässlich der 39. Kommandeurtagung der Bundeswehr am 09. April 2002 in Hannover, p. 4.

35 "Berlin/Bonn intern, Ein Drittel der Bundeswehr gebunden,"*Soldat und Technik* no. 1 (January 2002), p. 6; "Auslandseinsätze: Die Bundeswehr stößt an ihre Grenzen," p. 2.

36 Rudolf Scharping, "Das Ansehen ist weiter gewachsen," Interview des Bundesministers der Verteidigung vom 13. Februar 2002, p. 3, 5; Interview des Bundesministers der Verteidigung mit der Frankfurter Allgemeinen Sonntagszeitung zum Bundeswehreinsatz in Afghanistan vom 16.12.2001, *Bundeswehr* online, 17 December 2001, available at http://www. bundeswehr.de/news/reden/reden/_minister/011216_fasz_afghanistan.html, pp. 1, 2.

37 Karl Feldmeyer, "Military Says Government Is Out of Touch With Reality," *FAZ.NET F.A.Z. – English Version, 10 April 2002*, available at www.faz.de – search for military, p. 2; Harald Kujat, Rede des Generalinspekteurs der Bundeswehr anlässlich der 39. Kommandeurtagung der Bundeswehr am 09. April 2002 in Hannover, p. 5.

38 Karl Feldmeyer, "Military Says Government Is Out of Touch With Reality," pp. 2, 3.

39 Rudolf Scharping, Rede des Bundesministers der Verteidigung bei der Sondersitzung des Bundestages zu den Terrorangriffen in den Vereinigten Staaten am 19. September 2001, *Bundeswehr* online, 20 September 2001, available at http://www.bundeswehr.de/news/reden/reden/_minister/010919_sondersitzung_bt_terror.html, p. 1.

40 Kofi Annan, Rede des Generalsekretärs der Vereinten Nationen vor dem Deutschen Bundestag am 28 Februar 2002 in Berlin, *Information für die Truppe, Zeitschrift für Innere Führung*, no. 1 (1st quarter 2002), 74.

III

National Perspectives

GERALD WRIGHT

Unspent Currency: Peacekeeping and Canada's Political Role

Introduction

OSNIA will not live in the Canadian imagi-
nation as Vimy does or even Dieppe. The
size of the Canadian contribution, dispatched to a part of the world where
Canadian interests were hard to discern, was nonetheless remarkable.
When the UN Protection Force in Croatia (UNPROFOR) was set up in
early 1992 Canada sent 1,200 soldiers and approximately 45 RCMP
officers to the area. In short order, the need for an international
response to the fighting in Bosnia-Herzegovina also became evident.
When the call went out for further contributions Canada most definitely did not head for the washroom. Despite having to fight a continuing battle with the budget deficit, the government provided
another battalion of 1,200, with the mission of facilitating the delivery of humanitarian assistance. For an extended period only France
had more peacekeepers in the field, and to this Canadian contribution had to be added other forms of assistance, including the provision of over thirty-six million dollars in humanitarian assistance
during the Mulroney prime-ministership. Since that time Canada has
been represented in IFOR and SFOR and, though critics have suggested that its efforts have been flagging,[1] in carrying out the civilian
aspects of the peace agreement negotiated at Dayton.

The Bosnian conflict raged over more than three frustrating years.
In my view, the events were so overwhelming that not enough time

GERALD WRIGHT, Skelton-Clark Fellow at Queen's University, 2001–2002, was
Special Advisor to the Secretary of State for External Affairs, 1992–1993. The
author wishes to thank Dan O'Meara for his comments on an earlier draft of
this paper.

was taken by ministers and officials to ask what were the real possibilities of changing the situation and what was really at stake here for us. Once the situation on the ground had changed to a degree and outside pressure had been brought to bear, the conflict ended, whether permanently or not no one knows. This in itself told us a lot about what was driving the parties and how they could be influenced, as well as about what could be expected from the allies. Dayton gave us a glimpse, albeit imperfect, into the internal dynamics of the situation. Looking back, until the conditions that brought about Dayton were achieved, the range of options available to decision-makers appears pretty narrow, suggesting that lessons for the future should be more nuanced and less sweeping than some statements of commentators have been. The protection of individuals, peacekeepers or civilians, which was often held out as the goal of Canadian policy, should not be downplayed but a more important objective was restoration of peace and stability. In that perspective, Canada's role was not productive, was maybe even counter-productive. Secondly, Canada, though a giant as a peacekeeper, was almost, but not quite, a pygmy as a political actor. The currency of political influence bought by the peacekeeping contribution remained unspent. The role that Canada should have played, and particularly the central place that the United States should have occupied in its strategic calculations, was not clearly recognized at the time. That these factors should loom so large only in retrospect does not detract from their importance as lessons to be learned from the Bosnian crisis.

Floundering in the Quagmire: The West Tries to Cope with the Bosnian Conflict

MANY OBSERVERS have concluded that the West should have intervened forcefully at a much earlier date. (That is presumably also their prescription for ensuring against a repeat performance of the tragedy). Richard Holbrooke blames, among other factors, "the inadequate American response to the crisis." What should have happened, in his view, is what, in the end, did happen, though long after the damage had been done.

The Yugoslav crisis should have been handled by NATO, the Atlantic institution that mattered most, the one in which the United States was the core member. The best chance to prevent war would have been to present Yugoslavia with a clear warning that NATO air power would be used against any party that tried to deal with ethnic tensions by force.[2]

It is hard to argue against this opinion. Better to be in at the beginning, before the wanton destruction of human life, homes and infrastructure, and before ethnic passions have a chance to be fired by the harrowing evidence of havoc wrought upon one group by another. Better to get there before the rag tag militias and bandits have been formed into fighting forces and fed with weapons and ordnance from the stock of the Yugoslav Army or Iran and other Muslim countries.

Critics who contend that the response at the beginning was weak-kneed become even harsher when they condemn the manner in which western governments, and particularly the members of the Security Council, conducted themselves between 1991 and 1995. In a nutshell, these governments' reach is held to have exceeded their grasp. The unrealistic mandates that were handed to peacekeeping forces, force levels that were loudly proclaimed but were, practically speaking, unattainable, and the sadly misnamed "safe areas" are cases in point. UNPROFOR itself, as the international community's sole surrogate instrument for ending the conflict and restoring peace, was allowed to carry too heavy a load of expectations. The bankruptcy of the strategy of substituting rhetoric for action appears to have been conclusively demonstrated by the massacre of innocent civilians, allowed to believe that they could count on the protection of the UN.

It is easy to condemn the decisions of western governments that did so little to stop, may even have helped perpetuate, catastrophe in Bosnia, but that gives no guarantee against a repeat performance. There is little value in stating what should have been done if that could not conceivably have been viewed as a reasonable course of action at the time. Who is so prescient as to be confident that nationalist stirring will erupt in full-blown conflagration? Abandon the benefit of hindsight, get inside the mindset of the main actors and ask whether it would, indeed, have been possible to take a radically different tack.

The policy paralysis of the early nineties was made up of a number of ingredients. There was a mismatch between diplomatic initiative, which the Europeans wanted and which the North Americans were prepared to let them have, and the military capability required to intervene decisively in the conflict, which belonged solely to the Americans. Diplomacy was, and remains, what you do first when conflict first breaks out and it is doubtful that too many believed in 1991–1992 that the moral and political foundations had been laid for a military response. That was not a risk worth taking as long as there was a chance of restoring stability by talking to the parties and, indeed, the success, albeit shaky, that Cyrus Vance achieved in Croatia must have kept this hope alive.

The attitude of the United States came to be central to the way everyone else regarded the problem. Once the hopes of a diplomatic solution wore thin, ground troops were thought necessary to break the stalemate but every government agreed there was no prospect of an expeditionary force because of the obvious disinclination of the United States to entertain such an involvement. There is only so much that a new US administration can take on. Bosnia was no match for the Clinton administration's domestic program when it came to competing for a place on its political agenda. Even US advocates of military action thought it would require building a coalition of allies, not an easy task with the UN Security Council and NATO deadlocked.[3]

The allies of the United States were hardly clamouring to change that country's mind. Governments had to weigh in the balance the possibility that premature intervention would worsen the conflict, in this case helping it to overflow the boundaries of Bosnia (and Croatia). The prospect of intervention was feared to be encouraging combatants to hang on and refuse to accept peace terms. If there were intervention, it would simply ratify a disgracefully unfair partition of the country. Moreover, though the sanctity of sovereignty was much diminished, it was still considered prudent to stay out of other people's business. France's President Mitterrand was less interventionist than his successor, Jacques Chirac, would prove to be. Europeans argued that the Yugoslav situation was essentially a civil war. As far as Canada was concerned, it could have been regarded as "a quarrel in a far-away country between people of whom we know nothing." At an External Affairs meeting on Yugoslavia, Neville Chamberlain's words were repeated by one senior policy maker.[4]

The European allies were watching each other as much as circumstances on the ground. The United Kingdom and France were greatly influenced by the evolving role of the European Community (which had not yet become the European Union), the EC's relationship to NATO and their own status within the Community. They were motivated to contribute to peace operations in order to qualify for a seat at the table and vie for influence as the Community sought to test its fledgling capability in foreign affairs. Though they were not immune to its tragic dimensions, the conflict in the former Yugoslavia provided a theatre in which to continue their strategic game.

What western governments knew about the conflict was that it was being carried on by people whose attitudes had been shaped by a very different historical experience from that of most North Americans and West Europeans. We could not expect them to react as we would. This culturally based caution may, at times, have led to making incorrect judgements. For example, the expectation that heavy bombing would only embitter the Serbs further and drive them into more extreme and violent behaviour turned out be dead wrong in 1995. But until that time there was much scepticism that bombing would do the trick and, in retrospect, that scepticism appears entirely rational. News reports that the parties were sufficiently bloody minded to position bombing targets in close proximity to schools and hospitals had a considerable impact on thinking in the Canadian government and probably other governments. The view that we were up against people whose values and attitudes we did not entirely understand and about whom we could not easily make assumptions ranked high among the operational beliefs in western foreign ministries, including Canada's, and it strongly advised going very carefully.

Also contributing to paralysis was the failure of military establishments in the NATO countries to come up with a concept of usable military power to tackle ethnic strife in a decidedly inhospitable environment. Military leaders, particularly those in the Pentagon, were a drag on taking assertive action and they remained so throughout the war. The Balkans were portrayed as Europe's Afghanistan, an impossible theatre of military operations. The views of Colin Powell were in the ascendant. Such views played directly to a public that was scarred by the memory of Vietnam and were fortified by the antiseptic experience of the Gulf War.

As the intractability of the situation grew more evident, critics castigated the moral indifference and pusillanimity of the West. "Today's equivalent of Chamberlain is the Vance-Owen rejection of the use of force to stop the killing," Zbigniew Brzezinski charged.[5] It became evident that none of the principles enunciated by the London Conference in September, 1992 was being respected, that gains won by force were not being rolled back, that the infamous ethnic cleansing had not been stopped, that conditions in the camps were no better.

The Canadian government too wrestled with the developing dilemma. UNPROFOR membership had originally served as a validation of Canada's status as a G-7 member, a status that Brian Mulroney prized highly.[6] That explains why Canada actually broke its own guidelines for peacekeeping commitments with the decision to extend the UNPROFOR mandate in 1992. As the situation worsened it appeared there was no practical way to escalate the response. Mirroring the Pentagon, National Defence constantly reiterated the impossibility of successfully fighting a war in the former Yugoslavia without, at very least, being in possession of overwhelming force. This attitude carried over to the conduct of the peacekeeping operation. National Defence exhibited near paranoia that plots would be hatched to use the peacekeepers in a manner inconsistent with their equipment, deployment, training and mandate. It is hard to exaggerate the impact that this had on ministers who, though irritated by it, were not so brazenly Churchillian as to go against the military professionals' advice.

Throughout his last year as prime minister Mulroney demonstrated an eagerness for finding a way out of the Yugoslav quagmire. The internal debates of his government, however, showed how it was caught between wanting to act in response to the popular revulsion over events in the Balkans and fearing that almost any military intervention within the realm of reasonable possibility was fraught with enormous dangers. The frustration in the Langevin Block and the Pearson Building became almost palpable in the late spring of 1993. The split between National Defence and External Affairs grew wider as the former pleaded its lack of capability to undertake more aggressive forms of military action and External Affairs Minister Barbara McDougall, at the same time as asserting the importance of the peacekeepers' safety, began to wonder aloud whether they could not be employed in more muscular fashion to score at least a few successes at the local level.

Canada's role as a major contributor of peacekeeping forces compounded the conundrum confronting the government. The Yugoslav experience was a lesson in the limitations and pitfalls of peacekeeping. Inadequacies at the organizational level were evident, particularly with respect to financing of missions (Canada felt hard done by on this score because too much of the burden was borne by contributors directly and too little by the UN, which allocated its share of peacekeeping costs to members according to a formula), and to the careful cost-benefit analysis that, Canadian officials came to believe, the Security Council should undertake before authorizing a mission. On the ground, peacekeeping forces were, on occasion, shown to be incapable of getting convoys through to their destination, constantly vulnerable to accusations of favouring one side over the other, and perhaps even in danger of being held hostage, as happened briefly to General Morillon and a handful of Canadian troops in Srebrenica in March, 1993, and again in May, 1995 when several hundred peace-keepers were handcuffed to trees and telephone poles. The UN came dangerously close to sharing General Mladic's aim: forestall air strikes. When you reflect on how often assertive action was abandoned or watered down because the peacekeepers would have been vulnera-ble to retaliation, it is hard to avoid the conclusion that their presence came to stand in the way of ending the conflict. "Man is neither angel nor brute," said Pascal, "and the unfortunate thing is that he who would act the angel acts the brute."[7]

But once Canada and its peacekeeping partners were stuck in the quagmire it proved extremely difficult to get out. The irony of trying to pacify ethnic conflict is that by the time the hopelessness of the task is realized the escape routes are treacherous. This was true both in terms of the practical task of facilitating the withdrawal of peacekeepers from the area and in term of the public uproar that would have been created by abandoning the scene. Withdrawal was seriously contem-plated in 1995 at the time of the Srebrenica horrors but at the second London conference called by Prime Minister John Major decisions were taken that led through Operation Deliberate Force to Dayton.[8]

By this time the "CNN effect," which had been building throughout the war, was a major driver behind developments in the Yugoslav drama. Public horror at what was going on influenced both the content and the timing of NATO governments' reaction. In so far as the media were on the spot to broadcast the spectacle of savagery, democratically elected governments of societies with highly developed sensibilities had little choice but to engage the issue. But what should have been a measured and consistent strategy of applying force to achieve a politi-cal outcome became instead a sharp correction in course.

Whatever the recommendation for action to break the impasse prior to Dayton, there were always convincing arguments against it. It would have taken a cataclysm tantamount to a World Trade Center attack to galvanize military and civilian bureaucracies and overcome the many objections to assertive action. Something similar would have been required to shake public queasiness about taking casualties. There is a lot of weight to the argument that international crises must "ripen" until the major powers will be motivated to tackle them.[9] Let us not, there-fore, discount the political challenge of moving decisively in situations such as Bosnia. Nor is it wise to set too much store by new guidelines, governing the initiation of peace support operations or national contributions to such operations, however much these may be the product of zealous inquiries into past failures. The UN may refine its concepts of peacekeeping and peace enforcement, and Europe may equip itself with more effective military instruments, but unless we learn how to mobilize political energies in the absence of an unambiguous and immediately perceived threat, future Bosnias will be left to fester as before.

When trying to discover the cause of terrible outcomes it is altogether too common to invoke weakness of political will, much as the Gang of Four used to be trotted out to explain every ailment that ever afflicted China. That is hardly useful counsel for those trying to avert such outcomes. Post mortems of Bosnia have to take into account the context from which the decisions of western governments emerged. Those decisions were subject to the constraints and imperatives of democratic politics. There was the constant jockeying for position with allies, there were competing domestic objectives, there were divergent bureaucratic interests and perceptions, and there was maddeningly complex public opinion that set clear limits to what could be attempted but, at the same time, demanded that something must be done. If that is understood our expectations of averting more Bosnias will be more realistic. That in itself would be a step forward. After all, were not unrealistic expectations partly responsible for Bosnia's disaster?

Canada's Political Role

CANADA'S PEACEKEEPERS could not have done much to alter this situation. Canada could, however, have tried to use the leverage provided by its peacekeeping contribution to exert influence over its allies and thereby gain through diplomacy what could not be achieved in the field. Such a role would have been aimed at an expansive conception of the national interest, reviving the voluntarist strain in Canadian foreign policy, and would have gone beyond the provision of peacekeeping services. The government would have eagerly solicited invitations to participate in monitoring and decision-making bodies. The crisis would have been exploited as an opportunity to demonstrate Canada's diplomatic expertise, set precedents acknowledging not just the right of Canada to be consulted but also the right to a seat in the councils of the major powers, and define solutions that drew from the Canadian experience of moderating discord. From the prime minister on down every effort would have been made to keep Canada's profile high by means of an active diplomacy. It would have been accepted, of course, that there were limits to the government's reach and resources but the emphasis would have been on compensating for those limits with solid intellectual input and faultless execution. Following the example set by Canada's early postwar foreign policy planners, it would not have been considered presumptuous or overly ambitious to volunteer for the gravest responsibilities or propose a design for a settlement of the conflict.

This is the outline of a foreign policy role that inspires one point of view in the current foreign policy debate, the role of "an activist, imaginative middle power, reflecting our tradition of compromise, conscious of our limitations but alive to our potential."[10] Policy makers would, however, have asked themselves what purpose would be served by Canada undertaking such a role in the Bosnia case. As we have seen, margins for manoeuvre were tight and, for a long time, a settlement of any kind could not be expected. In such circumstances, did Canada even try to exert influence?

Canada did play a political role during the Bosnian crisis. That role was a muted one for reasons that were mainly, though not entirely, of Canada's own choosing, fell short of the standard set above and was pursued even less aggressively after the advent of the Chrétien government. Canadian diplomacy focused on the allies and barely touched the adversaries. There were sporadic contacts with the warring parties (never, so far as I am aware, with the Bosnian Serbs) that were intended to keep up the pressure to come to the bargaining table but did not fulfil any distinctively Canadian strategy or goal. The argument that Canada consistently pressed with other London Conference powers, particularly the United States, was that military action of any kind should not be undertaken if it would endanger, in any way, the safety of the peacekeeping troops already on the ground in the former Yugoslavia. The public had to be constantly reminded that this was Canada's first preoccupation, particularly as impatience mounted over the failure of UN measures to end the crisis and the demand arose for a more robust response. On his farewell visit to London Prime Minister Mulroney chided US Senator Joseph Biden for criticizing the Western powers' caution on Yugoslavia. "How could you be bombing the Bosnian Serbs while leaving British peacekeepers on the ground in parts of Bosnia?" he reminded British reporters.[11]

The argument had to be repeated often as new proposals for nudging the conflict towards a resolution were entered into the policy mix in New York and Geneva: the "no fly zone" in Bosnia, the proposal for "safe areas," and the later US initiative to launch massive air strikes in defence of Sarajevo. In turn, each of the proposals was greeted with scepticism by Canadian officials and each was the subject of considerable diplomatic efforts intended to ensure that the form in which it was eventually adopted would take due account of the safety of the peacekeepers. Fortunately, there were allies with peacekeepers in the field who, much of the time, looked at the question in the same way as Canada. There were, however, times when Canada, on its own, balked at Washington's plans. In regard to the air strikes, which became a major issue during the period of the Campbell government, Canada was successful in getting an UNPROFOR "sign off" before bombing would commence, but not without incurring serious, albeit temporary, acrimony on the part of the Americans.[12] (That decision had to be reversed before Operation Deliberate Force could begin on August 30, 1995.)

The government bore, of course, responsibility for its peacekeepers but the single-minded pursuit of their safety carried overtones of domestic politics. With a federal election in the offing, the public's perception mattered a great deal. It was considered imperative not to be perceived as abdicating responsibility for the troops on the ground. In that connection, the frequent public statements, both before and after his retirement, by Major General Lewis Mackenzie, the former commander of the UN force in Sarajevo, created a lot of unease. His trip to the Federal Republic of Yugoslavia and meeting with some of the principals, including Radovan Karadzic, sounded an alarm. Who would the public perceive to be occupying the driver's seat? The visit which Mrs McDougall paid to Yugoslavia in May, 1993, succeeded in attracting media attention to both the government's own actions in respect of the crisis and to the, theretofore little reported, activities of Canadian peacekeepers in the field. The importance of being seen to be in control was all the greater because Canadian lives were at stake and the government was under attack for having put those lives at unnecessary risk through bad planning, poorly drafted mandates and failure to provide equipment appropriate to the task.[13]

Canada also argued against lifting the arms embargo for Bosnia. The rationale for this was that permitting Bosnia to arm itself from abroad, in order to be on a par with its adversaries, would simply worsen the fighting and make a peaceful resolution more difficult. Within government, the point was also made that the Bosnians were untrained in the use of heavy weapons and that the interval between lifting the embargo and deploying these weapons would give the Serbs every incentive to raise the ante through military action. This stand pitted Canada against the Clinton administration when it came into office, and against mounting congressional support for lifting the embargo, but it evoked very little debate at home, apart from the protests of Bosnian organizations.

Further, Canada took some initiatives bearing on the resolution of the conflict. Noteworthy was Mrs McDougall's strenuous and consistent advocacy, beginning with her speech to the 1992 London Conference, of an international court to hear cases of war crimes in the former Yugoslavia. Many concerns about this proposal were raised within the government. How would the laws applied by such a tribunal be made consistent with the different, and sometimes conflicting, systems of domestic law prevailing in the participating states? What real chance was there that those chiefly responsible for the tragedy would be apprehended and brought to justice? Why would they not be expected to bargain for their own immunity as part of an eventual peace settlement? The argument used to overcome these objections was that the preparation of legal machinery and the carrying out of UN investigations for this purpose would have a sobering effect on the perpetrators of the Yugoslav tragedy. No one could have been confident at the time that this argument would hold water but the process set in motion – and impelled particularly by a conference of legal specialists in Vancouver that was financially supported by the government – was one that turned out to be a major advance in the application of international law to military conflicts.

A few modest steps do not, however, amount to an energetic political role. Part of the problem was that Canada did not carry the clout that might have been expected on account of its contribution to resolution of the conflict. Since Pierre Trudeau withdrew half Canada's NATO contingent from Europe in 1969, claims and counter claims have been made about whether putting troops on the ground buys influence and access, and how much. Bosnia is an interesting test case that yields an ambiguous conclusion.

In a message from Brussels, Jim Bartleman, Canada's NATO Ambassador, expressed relief that having 2,600 peacekeepers in the former Yugoslavia had made life easier for him with his colleagues on the NATO Council. (He had been embarrassed by the recent withdrawal of Canadian troops from Lahr and Baden.) But the peacekeepers were not an automatic admission ticket to the most important meetings. There was a continual problem of being excluded from meetings of Western governments on the former Yugoslavia or left "out of the loop" when important consultations were being conducted by telephone. Getting into the loop was made more complicated because the locus of consultation and decision-making moved around and participating countries varied often from meeting to meeting. More important, Canada had not gained the allies' acknowledgment that by right it owned a place in their councils.

The energies of the minister, and particularly of the Canadian ambassadors in New York and Geneva, were heavily concentrated on trying to gain a seat at the table. Time and again Barbara McDougall had to place telephone calls to the UN Secretary General, the US Secretary of State or the British Foreign Secretary. Time and again Ambassador Gerry Shannon in Geneva had to seek meetings with Cyrus Vance or his senior staff to make sure that Canadian views were taken into account. On her visit to Geneva in December, 1992, McDougall managed to organize a dinner meeting with Vance, David Owen and Douglas Hurd. These efforts did meet with a considerable degree of success. Hurd, in particular, appeared to understand that the size of Canada's contribution justified a right of consultation. David Owen was of the same view. According to his memoir, he made a point of keeping Canada, with "its unrivaled expertise of UN operations," fully informed of the views of the International Conference on the Former Yugoslavia.[14]

It was nonetheless a never-ending battle. The issue arose again during the short-lived Campbell government when Canada was temporarily left out of US consultations concerning the plan to use air strikes to push the Bosnian parties into a deal. It arose yet again just as the Chrétien government was coming into office when the European Council issued a declaration calling for "the use of all appropriate means to support the convoying of humanitarian aid", a choice of words that alarmed Canadian policy makers. Part of the problem was of Canada's making. The inclination of even close allies, such as Britain and France, to by-pass consultations with Canada on occasion was probably magnified because of the Chrétien government's flaccid approach to the crisis.[15] Not much clout was going to be accorded to Canada when its government was encouraging uncertainty about whether its peacekeeping commitment would be renewed.

A political role hampered by lack of clout and focused solely on the protection of the peacekeepers was decidedly stunted. There is no evidence that the government had any intention to expand it. The government laid greater stress on the manner in which the conflict should be resolved than the design of a desirable outcome. Only when the situation of the Bosnians came close to total defeat did it begin to be suggested that one of Canada's aims should be to ensure at least some kind of future for Bosnia. Notwithstanding Canada's own experience of ethnic diversity, Canadian officials did not invest much time or resources in thinking through the issue of Bosnia's survival as a multi-ethnic state.

What was noticeably missing from Canada's policy stance was a sustained attack on the main issues. For example, on direct intervention to force a settlement in Bosnia the government sounded an uncertain trumpet, occasionally throwing out an idea but refraining from the investment of energy needed to drive the point home. In his Harvard speech of December, 1992, the Prime Minister, in answer to a question, aired the suggestion of a UN enforcement action similar to that undertaken to regain Kuwait from Iraq. In his London speech of May, 1993, he went so far as to propose criteria for military action, but neither proposal was followed by sustained diplomatic activity. At the same time, policy makers came increasingly to believe that the credible threat of military action was essential to bring the parties to the table. That had to be left to the United States. When the Clinton administration failed to make good on its early intimations of a more aggressive posture towards the Serbs, they were quick, within their own walls, to criticize the administration's weakness of will.

Lacking was the intellectual input that would have lent weight to Canada's interventions. The significant investment that Canada made in the Yugoslav conflict was not governed by a thought-through conception of the desirable political outcome and how to get there. Policy makers did not attempt a deeply considered diagnosis of the problem or the development of a set of strategic objectives. Meetings on Bosnia were taken up with checklists of who was doing what. No interdepartmental working group formed of the two departments most directly concerned, National Defence and External Affairs, existed to come up with proposals for a resolution or to subject them to critical analysis. The official Canadian position was that the Vance-Owen process, rather than the Vance-Owen plan which did not command much confidence in Ottawa, was the way to achieve a peaceful outcome negotiated between the three warring parties.

Ironically, when the opportunity arose to get admitted to the first tier of allied partners the government hung back. It is hard to believe that the size of the Canadian contribution of peacekeepers, combined with an all-out diplomatic effort, would not have won a seat on the Steering Committee of the London Conference or, more significantly, in the Contact Group that was set up in 1994. (The government may have been content to have the press spread the impression that Canada had been deliberately excluded from the latter.) That would have solved the problem of access, at least until the United States began to "end run" the allies. The government was, however, not interested in making such an effort. The break-up of Yugoslavia and its aftermath were, after all, viewed as Europe's problem at the start. What interest had Canada in embroiling itself in intense diplomatic activity with other governments, most of which were driven by concern for the future shape of Europe as much as by concern for Yugoslavia? As far as the Canadian public was concerned, support was not building around a clearly defined point of view. There was a steady drumbeat of criticism from the organizations of Serbs, Croats and Bosnians, but their influence did not appear to extend beyond their respective ethnic groups. There was thus no political incentive to identify Canada further with the conflict. Moreover, Canadian resources were stretched to the limit already. During the Mulroney era, the government was at war with itself, for the desire to behave as a G-7 country clashed with the priority attached to fiscal responsibility and a wariness about allowing fuzzy internationalism to result in further commitments.

The Bosnia case prompts us to reflect on how a political role and a peacekeeping role can be kept going in tandem. Canada was subject to conflicting pushes and pulls, wanting to be acknowledged as a front line player at times but at other times content to go to the sidelines. The government was pulled in the direction of greater diplomatic and political activity by its peacekeeping responsibilities but kept out of some of the decision-making by its allies.

On another occasion it might prove impossible to contribute troops and not both seek and accept a political role that is at least commensurate with the contribution. An electorate insisting on accountability and sensible management of the risks of peacekeeping operations is going to require a government to demonstrate that it is exercising control to the fullest extent possible. That control is likely going to be inseparable from participation in the political direction of the effort. A fortiori, if peacekeeping becomes peace enforcement the inconsistency between military and political efforts will become blatant. Why should a government not support its men and women in the field by exerting every instrument at its command in the direction of an outcome that will get them out of harm's way and bring them home?

Canadian Interests

THE TEST of whether or not Canada should have played a more active political role is to ask how that would have advanced Canadian interests. Other governments were inclined to see their core interests engaged by the crisis, whereas Canadian governments appeared to regard peacekeeping chiefly as a voluntary contribution to international stability, aid to bolster the international milieu but bearing little relation to "possession goals" beyond the enhancement of G-7 member status.[16] Was there more at stake for Canada than was realized?

The safety of the peacekeepers was just one interest that can be discerned in the Bosnian case. Surely it should have been a higher priority objective of Canadian policy that multilateral management approaches and multilateral institutions prove successful in containing and reducing conflict and thereby become entrenched as bulwarks of the new post-Cold War order. Integral to the success of the multilateral principle was the adherence of the United States, cognizant of the importance of acting in concert with its allies and bent on working with them to develop principles that would command general respect in the new order. Canada's effectiveness can be measured in terms of how well this interest was preserved and extended.

Domestic politics pushed the peacekeepers up the order of priorities. Pursuing their safety to the exclusion of other policy goals, however, fitted poorly with a wider interest in the controlled and discriminating application of American power. As a NATO member, Canada eventually went along with military action intended to bring the Serbs to heel. That was after a series of stands, often taken in good company but opposed to the kind of decisive action that would help end the conflict. If Canada's image in the eyes of US policy makers was altered at all by the experience it was to lump us in with the lesser powers that were incapable of sharing the world view and sense of responsibility of the United States. These were not governments whose political weight required that attention be paid to them, or whose advice was so sage that it had to be solicited. Sooner or later, they could be relied upon to provide minimally necessary support and meanwhile it was better to lead by fait accompli rather than take them step by step through the incubation, development and application of policy.

Hardly surprising, therefore, that the principle of multilateralism, and the attachment of the United States to that principle, emerged from the conflict badly frayed. During the march to Dayton the US set store by the alliance not because there was genuine acceptance of advance consultation and policy coordination but because the imprimatur of alliance approval was highly valued. That was worth making a diplomatic effort to achieve but the model of alliance behaviour that survived in the minds of US policy makers was one in which initiative and control belonged to them and all that was left to the allies was the exercise of legitimation. Ploughing ahead on their own had brought success, thus inclining them to practice multilateralism on a symbolic level only. The assertion of US power that brought an end to the Bosnian crisis, in the Europeans' own back yard, also defined the relationship of the US with its allies in the minds of the Americans most involved. The trend of US foreign policy since has cast the significance of the Bosnian crisis in higher relief.

Canada did not seize the opportunity afforded by Bosnia to build a reputation as a political actor that could not be discounted and would have to be consulted. Such an initiative would have begun by using the peacekeepers as leverage to gain guaranteed access to the allies' councils. It would have required a campaign to increase the public's appreciation of how critical it was to resolve the Bosnian crisis and thereby shore up the domestic base for an activist political stance. Further, it would have required a sympathetic effort to enter into the Americans' strategic perspective but not necessarily agree with their policies, develop a clear picture of a desirable outcome but possibly challenge their view what the outcome should be, refrain, if possible, from being a drag on decisive action but not endorse automatically every US initiative. The goal should have been to establish a purchase on the attention of the US government that could be used in future crises, not just to tackle the crisis at hand, however dramatic and harrowing it may have been. Multilateralism prevails not because of a one-shot experience but because of an accumulation of respect and familiarity and the working arrangements to which these give rise.

An active political role is a must in such circumstances because the battle between unilateralism and multilateralism in the United States is one of immense consequence for Canada.[17] Breathing life into American multilateralism is a time-honoured Canadian strategy that will look even more compelling as the two countries are thrown into closer integration and the weight of US decisions is felt north of the border to an even greater degree than has recently been the case. That means pursuing the aim of trying to have an impact on international affairs chiefly by influencing the United States, in preference to playing a distinctive role that side-steps the exercise of American power. It will be objected that the US is impervious to influence. It is easy to be intimidated by the weight of competing forces and the intensity of political debate in the US, and thus to assume that there is nothing to be done but watch and adjust to the outcome. Yet allies retain a sign-off which is not devoid of meaning, and they can often find influential support for their views from American politicians outside the executive branch.

Multilateral decision-making should not be equated with governments moving in lock step. Leadership by one or two governments is necessary, as even Canada, whose actions have occasionally appeared contrary to its professions of the multilateral principle, has found.[18] Even when US administrations accept that their decision-making must be carried on through wide consultation and policy coordination, the practice of multilateralism can go off the rails. Global responsibilities weigh heavily on US decision makers and avowed multilateralists among them are sometimes tempted to think that going it alone is the only way to spur less heavily burdened allies to get a move on.

That is where allies who can be effective advocates and interlocutors on the central issues come in. They can hold in check the temptation to act unilaterally and reinforce the assumption that allies represent sources of influence and opinion that must be taken into account. They have to grasp the superpower's mentality sufficiently well to be able to shape their arguments in a manner that appeals to the superpower's instincts. Canadians need a "sense of power"[19] and a willingness to play an active political role if they are to project the confidence and world-view that will help cement the US attachment to multilateralism. Most important, they must be guided by the realization that the United States will not take multilateralism seriously if it cannot take its potential partners seriously.

Notes

1 See John Graham, "Black Past, Grey Future?" *International Journal,* 53 (Spring 1998), 204–220.
2 Richard Holbrooke, *To End A War* (New York: Random House Inc., 1998), p. 28.
3 George Kenney and Michael J. Dugan, "Operation Balkan Storm: Here's a Plan," *New York Times,* 29 November 1992.
4 This is the author's recollection of a departmental meeting in which he participated as a ministerial staff member. One wing of External Affairs, headed by the then

Under Secretary, was inclined against taking on more peacekeeping commitments, arguing that these could not be justified in terms of Canada's national interests and that economic objectives were a much higher foreign policy priority.

5 *New York Times*, 22 April 1993.

6 A factor that weighed heavily in his thinking was his personal relationship with the White House and the access that afforded him to pursue Canadian interests in the bilateral relationship with the United States. This undoubtedly drove his decision to commit forces to Somalia in early 1993, a decision that External Affairs officials, had they had any role in it, would have firmly opposed. He was by no means the first prime minister to undertake an overseas commitment prompted by wider political considerations. Lester Pearson, mindful of the irons Canada had in the fire with Washington, agreed to send a force to Cyprus under pressure from President Lyndon Johnson.

7 Blaise Pascal, *Pensées*, Section IV, No. 358.

8 This is not to discount the effect of the Croat-Muslim offensive, which occurred at the same time as both the NATO bombing and Richard Holbrooke's diplomatic initiative, and which can be credited to the Washington Agreement of 1994 between Muslims and Croats. That the Serbs were pushed back somewhat certainly improved the chances of an agreement between the parties.

9 Dana H. Allin, *NATO's Balkan Interventions*, Adelphi Paper 347 (London: The International Institute for Strategic Studies, 2002), p. 33.

10 Andrew Cohen, "The Ghost of Canada's Past," *Ottawa Citizen*, 4 December 2001.

11 Stephen Ward, Canadian Press dispatch, 11 May 1993.

12 It was reported that Canada, apparently alone among the NATO countries, had stood in the way of a US plan to wage air strikes against Serbian forces. *New York Times*, 3 August 1993.

13 The government's handling of its peacekeeping responsibilities was, indeed, momentarily shaky when General Morillon's request to send Canadian troops to Srebrenica arrived. The implications of the "safe area" concept were not understood and there was a reaction of horror at the thought that approximately one hundred Canadian troops might be taking responsibility for the lives of thousands of Bosnians. Lloyd Axworthy, the Opposition critic for external affairs, attacked the government for having undertaken the commitment. It developed that, whatever General Morillon may have told the inhabitants of Srebrenica, Canadian troops were not expected to defend the town if attacked. When Canada was successful in getting allies to share some of the responsibility the commitment appeared manageable.

14 David Owen, *Balkan Odyssey* (New York: Harcourt Brace & Company, 1995), p. 206.

15 "Like a jazz musician improvising a tune, Prime Minister Chrétien is sounding the first notes of a Canadian retreat from Bosnia." Paul Koring, "Canada, UN may no longer be in tune," *Globe and Mail*, 13 January 1994.

16 These two types of foreign policy goals are defined in Arnold Wolfers, *Discord and Collaboration* (Baltimore: The Johns Hopkins University Press, 1962), pp. 73–74.

17 See Joseph S. Nye Jr., *The Paradox of American Power: Why the World's Only Superpower Can't Go It Alone* (New York: Oxford University Press, 2002), pp. 154–163.

18 An example would be Canada's unilateral decision in 1970 to extend its jurisdiction over Arctic waters by means of the Arctic Waters Pollution Prevention Act.

19 This term is taken from Carl Berger, *A Sense of Power: Studies in the Ideas of Canadian Imperialism* (Toronto: University of Toronto Press, 1970).

DAVID HALE

The United States and Bosnia: Missing Pieces in the Jigsaw Puzzle

I Introduction

THERE ARE three key questions about America's role in Bosnia-Herzegovina over the last decade. Why did it take the US so long to become involved? Why has the US been involved in the particular manner it has? When and under what circumstances will the US leave Bosnia? These are the questions addressed in this chapter.

The pressures and constraints of American public opinion have shaped policy on Bosnia. US participation in international efforts to manage the conflict was primarily diplomatic and military. But since the Dayton Accords the limitations of the public mandate have prevented two missing pieces from being put in place. Two key areas, that would more easily permit the US to withdraw, have not adequately been addressed: first, the corrupt Bosnian leadership has not been purged; and second, a thorough economic plan has not been developed. They are the missing pieces in the jigsaw puzzle. If the US is to be fully successful in Bosnia, closer examination of the leadership and stronger economic support is essential. Any pullout with these two items left undone runs the risk of a resumption of violence. The matter is now more urgent because, with the war on terrorism, Washington is actively seeking a viable exit strategy or at least a lessening of its Bosnian commitment.

Colonel DAVID D. HALE JR, United States Army, was Visiting Defence Fellow at the Centre for International Relations, Queen's University, for the academic year 2001–2002.

II US Involvement Prior to 1992

URING the Cold War, the US and the West granted Yugoslavia a special status in order to use it as a strategic means to contain Soviet communism. Josef Broz Tito – half Croat, half Slovene – seized power by fighting the Nazis to a standstill and held power for an astonishing 35 years. In 1948, Tito made an historic break with the Soviet Union. From then on, the West was ready to overlook all other problems with Yugoslavia because of its strategic importance.[1] After the fall of the Berlin Wall and collapse of the Soviet Union, however, Yugoslavia was no longer of the same significance to Western interests.[2] Its collective leadership ignored all the careful checks and balances Tito had established and pushed Yugoslavia toward disintegration.[3] The conflict in Yugoslav was not inevitable; it could have been prevented.[4] While historically rooted ethnic rivalries came to drive the conflict, many see economics as the root cause. In the 1980s there was a significant economic downturn in Yugoslavia. Attempts at internal economic reform, led by the federal government, ended in failure. The leadership in Bosnia – as in other republics of federal Yugoslavia – sought to use nationalism and to blame other ethnic groups for the economic problems.[5] Ordinary Bosnian Serbs came to believe that they were under threat.[6]

In the spring of 1991, the Yugoslav crises became acute, with the Slovenian and Croatian leaderships pushing for outright independence. In June, when Secretary of State James Baker was in the Balkans he told all the entities, "Do not take steps not agreed upon by the others."[7] The leaders of Yugoslavia took Baker's words to mean the US would not become involved, thereby opening the door to the conflict. Shortly after Baker's visit, Slovenia and Croatia declared independence, and war broke out, first (and briefly) between Slovenia and the federal armed forces (JNA). Baker's misreading of the situation – he famously claimed "we don't have a dog in this fight"[8] – probably caused the Americans to be less attentive to the problem than they might otherwise have been.

In September 1991, the Yugoslav federal president sent a letter to the UN requesting peacekeeping forces for the situation in Croatia. The UN Security Council passed resolution 713 on 25 September. An arms embargo was placed on the whole of Yugoslavia.[9] In November 1991, the UN moved to take the lead from the European Community (EC) in mediating a resolution to the dispute. The UN would be responsible for protecting civilians in the UN protected areas in Croatia and the Yugoslav Army would withdraw to Serbia.[10] On 7 April 1992 the passage of UNSC Resolution 749 authorized full deployment of the UN protection force (UNPROFOR) to three UN protected areas in Croatia.[11]

In mid-December 1991, Germany announced that it would recognize Croatia and Slovenia.[12] There were three main reasons for Germany's decision. Many Germans felt that, having just achieved reunification and, with it, full sovereignty, they could not then turn around and deny the right of self-determination to others. Second, Germany, as a Central European power, would likely bear the consequences of any ensuing conflict in the Balkans more than most. Third, German public opinion was staunchly pro-Croat because, unlike Serbia, it had been under German sway in the past.[13]

The German government also argued that internationalizing the Croatian problem would open the way to negotiations. Given the actions of the Serb leadership and the JNA, many in the West viewed Belgrade as the problem. If the republics became recognized as countries, the conflict would no longer be defined as domestic, and there could be serious negotiations among the leaders under international auspices.[14]

Much of the world, the United States included, feared recognition would have the opposite effect. Britain, France and the rest of the EC reluctantly followed German recognition of Slovenia and Croatia as independent countries, on 15 January 1992. But Washington did not follow suit, fearing that it would egg the Serbs on in their war against Croatia.[15] The UN Secretary-General had launched a mediation effort under former U.S. Secretary of State Cyrus Vance and European Union mediator Lord Owen, which led to a cease-fire agreement in Croatia and the deployment of the first UN peacekeepers during the winter of 1992.[16]

Ambassador Zimmerman eventually advised the US Secretary of State James Baker to recognize Slovenia and Croatia.[17] By that time, given events on the ground, recognition of these entities may have seemed like a necessary step in halting the violence. But rather than solving the problem, it only morphed it into another form.[18] In March, Bosnia in turn declared independence, following a referendum. In the end, the Americans felt that recognition of Croatia also forced recognition of Bosnia, for many of the same reasons. By recognizing Bosnia, they reasoned, they could help negate the potential of military involvement by the JNA. On 6 April 1992, the US recognized all three (Bosnia, Croatia and Slovenia). At the same time, meeting in Lisbon, the EC recognized Bosnia.[19] Slovenia and Croatia had sparked the disintegration of Yugoslavia. Slovenia departed relatively unscathed while, in early 1992, the situation in Croatia stabilized, at least for a while. From that point on Bosnia became the problem.

From the beginnings of the Yugoslav conflict until late 1992, the US stayed in the background, leaving attempts at international intervention to the Europeans working through the OSCE, the EC and the UN. In his memoirs, Republican Secretary of State James Baker explained this decision: "It was time to make the Europeans step up to the plate and show that they could act as a unified power. Yugoslavia was as good a first test as any."[20] This is the principal reason why the US did not become involved until later; it waited for Europe to solve the problem.

III US Involvement: 1992–1993

THE WAR in Bosnia-Herzegovina was fought from 1992 to 1995 among Bosnia's three major ethnic and religious groups: Bosniaks (Muslims), Serbs (Eastern Orthodox Christians), and Croats (Roman Catholics). Bosnian Serbs and Croats fought for and declared the establishment of ethnically pure states separate from Bosnia, while Bosniaks fought for a unified, multiethnic Bosnia.

In 1992 and 1993, two different US administrations considered involvement in the Balkans. Given the indifference of the American public, the collapse of the Soviet Union, the war with Iraq and its aftermath, the US remained limited primarily to a diplomatic role. As the violence escalated, the US and the rest of the international community had three choices in Bosnia. They could attempt to seal the borders and prevent the conflict from spreading to the rest of the Balkans. They could intervene with military force, in effect becoming an army of occupation, and attempt to force a solution. Or they could maintain just enough involvement to avert the worst effects of the war on the civilian population.[21] These three choices would remain throughout the conflict in Bosnia.

The first choice was nearly impossible because there was not sufficient international support. The West shied away from the second choice of massive military involvement because of cost and risk to troops. Estimates suggested that anywhere from 100,000 to 500,000 troops would be required. Many critics referred to the Nazi experience in World War II. For its part, the US did not want another Vietnam and was still trying to get Europe to handle the problem. The US was not entirely alone in being reluctant. Some in Britain likened Bosnia to Northern Ireland. The European Union and later the UN therefore chose the third alternative, allowing the war to continue while dampening its worst effects.[22]

For both administrations, it must be stressed, the perception during this period was that the Balkans were not a region of vital national interest to the US. The government's actions were carefully restrained and limited, widely observed and reported upon by the media, and sensitive to public opinion in the United States.

In 1992 Vance and Owen had developed a plan for peace based on a complex division of Bosnian territory among the three ethnic groups.[23] Upon taking office in January 1993, President Clinton had appeared to be indifferent to the Vance-Owen peace plan for Bosnia and unwilling for American forces to be involved.[24] This is one of the reasons why there were no American troops as part of the UN protection force.[25] He also probably felt there was too much risk to the soldiers on the ground. Nevertheless, in May 1993 U.S. efforts helped gain the parties' agreement to the Vance-Owen plan, although the Bosnian Serbs subsequently renounced the accord.[26]

In early 1993, President Clinton read *Balkan Ghosts: A Journey Through History*[27] which left its readers with the sense that nothing could be done by outsiders in a region so steeped in ancient hatreds. For this reason and others, Clinton and his advisors believed that a diplomatic solution was the only real option. He was only willing to use air power to aid in those negotiations. The problem here was, first, to determine how, and indeed if, air power could lead to constructive negotiations, and second, to persuade the NATO allies with UN peacekeepers on the ground that this option would not put their people at risk.[28]

Starting in 1993, however, the US began to look to the unfolding events in the Balkans and begin to reconsider its role – and that of NATO – in crisis management in support of the UN. Also in 1993, because of pervasive media coverage – sometimes called the "CNN effect" – the American public began to feel that US leadership was needed in the form of diplomatic negotiations, although it still strongly opposed putting US troops on the ground. In late 1993 and early 1994, therefore, the US administration conducted a reevaluation of its policy.

IV   US Involvement in Bosnia: 1994–1995

IN 1994 and 1995, the Clinton administration worked in support of the UN effort in the Balkans and focused NATO's efforts on maintaining the peace in the region.[29] NATO developed detailed plans for extraction of the UN forces in Bosnia. In the course of this planning, military planners and administration officials came to realize that in the course of an extraction operation the risk to US lives could be great.[30] Moreover, although the US did not see the Bosnian conflict as a direct threat to its own national survival, there was concern that it could result in the collapse of several European governments; it therefore became more than simply a matter of humanitarian intervention.[31] The viability and survival of NATO as an entity became an important issue. This was one more consideration that caused the US to change its policy and begin to take a lead role in the negotiations.

In early 1994, the US decided to support a modified Vance-Owen peace plan. The US revisions included: less land to Serbs; stronger guarantees from Balkan leaders; the mobilization of European, Canadian and US troops under NATO control rather than the UN; stricter sanctions against truncated Yugoslavia; and the setting up of war crimes trials for Serbs and Croats.[32]

Toward the end of 1993, Secretary of State Warren Christopher proposed a "lift and strike policy."[33] This policy would involve lifting the arms embargo, primarily to benefit the Muslims, and using NATO air strikes against Serb forces. Such proposals, in one form or another, continued to be espoused over and over again, particularly by members of Congress,[34] up until Dayton. The arms embargo did not hurt the Serbs as much as the other parties because in the former Yugoslavia most of the arms industry plants were in Serbia or under Serb control. The Serb forces operated with considerable local autonomy, and had large, well-dispersed and concealed arms caches. They could largely dictate their own weapon and ammunition consumption rates and were not very susceptible to air attack either.[35]

Clinton was caught in a quandary with the embargo. The United Nations Security Council had imposed it. Lifting it would require the unanimous consent of the five permanent members. Of the five, Russia, Great Britain and France opposed lifting it. Any one of them could veto such an action and the embargo would remain. Therefore, Clinton only had the option to not enforce the embargo, which he decided to do in November 1994, but only after a great deal of pressure was put on him domestically.[36] The Republican-controlled US Congress submitted a bill to lift the embargo, which did not pass.[37]

Despite the embargo, arms continued to flow to the Muslims from a number of sources in the West and Middle East. But the embargo had to be lifted to make the arms shipments greater, less difficult and part of public policy.[38] Arming the Muslims and conducting air attacks on Serbs and Croats (by this time also fighting the Muslims in western

Bosnia) were viewed by the US as complementary measures. Neither would end the problem if used in isolation.[39] Despite allegations by some allies, the US never implemented "lift and strike" in any manner that was meaningful diplomatically.[40] In the first place, it was difficult to identify targets on the ground. The Serbs were not concentrated in such a manner as to provide targets vulnerable to air strikes. More importantly, no one had really addressed what would be done if the bombing were not effective.[41] But air attacks remained highly desirable to Clinton because he could appear to be doing something decisive with low risk to American lives. Clinton's use of air power to help him on the domestic front was a frequent feature of his policy in the region.

A mortar attack on the Sarajevo market on 5 February 1994 killed at least 66 people and injured more than 200.[42] It galvanized the administration into further action, prompting a NATO ultimatum that same day on a weapons exclusion zone around Sarajevo. NATO demanded all artillery be withdrawn 12 miles from the centre of Sarajevo.[43] UN observers reported a dramatic increase in compliance efforts after the Bosnian Serb leader Radovan Karadzic met with a senior Russian envoy and announced his nationalist forces would meet the NATO demand. [44]

US mediation resulted in the establishment of the Federation (Muslims and Croats) in March 1994. For a year prior to this, the Bosniak and Bosnian Croat armies had been fighting each other in west and central Bosnia. The Washington Agreement on a Federation led to a cease-fire between these two armies that held for the balance of the war.[45]

In May 1994, the United States, France, Britain, Germany and Russia established a five-nation Contact Group, with the goal of brokering a settlement between the Federation and the Bosnian Serbs. The Contact Group based its efforts on the objective that Bosnia would remain a single state and would consist of the Federation (Muslims and Croats) and a Bosnian Serb entity. Further, these two entities would be linked via mutually agreed constitutional principles, which would spell out relationships with Serbia and Croatia proper. The Contact Group was extremely important to the US in carrying out its policies for a number of reasons. It enabled the big powers to reach a common position in advance of negotiations with the parties to the conflict. It reduced the number of political allies the US had to persuade – making it an easier task than trying to sway the entire UN or even all of NATO's member nations. So decisions could be made far more rapidly. It by no means meant that the pursuit of national self-interest by the nations involved was diminished, or friction eliminated

– far from it. The Contact Group did, however, give the US greater leverage on the other powers involved as well as on the main parties to the conflict in on the ground in Bosnia.

For example, at the meetings sponsored by the Contact Group in Geneva (September 8, 1995) and New York (September 26, 1995), the Foreign Ministers of Bosnia, Croatia, and Serbia (now also representing the Bosnian Serbs) agreed to basic principles for a settlement in Bosnia. These included constitutional structures, free and fair elections, and respect for human rights. The Contact Group endorsed a plan devised earlier to leave 51 percent of Bosnia under control of the new Muslim-Croat Federation, while awarding 49 percent to the Bosnian Serbs.[46]

Although the US mediated peace talks between Serb and Bosnian forces, and a truce was signed on January 1, 1995, the war continued during the spring of 1995 when the Croat army attempted to retake territory – both in Bosnia and in Croatia – held by Serbs since the beginning of the conflict.[47]

In July and August 1995, two key events, the massacre at Srebrenica and a second shelling of the Sarajevo market, forced the administration to take more drastic measures. On 11 July 1995, Bosnian Serb forces overran the safe area of Srebrenica and by 14 July evicted thousands of Muslim refugees, while detaining Muslim men, as well as Dutch UN forces.[48] Subsequently some 7,000 Muslims were massacred. Many argue that the fall of Srebrenica could have been prevented and that there had been a collective failure of the United States, the United Nations, and NATO in to stop the massacre. The fall of Srebrenica was highly significant because it turned Western opinion[49] and underlined once more the ineffectiveness of the UN.[50]

In late July, President Clinton decided that the changes on the ground and the new resolve displayed by member nations of NATO provided the basis for an all-out diplomatic effort to end the conflict. In early August, he sent his National Security Adviser, Anthony Lake, to present a US peace initiative to NATO and the Russians.[51] The evidence of continuing atrocities, culminating in Srebrenica, had changed American public opinion sufficiently to force the administration to do something to stop the violence.

The shelling of the Sarajevo market on 28 August 1995 killed 38 and injured at least 80.[52] This second shelling had a more pronounced effect than that of February 1994, in large part due to the steady stream of print and television reports, throughout 1994 and 1995, of atrocities, concentration camps and mass gravesites. The bloody results of this incident were televised around the world in minutes. The images provoked the first engagement of NATO in European hostilities since it was founded four decades earlier and the first involvement of US forces in combat in Europe since the beginning of the Cold War.[53]

The first serious test of NATO resolve in the post-Cold War era was the successful conduct of US-led NATO air strikes against Bosnian Serb forces in August and September 1995 in support of UN peace-making efforts. Although initiated in response to the Bosnian Serb shelling of the Sarajevo marketplace, Operation Deliberate Force was the culmination of events and related planning over a long period. Confirmation of Bosnian Serb complicity in that attack led two days later to the unleashing of an 11-day campaign of coordinated NATO air strikes against approved Serbian targets in Bosnia-Herzegovina. This was a very different use of air power than in the previous years. The objective of this campaign was to protect the remaining UN protected areas, such as Sarajevo. These areas were particularly vulnerable to Serb artillery. This air campaign would also serve to protect UN peacekeepers in those areas as well as civilians. It was more difficult for the Serbs to use the peacekeepers as human shields as they had done in the past, because most of the UN forces had been moved away from direct contact with them. The purpose of the operation was to deter further Serb attacks against declared UN safe areas and to respond as necessary to any such attacks until they ceased.

V The US Domestic Situation in the Run-up to Dayton

IT IS very important to understand the domestic situation that President Bill Clinton faced prior to Dayton. During its first year in office, the Clinton administration could claim its problems were inherited from the Bush administration. President Clinton was not able to fulfill his campaign promises in regards to Bosnia, Somalia and Haiti. For example, the Bush administration had sent troops to Somalia for the limited purpose of distributing food. The Clinton administration's ambassador to the United Nations, Madeleine Albright, stated it was "for the restoration of an entire country." Similar promises were made in both the cases of Bosnia and Haiti by the Clinton administration.[54]

These campaign promises reflected the convictions of Anthony Lake, the campaign's foreign policy coordinator who became Clinton's national security advisor. The policies he authored were aimed at relieving the suffering caused by ethnic cleansing in Bosnia, starvation in Somalia, and oppression in Haiti. The foreign policy of the US has historically centred on American interests, defined as developments that could affect the lives of American citizens. Nothing, except the flow of illegal immigrants from Haiti, that occurred in these three countries seemed to fit that criterion. The Clinton interventions seemed intended to promote American values.[55] This dramatically affected the mandate the administration had to work under.

Taking the examples of the three military interventions in Bosnia, Somalia, and Haiti, we see a shift from traditional American interests to the international periphery, looking at small, poor, weak countries far from the crucial centres that had previously dominated American foreign policy during the Cold War. Clinton could no longer rely upon a Cold War umbrella to legitimize many decisions and actions, as previous administrations had done. Public support, which seemed easier to command in the past, was difficult to keep in the post Cold War. Some critics claim Clinton's foreign policy failed because it did not command public support.[56] Clinton learned from this experience.

In the Congressional election of November 1994 the Republicans won by a landslide. Clinton was very concerned that he would be a one-term president like his predecessor, George Bush. On the domestic front, he was fighting for political survival, with the failure of his Medicare reforms. On foreign and defence policy, his relationship with the military was in bad shape, and the American public perceived Somalia, Rwanda and Haiti as failures.

While a success in foreign policy might not be enough to turn his political fortunes around, doing something decisive and effective about Bosnia might at least help change the image of his foreign policy among the American people. But Clinton was in a quandary here: the cost and risk of using American troops to force a solution on the ground was not an option for him because after Somalia the loss of American lives was still believed to be unacceptable to the public. He understood that if he did not come up with a solution, the viability and the very existence of NATO might be threatened. The smaller countries of NATO had a huge investment in the alliance; if NATO were discredited or disbanded it would have large negative impact on those governments.

Driven by these concerns, in 1994 the US administration began to come to grips seriously with Bosnia. From late 1994 through 1995 the US attempted to bring to bear all of the elements of national power to solve the problem, but in no single area could the US employ the full force of those powers without restrictions. It was a maddening balancing act. The US could use force but not too much, mainly restricted to air strikes but even with this there was a difficult problem of peacekeepers on the ground in Bosnia that would be used as human shields. The US could use economic power but again with some restrictions. The Russians viewed lifting the arms embargo in favor of the Federation (Muslims and Croats) and to the detriment of the Serbs as unacceptable. The US could use diplomatic power but their allies were not always pliable and the warring parties could often frustrate diplomatic initiatives by their actions on the ground. Even in the area of information there were restrictions because making it known that the US knew something could deny the future use of that source of information.

One of the reasons it took so long to apply military force prior to the fall of 1995 was that there was widespread concern that military action of any sort would impede the flow of humanitarian aid. The United States provided important political, financial, and personnel support to organizations participating in the operation, as well as to the international community's economic reconstruction program for Bosnia.[57]

The US had to find a diplomatic solution that would ensure there were no American casualties. Attempts by the UN and the international community throughout the war to stop the fighting and mediate a settlement were unsuccessful until 1995, when Federation military successes on the ground and NATO air strikes changed the balance of incentives and brought the warring parties to Dayton. US-led negotiations culminated in a cease-fire in October 1995 and the Dayton Accords in December.[58] Assistant Secretary of State Richard Holbrooke was the head negotiator; he probably obtained the best deal he could under the circumstances – given restrictions on the use of force, and the delicate situation on the ground and in the alliance. Dayton was not a complete victory for anyone, but the agreement did serve the US national interest in stopping the violence and preventing it from spreading.

The Dayton Accords declared that Bosnia was to be a single state consisting of two entities that were created during the war: (1) the Bosnian Serb Republic, known as Republika Srpska, and (2) the Federation, an entity that joins together Bosniak and Croat controlled areas of Bosnia. Most areas within Bosnia, with the exception of central Bosnia, were populated and controlled by a predominant ethnic group as a result of population movements during the war.[59]

The US would lead a coalition force, including European, Canadian and US ground troops, into Bosnia but there would be many restrictions on what the force could do. According to agreements made with its allies, the US would not be the lead in the civil implementation of Dayton.

As important as what was achieved by the Dayton Accords, is what was not achieved. Although the leading element of the NATO-led Implementation Force (IFOR) force in Bosnia, the US was not in a position to act as an army of occupation. Since Americans did not have total domination of the political and leadership structure there were two things they could not put in place. First, there was no overall plan to investigate the leadership in Bosnia and make a judgment on their worthiness as leaders. Given that the leaders of the three warring parties had signed the Dayton Accords, there could be no immediate prospect of something like the "denazification" process conducted in Germany after World War II.[60] Unlike Germany, none of the parties had been defeated, and Dayton was not an imposed peace. Thus NATO was not an occupying force, and it could not remove and investigate the leadership.

Second, there could be no equivalent of the Marshall Plan for Bosnia, in the sense of an economic development program conceived, administered and paid for by the US.

The US domestic situation would not permit President Clinton to make the peace operation in Bosnia appear like a US-only show. The presence of other countries provided legitimacy to the mission, clearly showing an international commitment. It also lessened the cost on the US so the President could demonstrate that the US was not being taken advantage of by its allies. Russia became important here both because of proximity and long-standing relationship with the Serbs. Russia, often part of the problem, would have to be part of the solution. Washington and Moscow set up a Russian unit in Bosnia and settled NATO's command role. Russia did this to bolster its image at home and internationally.[61] All of this allowed President Clinton to claim that the Europeans were shouldering a good share of the burden and the risk – which was true – but it also meant a more fragmented management of the international recovery program for Bosnia.

By taking the lead on the military side, however, Clinton could demonstrate that he was being decisive and in control for the benefit of US national interests. The need for US control was clear, because it was believed that domestic opinion would not have permitted US soldiers to be commanded by foreign officers. The American electoral timetable also dictated the Dayton provision that IFOR should only be on the ground for one year, so that success could be declared and the US troops brought home by the end of 1996. Accordingly, the diplomatic community rushed to hold elections within one year.[62]

Civil implementation of Dayton was an important issue, particularly given attitudes in Congress with respect to burden-sharing with allies. The Office of the High Representative (OHR) is the lead international civilian agency in Bosnia-Herzegovina.[63] By creating this body to oversee and coordinate the work of the UN, the EU, the Organization for Security and Cooperation in Europe and other entities,[64] Clinton demonstrated to his allies and the US public that this was clearly not a US-only show. All these considerations help explain why the US became involved in Bosnia in the manner that it did.

For the Clinton administration, and for US interests, the outcome of Dayton was not completely satisfactory. By sharing the risks and the burdens, America shared some of the power to make decisions. The OHR has had a very difficult time implementing the civil side of the Dayton Accords. For some in America and elsewhere, Dayton also raised ethical issues, since the US had negotiated with persons indicted for war crimes. Dayton succeeded in stopping the violence and preserving the integrity of the Bosnian state, but the need for compromise meant that the goals stated in the Accords were often so nebulous that a clear exit strategy could not be easily defined.

V US Involvement Since 1995

THE CURRENT SITUATION on the ground in Bosnia at the moment is stable, but less than ideal in many ways. The most important conclusion drawn by the international community from the early years of its presence there is that withdrawal is impossible without confronting the issues of local leadership and economic reconstruction.

The international operation to implement Dayton had four key objectives. It was to: (1) provide security for the people of Bosnia; (2) create a unified, democratic Bosnia that respects the rule of law and internationally recognized human rights including cooperating with the war crimes tribunal in arresting and bring in those charged with war crimes to trial; (3) rebuild the economy; and (4) ensure the right of people to return to their prewar homes.[65] It was not, however, to intervene to replace the political leadership of Bosnia or of its two entities.

Every country in IFOR and its successor, SFOR, retained command of its national forces. Some problems arose because countries sometimes had differing rules of engagement. For example, the Canadian

Forces were not allowed to use deadly force in riot control.[66] This was significant because at one point in the summer of 1997 a riot took place in the contested town of Brcko, whose aim may have been to cause American fatalities and force the US to withdraw from Bosnia. The local SFOR commander could not have used Canadian forces to control the riots due to their rules of engagement. Nevertheless, most of the time NATO forces attempted to use intimidation through their presence instead of force.[67]

The US views peacekeeping missions differently from other countries. The table below provides a brief comparison between the US and Canada.

Canadian	US
Canada had an extremely bad UN experience with restrictive rules of engagement. They could not use their weapons except for force protection.	Did not enter Bosnia with Canada but much later as a part of NATO.
Deployed with minimum weapon capabilities. No tanks, artillery or air support.	Deployed with maximum weapons and intelligence capability. Approached deployment as a "warfighter" task.
Attitude: negotiation and mediation. No matter how much delay in operations. Viewed as a humanitarian mission.	Attitude: Operations first. Negotiations and mediation preferred but not at the expense of operations.
Sought perception by the civilian population in both Bosnia and Canada is a "kinder and gentler" army, not warfighters. There to "smooth things over."	Desired perception by civilian population in both Bosnia and the US as "show of force." Use flak vests, Kevlar helmets, tanks, artillery, and Apache attack helicopters. Prepare to escalate if necessary.
No special operations of an offensive nature. Defensive in nature only.	Use special operations: capture war criminals[68] and determine "bad guys" in population. Aggressive in nature.

These differing perspectives and capabilities make it difficult to carry out policy with allies and often even to agree on that policy in the first place. The US applies great resources toward any operation because it can, and because it is US doctrine to use overwhelming force and capabilities to intimidate adversaries. This has important strategic as well as tactical implications.

From December 1995, when the US ground troops entered Bosnia as part of IFOR, large-scale violence ended. Small-scale violence continued for a while, but at a level acceptable to the international community.[69] To separate the former warring factions as the initial force was tasked to do was relatively easy. That was accomplished in the first few months on the ground. The main problem was the government structure, leadership and economics – in other words, the civil implementation of Dayton.

The Americans set a deadline of twelve months for their involvement on the ground. Everyone, including the Americans, knew they could not possibly make this deadline. The deadline was set for reasons of electoral advantage for Clinton, who was facing reelection in November 1996. If American troops were to stay in Bosnia beyond the twelve-month deadline, it would have to be for a reason acceptable to the American electorate. The official position thus became that all of the military objectives of Dayton had been achieved but that the civil implementation, something for which the Americans had minimal responsibility, was lagging and that the NATO force with other allies would have to stay. The force was re-named Stabilization Force (SFOR) to show that there had been progress made. This approach by the Clinton administration effectively removed Bosnia as an electoral issue.

The elections held in Bosnia in 1996 only reproduced the old patterns of nationalist leadership in the three ethnic communities. The extreme nationalism that precipitated and grew out of the war had made ethnic identity a critical factor in many aspects of Bosnian daily life, and the violence, fear, and collapsed social structure that resulted from the war had eroded support for pluralism. American pressure for early elections had backfired, as many officials in the State Department and elsewhere subsequently acknowledged.[70] But even after it was clear that the US would have to stay in Bosnia longer than 12 months, there was no immediate strategic reassessment to make possible either an investigation and reform of the leadership or the implementation of a comprehensive economic plan. Since then, however, leadership has been improved through further elections, through decisive action by the OHR in dismissing corrupt and anti-Dayton officials, and through the detention of many accused war criminals. This divided country remains dominated by parties conducting politics largely along the divisive lines of ethnicity and nationalism. There are many international officials in the country working to resolve this state of affairs and to improve the situation for the media. In both fields, however, the going is tough, as events demonstrated last year.[71]

The security situation is good, in the sense that renewed war among the three ethnic groups is very unlikely. But ethnic intolerance remains strong throughout Bosnia. War would not immediately break out if SFOR were to suddenly withdraw, but small-scale violence might well escalate over time.[72] While much progress has been made in identifying and capturing those believed responsible for war crimes, former Bosnian Serb leader Radovan Karadzic and the former Bosnian Serb General Ratko Mladic remain at large.[73]

The economic situation remains bleak. For most years since Dayton the economy has only two growth areas – corruption and international aid. The black and gray markets continue to thrive, while aid is tapering off because of donor fatigue and new priorities both in the Balkans (Serbia) and elsewhere (Afghanistan). There is still no rule of law sufficient to attract outside investment. There has been much rebuilding, but the economy was very interdependent with the rest of Yugoslavia, and those links will take a great deal of time to repair.[74]

VI The future of US Involvement in Bosnia

FOR SOME TIME, the Americans have been looking for an exit strategy from Bosnia.[75] In theory, the US could pull its troops out, but Europe needs American leadership in Bosnia, and perhaps America needs to be there for its own reasons. Even if the US and NATO eventually hand off the leadership of peacekeeping duties to the European Union (EU), some sort of US presence will likely still be required.

In 1997, out of frustration over the lack of progress in civil implementation of Dayton, the US tried using the US military to aid in the civil implementation of the Dayton Accords. It tried to have the US military to help coordinate the international and non-governmental agencies working in Bosnia. The effort was not successful. The OHR remains in charge of civil implementation. Under the OHR, the

United Nations High Commissioner for Refugees is still in charge of returning the refugees to their homes. The Organization for Security and Cooperation in Europe is still in charge of elections and democratization. The failed American effort to challenge these arrangements represents the frustration some in the US government feel over the lack of progress on the civil side of Dayton. The view of some in the US government is that the people assigned to the UN, the OHR, the OSCE and other organizations have little incentive to succeed. Many of them are not career civil servants but contractors hired just for Bosnia, with some significant responsibilities. Success in this job risks putting them out of work.[76] Even if it is only true for some, this claim hints at a degree of continuing tension between US officials and the rest of the international community in Bosnia.

The OHR, with US backing, continues to remove corrupt leaders by the means at its disposal. In the last three years, as well, there has been increased emphasis on arresting persons indicted for war crimes (PIFWCs). Earlier, the challenge was that if SFOR troops on the ground were tried to arrest these persons, they could be the target of bombings and other attacks. In 1997, some of them were attacked when British forces arrested the first person indicted for war crimes. The attacks were done in such a manner that forces were not harmed but a clear message was sent. For that reason, the countries involved in such operations appear to bring in outside personnel. These operations have met with considerable success.

The US and the rest of the international community continue to support free and open elections in Bosnia. Many of the candidates, particularly at the local level, are able to influence the local economy or their constituents through money acquired from the black market or organized crime activities. As a result, some corrupt people continue to be elected. Nevertheless there is progress.[77] More reformist and ethnically inclusive leaders have been elected at the municipal, entity and national levels. Meanwhile the OHR continues to remove corrupt or uncooperative personnel from office.[78]

Coordination of economic development under the OHR has not been all that successful. One response to the economic problem was the EU's initiative, on 10 June 1999, to create the Stability Pact for South Eastern Europe. There has been some progress since then, at least in the region as a whole.[79] But the lack of a comprehensive economic plan for Bosnia – one of the two missing pieces - has something to do with the other missing piece. A large portion of the aid that is pumped into Bosnia winds up on the black market or is siphoned off for the enrichment of the leadership. But trying to fix the problem by bypassing members of the legitimate elected government is problematic.

The US finds itself in the position that neither of the two missing pieces that keep it in Bosnia is under its direct control. The US has significant potential influence on both governance and economic development, but is hamstrung in its actions by the political agreements it made to put US forces in the ground in a low-risk manner. While the international community provides more economic support, the old Bosnian leadership still controls the purse strings in many areas.[80] In the end, however, the international community may accept simply the absence of fighting as victory.[81]

All of this helps to explain why the US is still in Bosnia and why it is involved in the manner that it is. The US will probably remain in Bosnia, although at reduced levels, for quite some time. Long-term peace missions are not unknown, after all. The American military remembers being given a temporary mission in Sinai, over 22 years ago.

VII Conclusion

IT TOOK the US a long time to become involved in Bosnia because of the expected cost and the constraints of US public opinion. It continued to view Bosnia as a European problem until 1993, when peacekeeping and negotiating failures by the EC and the UN, in conjunction with heightened media attention, changed domestic and international public opinion. The US was then obliged to take a lead role. However, because the American public was still not willing to risk American lives, the US could not risk ground troops. It was therefore primarily restricted to a diplomatic role and the use of air power.

In 1995, the media's reporting of atrocities stirred public opinion and to forced the US to intervene more decisively to end the violence. But the US administration believed that this had to be done at minimal risk to American lives. Through the use of diplomatic actions, air power and military support to change the situation on the ground, the US forced the leaders in the Balkans to negotiations in Dayton.

When the US entered Bosnia with ground troops in December 1995, it did not – and could not – enter as an army of occupation. For that reason among others it proved very difficult to enforce the civil aspects of the Dayton Accords. Transition to an effective multiethnic government has not yet occurred. A unified, democratic state that respects the rule of law and adheres to international standards of human rights has not yet been achieved. Although national, ethnic entity-level and local elections have been held, most institutions created to unify Bosnia's ethnic groups are not yet functioning. Bosnia remains politically and ethnically divided, freedom of movement across ethnic boundaries is still constrained and economic activity is still not at a desirable level.

The US has not been in a position to change the civilian leadership, despite the evidence that elections continue to put into office many politicians who are corrupt and hostile to the principles of Dayton. This reality in turn inhibits the development and implementation of a comprehensive program for economic development. The US will not be able to withdraw from Bosnia completely until the two missing pieces are put into the jigsaw puzzle. First, a more legitimate leadership must emerge, probably through a combination of diplomatic pressure and truly free elections. Second, comprehensive economic support and reform remain essential.

The US must remain engaged in Bosnia. US commitment in the form of diplomatic and military leadership has been vital to the success of the international presence in Bosnia, at least relative to the situation prior to the Dayton accords. US troop levels, and the total complement of SFOR, have been gradually reduced. US forces may be drawn down further in coming years, but a complete withdrawal would not be possible without dire consequences. There is a real risk in reducing the international presence while most of Bosnia's problems remain unresolved, but the temptation is there. An illustration: Washington recently sought to reduce US troop levels to 1,800, on the same day the reward for Bosnian Serb leader Radovan Karadzic was raised to $5 million.[82]

Notes

1 Richard Holbrooke, *To End A War* (New York: Random House, 1998), pp. 24–26.
2 "Yugoslavia: The Avoidable War," Canadian Broadcasting Corporation. Produced by Frontier Theatre and Film Inc. Broadcast in Kingston, Ontario, Canada, 14 February 2002.
3 Dawn M. Hewitt, *From Ottawa to Sarajevo: Canadian Peacekeepers in the Balkans* (Martello Papers, Queen's Centre for International Relations, Queen's University, Kingston, Ontario, 1998), p. 8.

4 Ibid., p. 7.
5 Warren Zimmerman, *Origins of a Catastrophe: Yugoslavia and Its Destroyers* (New York: Times Books, 1996), pp. 151–153.
6 Warren Zimmerman, "The Last Ambassador: A Memoir of the Collapse of Yugoslavia," *Foreign Affairs* (March-April 1995), pp. 2–3.
7 "Yugoslavia: The Avoidable War" (CBC Television).
8 Holbrooke, p. 27.
9 Foreign and Commonwealth Office, London. Background Brief, The Former Yugoslavia: Chronology January 1990 – 31 October 1996, November 1996, p. 1; Mihailo Crnobrnja, *The Yugoslav Drama*, 2d edition (Kingston and Montreal: McGill-Queen's University Press, 1996), pp. 205–206.
10 Major General Lewis MacKenzie, *Peacekeeper: The Road to Sarajevo* (Toronto: Harper Collins, 1994), pp. 151, 174.
11 UNPROFOR In Croatia, A Chronology of Events (1992–95), Zagreb, 28 March 1995 (Igor Ilic and Slavoljub Leko) http://www.hr/hrvatska/WAR/UNPF-chron.html.
12 Beverly Crawford, "Explaining Defection from International Cooperation: Germany's Unilateral recognition of Croatia," *World Politics* (July 1996), p. 482.
13 "Germany Flexes Its European Muscle," *U.S. News & World Report*, 30 December 1991, p. 27.
14 Interview with Dr Charles Pentland, Queen's University, Kingston, Ontario, 28 February 2002.
15 Steve Forbes, "Germany was right," *Forbes Magazine*, 20 January 1992, p. 25.
16 US Department of State, Bosnia Fact Sheet: Chronology of the Balkan Conflict, updated and released by the Bureau of Public Affairs, 6 December 1995.
17 "Yugoslavia: The Avoidable War" (CBC Television).
18 Interview by email with Mr. Collin A. Agee, Army Intelligence Master Plan, 19 February 2002.
19 "Yugoslavia: The Avoidable War" (CBC Television).
20 James A. Baker III, with Thomas M. DeFrank, *The Politics of Diplomacy* (New York: G. P. Putnam's Sons, 1995), p. 483.
21 Hewitt, p.4.
22 Ibid., p. 4.
23 "Yugoslavia: The Avoidable War" (CBC Television).
24 Colin Smith, "Clinton's Cavalry Rattles Its Sabers," *The Observer*, 14 February 1993, p. 13.
25 Ivo H. Daalder, *Getting to Dayton* (Washington: The Brookings Institution, 2000), p. 32.
26 US Department of State, Bosnia Fact Sheet: Chronology of the Balkan Conflict, updated and released by the Bureau of Public Affairs, 6 December 1995.
27 Holbrooke, p. 22 ; Robert D. Kaplan, *Balkan Ghosts: A Journey Through History* (New York: Vintage Books, 1993).
28 Manfred Wörner, Secretary-General of NATO, at WEU Assembly, Paris, 29 November 1993; NATO Press Release, p. 3.
29 Interview by email with Col. Fred Sundstrom, US Army Officer, NATO HQ in Brussels, Belgium, 13 February 2002.
30 Ibid.
31 General Wesley K. Clark, *Waging Modern War: Bosnia, Kosovo and the Future of Conflict* (New York: Perseus, 2001), p. xxiv.
32 Roger Boyes, "American Bluster Masks Qualified Approval for Peace Plan," *The New York Times*, 9 February 1993, p. 12.
33 Clark, p. 37.
34 Remarks by Senator Joseph Biden, Delaware, at a speech on 16 October 1997, Fairleigh Dickinson University, Teaneck, NJ.

35 Air Vice Marshal Tony Mason, *Air Power: A Centennial Appraisal*, (Bath: Bookcraft Limited, 1994, 1997, 2000), p. 182.

36 *http://www.fas.org/irp/congress/1996_cr/s960509a.htm* (The Congressional Record).

37 *http://www.fas.org/irp/congress/1996_cr/h960425a.htm*.

38 http://www.reagan.com/HotTopics.main/HotMike/document-9.23.1996.3.html.

39 Edward Mortimer, "Twin Track to Bosnia Peace: Air Attacks and Military Aid Are Complementary, Not Alternatives," *The Financial Times*, 12 May 1993, p. 18.

40 Telephone interview with James C. O'Brien, Principal, The Albright Group LLC, and former State Department Official, 26 February 2002.

41 Clark, p. 42.

42 http://www.washingtonpost.com/wp-srv/inatl/longterm/balkans/stories/market.htm.

43 Danica Kirka and Carol J. Williams, "Bosnian Serbs Withdraw Artillery around Sarajevo," *Los Angeles Times*, 18 February 1994, p. 2.

44 Federation of American Scientists, Congressional Research Service Reports, Military and National Security, Bosnia – Former Yugoslavia and U.S. Policy. http://www.fas.org/man/crs/91-089.htm.

45 Report of the Chairman, Committee on Foreign Relations, US Senate, *Bosnia Peace Operation: Progress Toward Achieving the Dayton Agreement's Goals* (United States General Accounting Office, May 1997), p. 3.

46 Mason, "Air Power: A Centennial Appraisal," p. 179.

47 http://www.tfeagle.army.mil/TFE/bosnia_history.htm.

48 *UN Chronicle*, 32:4, December 1995, pp. 4–8.

49 David Rohde, *Endgame: The Betrayal and Fall of Srebrenica, Europe's Worst Massacre Since World War II* (New York: Farrar, Strauss and Giroux, 1997).

50 *UN Chronicle*, 32:4, December 1995, pp. 4–8.

51 US Department of State, 95/11/01 Fact Sheet – Bosnia: The Road to Dayton, Bureau of Public Affairs.

52 http://www.cnn.com/WORLD/Bosnia/updates/august95/8-28/. The number of 35 was later revised to 38.

53 David Binder, "Anatomy of a Massacre," *Foreign Policy* (Winter 1994), 70–78.

54 Michael Mandelbaum, "Foreign Policy as Social Work," *Foreign Affairs* 75/1 (January-February 1996), 17.

55 Ibid., 19.

56 Ibid., 20–22.

57 Report, *Bosnia Peace Operation*, p. 3.

58 http://www.state.gov/www/regions/eur/bosnia/bosagree.html.

59 Report, *Bosnia Peace Operaton*, p. 3.

60 Multinational Division (Southwest) Briefing and Mission Analysis Update, "Pip and Braid," Headquarters Multinational Division (Southwest), 19 April 2001, provided by Colonel Rick Hatton, Deputy Military Representative, Defence Counselor on 21 November 2001 at NATO HQ in Belgium.

61 Julia Preston, "Russia sends peacekeeping troops to Bosnia-Herzegovina," *The Washington Post*, 18 February 1994.

62 Confidential interview with a high-ranking US State Department official, January 2002.

63 http://www.ohr.int/.

64 http://www.oscebih.org/mission/themission.asp.

65 Report, *Bosnia Peace Operation*, p. 2.

66 Interview, Colonel Hatton.

67 Clark, p. 101.

68 White House Office of the Press Secretary, "Participation of U.S. Forces in Apprehension of an Indicted War Criminal," 15 April 2001, http://www.white-

house.gov/news/releases/2001/04/20010416.html.

69 Interview with Edgard Vandeputte, Head, Crisis Management Section, Crisis Management and Operations Directorate, Defence Planning and Operations Division, NATO HQ, Brussels, Belgium on 22 November 2001.

70 Interviews conducted at the US State Department in January 2002. Senior officials asked not to be identified by name.

71 http://www.freemedia.at/wpfr/bosnia.htm.

72 Interview and emails with Dr Steve Saidaman, US Joint Staff, J5, Bosnia desk officer.

73 Interview with Mr Raffi Gregorian, Deputy Director of Bosnia Affairs, US State Department, 21 January, 1995.

74 Interview and emails with Dr Saidaman.

75 Interview with Mr Vandeputte.

76 Interview with Mr Nigel Thornton, former British diplomat in Bosnia and Kosovo, in Greece, 20 November 2001.

77 http://www.ohr.int/ohr-dept/presso/pressa/default.asp?content_id=7178

78 http://www.ohr.int/ohr-dept/presso/pressi/default.asp?content_id=3209.

79 http://www.stabilitypact.org/stabilitypactcgi/catalog/ cat_descr.cgi?prod_id=1806.

80 Interview with a high-ranking US State Department official, January 2002.

81 Interview with Mr Vandeputte.

82 CNN News reports on CNN.com on 4 March 2002.

LOUIS A. DELVOIE

Through Islamic and Other Prisms: Turkey and the Bosnia Conflict

THROUGHOUT most of the world that was paying attention, the Bosnian conflict and its attendant atrocities were viewed as a humanitarian disaster. Vivid televised and written reports of ethnic cleansing, displaced people, mass murders, rape and torture, all evoked sentiments of sympathy and disgust wherever they were seen or read. But if the reaction to the humanitarian dimensions of the conflict can be described as being almost universal and uniform, perceptions of its geo-political dimensions and implications varied greatly.

In much of the Western world, the disintegration of Yugoslavia and the subsequent Bosnian conflict were seen as new threats to the peace and stability of Western Europe, thus dashing so many of the hopes which had attended the end of the Cold War and the demise of the Soviet Union. They gave rise to widespread fears of massive refugee flows and of the spread of conflict to neighbouring countries. Western leaders became ever more aware of how their failure to manage the crisis was undermining the credibility of institutions such as the European Union (EU) and the North Atlantic Treaty Organization (NATO). What's more, it was becoming a source of division among the memberships of these institutions and a source of antagonism with Russia, to the detriment of the grand designs to create a new security architecture in Europe.[1]

LOUIS A. DELVOIE is a Senior Fellow, Centre for International Relations, Queen's University.

In much of the Muslim world, the Bosnian conflict not surprisingly gave rise to quite different concerns and reactions. It was perceived primarily as an attack on a Muslim population by non-Muslims, in this instance Christian Serbs and Croats, to which the West remained largely indifferent. In that sense, it was comparable to other issues of which the 51 member states of the Organization of the Islamic Conference (OIC) had long been seized – the victimization of Palestinian Muslims by Israeli Jews or the subjugation of Kashmiri Muslims by Indian Hindus. More broadly, it was seen as a challenge to the world-wide community of the Muslim faithful, the *ummah*, and a test of the solidarity and resolve of that community.

Nowhere were these two very different perceptions of the Bosnian conflict more sharply juxtaposed than in Turkey. On the one hand, Turkey's Kemalist legacy of secularism and Westernization, its long-standing membership in NATO and its seemingly endless quest for admission to the EU, all made it highly sensitive to Western concerns. On the other hand, Turkey's overwhelmingly Muslim population, its historical links to the Balkans and its membership in the OIC, all con-tributed to making it attentive to the preoccupations of the Muslim world. The policy dilemmas thus created for the Turkish government were compounded by circumstances or phenomena particular to the times: the reaction to the EU's rejection of Turkey's application for membership in 1989, Turkey's diminishing importance to the West as a security ally in the wake of the end of the Cold War, Turkey's residual concerns about Russian intentions, the growing dismay in the Arab world over the intensification of Turkey's relations with Israel and Turkey's role in the US-led coalition against Iraq.

This paper will briefly examine the emergence of the Bosnian con-flict as a Muslim issue, the reaction to it of the Muslim world and the policy issues which this created for Turkey as it once again struggled with its Western and Muslim identities and interests.

Bosnia: The making of a Muslim cause

IN THE WEST, the disintegration of Yugoslavia and Bosnia's descent into violence were usually portrayed as the re-emergence of centuries-old ethnic conflicts which had been held in check and concealed for over four decades by the realities and imperatives of the Cold War. The end of the Cold War and the Soviet Union's withdrawal from Central and Eastern Europe had in a sense removed this restraint and allowed age-old hostilities to re-ignite. It was quite simply a case of the "return of history." This view is strongly contested by writers who have made a close study of the history of Bosnia. They contend that there was a long tradition of accommodation and coexistence among the religious communities and nationalities in Bosnia, that it was in fact a tightly knit multi-ethnic community. In their view the roots of warfare lie not in ancient Balkan hatreds, but in the socio-political conditions which prevailed after the death of Tito and in the catalytic role played by the propaganda generated by leaders and elites on all sides of what came to be labeled an ethnic dispute.[2]

Whatever the historical truth concerning inter-ethnic relations in Bosnia over the centuries, there is little doubt that Serbian leaders used history selectively to vilify and demonize the Bosnian Muslims, and in the process helped inadvertently to turn a local conflict into one of interest to the Muslim world at large. One recurring theme of Serb propaganda was that the Bosnian Muslims were not only adversaries, but also traitors, since they were really Serbs who in Ottoman times had converted to Islam for financial reasons. Another (not entirely consistent) theme was that a substantial proportion of the Muslim population was the product of migration from Albania and elsewhere, that these people had no legitimate right to self-determination in Bosnia and that they were in any event part of some perennial anti-Serb and anti-European plot. In Serb eyes, one of the most damaging charges levied against the Bosnian Muslims was that during World War Two significant numbers of Muslims had supported the Nazi-inspired Croatian Ustasha state. Finally, Serb leaders were wont to recall that during the early 1970s, the Bosnian Muslim leader Alija Izetbegovic had published an "Islamic Declaration," advocating a united Islamic community from Morocco to Indonesia; this publication together with charges of illegitimate contacts with Muslim countries had led to Izetbegovic and some of his associates being imprisoned by the Tito regime on grounds of being traitors to Yugoslavia.[3]

If Serb propaganda and actions helped to turn the Bosnia conflict into a Muslim cause, so too did those of the Bosnian leadership. Early on in the conflict, Izetbegovic visited a number of Muslim countries in search of political and diplomatic support. In July 1991, he went to Turkey where he accepted an invitation to join the OIC. "Some regard this move as folly, for it allowed his political enemies thereafter to accuse Izetbegovic of Islamic fundamentalism."[4] Within Bosnia itself, Izetbegovic and his party, the Muslim Party of Democratic Action

(SDA), sought "to exploit the appeal of Islam to once secular Muslims brutalized by their Christian neighbours and abandoned by the Christian West."[5] But it was the Bosnian spiritual leader, Mustafa Effendi Ceric, who framed the issue in the broadest geo-political terms. In 1993, he wrote:

> What is occurring in Bosnia is not only a question for the Bosnians. The war in Bosnia is a global conspiracy against Muslims, this is something that all Muslims should know. What is occurring is not only the suffering of the Muslims of Bosnia, but humiliation for all the Muslims of the world.[6]

Casting the issue in these terms was clearly intended as an appeal to international Muslim solidarity and to the conscience of the Muslim *ummah*.

Perceptions in the Muslim World

THE INITIAL RESPONSE of many Muslim countries to the war in Bosnia was rather reserved. They felt no particularly strong affinity towards a distant European Muslim population, which was viewed as rather haphazard in its practice of the faith and clearly secular in its approach to the place of religion in society. While several Muslim countries did make generous financial contributions to the Bosnian government on humanitarian grounds, "they were seemingly reluctant to become entangled in what they basically saw as a European civil war on what they considered a wayward, backsliding Muslim population, despite heavy Serb propaganda alleging that Izetbegovic was striving to turn Bosnia into an Islamist fundamentalist state."[7]

Opinion within the Muslim world did evolve, however, as the record of atrocities committed against Bosnian Muslims became more graphic and more voluminous, and as the Bosnian leadership became more successful in its endeavours to mobilize international public opinion. This shift translated itself into a more pronounced outpouring of sympathy for the plight of the Bosnian Muslims and into expressions of hostility toward their tormentors, especially the Serbs. Equally importantly, however, it tended to focus attention in the Muslim world on the impotence or indifference of the West when confronted with the suffering of the Bosnian Muslims. Coming as it did in the wake of the Gulf War and of President Bush's proclamation

of a New World Order, this heightened interest in the Bosnian conflict on the part of the Muslim world almost inevitably gave rise to
questions regarding Western motives and to charges of Western double standards. Whether framed in terms of international relations or of
respect for human rights, these questions and charges in turn contributed to further mobilizing Muslim countries and their publics in
support of the Bosnian Muslims.

In an international relations framework, the main question was very
bluntly put by Professor Ali Mazrui of the State University of New York
in these terms:

> The West, under the leadership of the Bush administration, said
> to Iraqi aggression: 'This will not stand!' To end Iraqi aggression
> in Kuwait, the West and its allies bombed Baghdad and Basra. To
> end Serbian aggression in Bosnia, was the West in 1992 prepared
> to bomb Belgrade? If not, why not? Did the reasons include
> racism? Was it alright [sic] to bomb Arab populations thousands
> of miles away, but insupportable to bomb fellow Europeans next
> door? … Was it a failure of nerve on the part of the United States
> or Europe? Or was it a triumph of macroracial empathy?[8]

This analysis, of course, fails to recognize important differences
between the Gulf War and the Bosnian conflict. It also fails to note
that the US-led coalition in the Gulf War was operating, in part, in
defence of two Muslim countries – Kuwait and Saudi Arabia. Such
nuances, however, often got lost in the emotionally charged atmosphere created by reports of the atrocities committed by the Serbs in
Bosnia.

Beyond the issue of inter-state aggression and war, the question of
human rights also entered into Muslim perceptions of Western
responses to the Bosnian crisis. This was to be expected given that
many, if not most, Western countries had given a new prominence to
the promotion of human rights in their declaratory foreign policies in
the immediate aftermath of the Cold War. The questions and perceptions to which this gave rise are very clearly outlined by Professor Ann
Elizabeth Mayer of the University of Pennsylvania:

> There is a problem when the disparity between pious moralistic
> rhetoric about human rights and the actual policies pursued by
> Western foreign ministries grows too glaring. Especially in the
> case of conflicts in which Muslims are seen as the victims of non-
> Muslims' aggression and oppression, the Western failure to

intervene, to condemn and deter violations of Muslims' rights can severely aggravate anti-Western antagonism and prompt calls for jihads against Western influence.

There are all too many examples of Western indifference in the face of grievous rights abuses afflicting Muslims. Probably the most dramatic contemporary example is Bosnia, where the world stood by in the face of genocide and ethnic cleansing directed against Muslims, systematic mass rapes, incarceration in concentration camps, terror, torture and the like, and where the worst abuses were mostly carried out by the Christian forces of the Orthodox Serbs and Catholic Croats. The failure to organize measures to forestall the ghastly carnage and cruelties confirm the impression that the West does not care about human rights where Muslims are the victims and does not want Christians held accountable for violating Muslims' rights.[9]

The combination of the realities on the ground in Bosnia and of the perceptions of Western indifference to them led Muslim countries, collectively and individually, to formulate a variety of responses aimed at protecting the Bosnian Muslims and their interests.

The Responses of Muslim Countries

WHILE INITIALLY SLOW to react to the Bosnian conflict, the Muslim states represented in the OIC progressively adopted firmer and more comprehensive policy positions on the issue. Thus at a meeting held in Karachi in April 1993, the Foreign Ministers representing 50 member states of the OIC issued a communiqué which: (a) condemned the genocidal Serbian aggression (b) reaffirmed the sovereignty, independence and territorial integrity of Bosnia (c) requested the UN Security Council to act decisively under Chapter VII of the Charter and to use all necessary means to restore the sovereignty, independence, territorial integrity and unity of Bosnia (d) requested the UN Security Council to exempt Bosnia from the arms embargo imposed on the former Yugoslavia (e) urged member states of the OIC and other members of the international community to cooperate with Bosnia in the exercise of its right of individual and collective self-defence under Article 51 of the UN Charter, including the supply of arms (f) announced that member states of the OIC would jointly seek the expulsion of the Federal

Republic of Yugoslavia from the UN (g) called for the reconvening of the UN General Assembly session on Bosnia in the event the Security Council was unable to deal effectively with the Serbian aggression (h) requested the UN to expedite the establishment of an international tribunal to try those responsible for genocide and war crimes in Bosnia (i) appealed to all member states of the OIC to contribute generously to the humanitarian relief effort in Bosnia and (j) announced their decision to dispatch a ministerial mission of the OIC Contact Group to the capitals of the Permanent Members of the UN Security Council to explain the positions of the OIC and to seek agreement on necessary follow-up action.[10]

The member states of the OIC mounted an active diplomatic campaign in support of these positions and objectives. Numerous high level missions were dispatched to Western capitals, the United Nations, the European Union and the Organization for Security and Cooperation in Europe. Deliberately or inadvertently, the diplomatic activity of the OIC played on the fears of European governments that failure to achieve a settlement acceptable to the Bosnian Muslims would result first in military intervention by Muslim countries, and ultimately in the creation of "a Muslim state in Europe, especially one with close ties with fundamentalist Islamic countries."[11] The posture and activity of OIC member states also played into the calculations and interests of the Bosnian government and of the US administration:

> The determination of the Izetbegovic government to continue the fight rested upon the conviction that it could count on the physical and moral support of the Muslim world at large, as well as a guarantee of survival from the United States. The Americans, it was presumed, solicitous towards Turkey and their Middle Eastern allies, would not allow the imposition of a Carthaginian peace at the Muslims' expense.[12]

Despite episodes of hesitation on the part of the US administration, this generally proved to be the case and the US kept its initiatives "broadly aligned with those of Turkey and other Muslim states."[13]

In addition to their diplomatic endeavours, the member states of the OIC also provided more concrete assistance to the Bosnians. Through agencies such as Merhamet they supplied large quantities of food and other humanitarian aid. As the crisis deepened in the summer of 1993, seven Muslim countries offered to send a force of 17,000 volunteers to Bosnia under the auspices of the OIC, much to the embarrassment and annoyance of Western European countries which had largely failed to respond to the UN's appeal for an additional 7,500 troops to strengthen the UN Protection Force in Bosnia (UNPROFOR).[14] While the OIC's offer of a large force of volunteers was turned down, Muslim countries did make increasingly significant troop contributions to UNPROFOR. By 1995, the UN force included contingents from Pakistan (2,994), Turkey (1,469), Malaysia (1,547), Bangladesh (1,263), Egypt (434), Jordan (100) and Indonesia (8 observers). Out of UNPROFOR's total strength of 19,040, contingents from Muslim countries accounted for 7,815 soldiers.[15] Following the conclusion of the Dayton peace agreements and the demise of UNPROFOR, contingents from Egypt, Jordan, Malaysia and Morocco entered service with the newly established NATO Implementation Force (IFOR) in Bosnia.

The military involvement of OIC member states and of their citizens in the Bosnian conflict occasionally gave rise to problems and controversy. Given the obvious sympathy of Muslim countries for the plight of the Bosnian Muslims, could their contingents in UNPROFOR be relied upon to display the impartiality among the protagonists which was supposed to be one of the hallmarks of UN peacekeeping forces? This certainly appears to have been a serious concern among UNPROFOR commanders when deciding when and where to deploy contingents from Muslim countries.[16] Far more controversial, however, was the reported presence in Bosnia of fighters from countries as varied as Algeria, Sudan, Iran, Iraq, Turkey, Saudi Arabia and the Gulf Arab States. Said to be operating alongside units of the Bosnian Defence Force, some of these so-called "Islamic volunteers" were believed to be veterans of the Afghan campaign against the Soviet Union. Evidence regarding their numbers, nationalities and activities remains rather sketchy. What is equally unclear is the extent to which they enjoyed the support or approval of their own governments. What does seem clear, however, is that the presence of even limited numbers of these fighters, coupled with reports of arms shipments to Bosnia from Muslim countries, encouraged both Serb and Bosnian leaders to play the "Islamic card" in their dealings with Western governments. In both instances, the spoken or unspoken threat was that if the West did not side with them, Bosnia would become another Iran in the heart of Europe.[17]

In short, the OIC and the Muslim world played an active and not insignificant role in the unfolding of the Bosnian conflict, whether politically, diplomatically or militarily. Among the member states of the OIC, one of those most prominently involved was Turkey. Some have seen in Turkey's involvement little more than an opportunistic attempt to secure a new foothold in the Balkans and to curry favour with the United States.[18] In fact, the Bosnian conflict and the OIC role in it presented the Turkish government with a rather difficult set of policy dilemmas given the country's enduring linkages to both the Muslim world and the Western world.

Turkey: The Pull of Muslim Forces

THE STRENGTH of public opinion in Turkey was a major factor in determining the government's approach to the Bosnian conflict. In an overwhelmingly Muslim population, it was to be expected that there would be a sense of solidarity with the Muslims of Bosnia once it became clear that Serbs and Croats were planning to divvy up Bosnia, and that the Bosnian Muslims were the victims of a systematic campaign of atrocities committed by the Serbs. These sentiments of solidarity and empathy based on a shared religion became more pronounced, and were vigorously reflected in the Turkish mass media, as the conflict unfolded and as the West was increasingly portrayed as being indifferent to the suffering of the Bosnian Muslims. The Turkish government, composed primarily of secularist parties, was deeply concerned that this public opinion might translate itself into support for the Islamist Welfare Party, which was already showing signs of increased electoral strength. This in turn might pose a threat not only to the interests of the governing parties, but also to Turkey's secular tradition.[19]

In the general public, sentiments of religious solidarity were buttressed by historico-political factors. Bosnia had, of course, at one time been an outpost of the Ottoman empire and Turks had a residual interest in what took place there. More important, however, was the fact that many Bosnians had migrated to Turkey in the late 19th and early 20th centuries when their region fell under the Austro-Hungarian empire. Believed to number several hundred thousand, Turks of Bosnian origin took a particularly active interest in what was going on in their ancestral homeland. Together with other Turks emanating from the Balkans and the Black Sea region, they were "instrumental in creating a new domestic force in Turkey, namely the formation of foreign policy constituencies and lobbies representing different ethnocultural communities and interest groups within the population."[20] All in all, the domestic pressures brought to bear on the Turkish government in support of the Bosnian Muslims were considerable.

These domestic pressures were matched by those emanating from within the Muslim world, especially those deriving from Turkey's membership in the OIC. Turkey had originally joined the OIC in search of support for its position on the Cyprus question, at a time when most of its Western partners seemed more inclined to side with the Greeks on the issue. But its membership in the organization had never been free of controversy, for four main reasons: (a) Turkey was constitutionally a secular state and many in Turkey opposed its membership in the OIC (b) Turkey adopted very moderate positions on the Arab-Israeli conflict and maintained diplomatic relations with Israel to the dismay of most Arab member states of the OIC (c) Many Arab states remain very conscious of Turkish subjugation of the Middle East and North Africa under the Ottomans (d) Turkey was a member of NATO and had a clear Western orientation whereas most member states of the OIC were non-aligned, and some were deeply hostile to the West.[21] Turkey was thus always at pains to establish its credentials as a loyal member of the OIC, and in the process always had to contend with the pressures generated by less moderate members of the organization.

These pressures became increasingly evident in the circumstances surrounding the Bosnian conflict and the evolution of other aspects of Turkish foreign policy at the time. As the OIC's positions on the Bosnian conflict became more comprehensive and more pronounced, Turkey found itself faced with challenges on at least two fronts. On the one hand, the Turkish government was actively engaged in efforts to establish a sphere of influence in the newly independent Muslim-Turkic republics of the former Soviet Union. In this endeavour it was facing direct competition from Iran, which was pursuing a vigorous diplomatic campaign in the region, buttressed by its substantial oil revenues. "In the international Muslim context moderate Turkey could not afford to be demonstrably less concerned [about Bosnia] than extremist Iran."[22] On the other hand, the Bosnian conflict coincided in part with a period in which the Turkish government was intensifying its defence and intelligence relationships with Israel, at the instigation of the Turkish military. "Both Israeli and Turkish defence officials maintained that the close military and intelligence cooperation between the two countries was not directed at any third party, but there could be little doubt that they intended to send a message to regional 'troublemakers' such as Iran, Syria and Iraq with which Turkey had difficult if not bad relations."[23] These moves by the Turkish government were greeted with dismay and hostility on the part of many member states of the OIC, and this in turn constituted another reason for Turkey to try to salvage its credibility within the organization by supporting OIC positions on the Bosnian conflict.[24]

Turkey: The Pull of the Western World

THE DOMESTIC and international pressures resulting from Turkey's Muslim identity were matched by a series of influences deriving from its longstanding Western orientation. For successive Turkish governments this orientation had been seen as the key to the preservation of Turkey's security in a turbulent and often hostile neighbourhood, as well as the best hope for ensuring Turkey's economic modernization and prosperity.

Turkey's principal institutional link to the West is its membership in NATO and it therefore has a broad political vested interest in the continued existence and vitality of the alliance. It also retains a strong interest in the security and defence functions of the alliance:

> The demise of the Cold War, the bipolar world and the looming existential threat from the Soviet Union has ended the strategic consensus that prevailed within NATO for some forty years....
> Of all the members of NATO, it is Turkey whose security considerations have been least affected by the transformation in the international order. Turkey still has a large, well armed and potentially hostile neighbour to the north in the form of the Russian Federation, the successor state of the Soviet Union. The temporary security respite which was provided by the collapse of the Soviet Union has been reversed by the retention of Russian bases in Armenia and the agreement for Russian troops to return to Georgia. In short, Turkey once again has Russian forces on its border.[25]

Given its abiding political and security interests in the preservation of the alliance, Turkey was faced with three principal challenges when dealing with the Bosnian conflict in a NATO context: (a) to be seen to be playing a constructive role in the decision-making processes of the alliance (b) to ensure that NATO was seen in both the Western and Muslim worlds as a relevant and useful actor in the search for a solution and (c) to try to avoid any irreparable damage being done to the alliance as a result of policy differences between the United States and some of the major European members of NATO.

The economic dimensions of Turkey's Western orientation also played into the Turkish government's policy-making process. The Bosnian conflict, and the possibility that it might give rise to a wider Balkans conflagration, represented a direct and immediate threat not only to Turkey's geo-strategic interests, but also to its all-important communications and trading links with Western Europe.[26] This in itself was a major consideration given the ever-parlous state of Turkey's economy. Equally important, however, was the longer-term question of Turkey's candidacy for membership in the European Community/Union (EC/EU). At the time the Bosnian conflict erupted, Turkey was still trying to digest the EC's formal rejection of its bid for membership in December, 1989. The Turkish government was also well aware that:

> Developments in the east had outpaced whatever meager prospects Turkey might have enjoyed in western European eyes. The rebirth of 'a Europe free and whole' pushed 'Turkey the stepchild' to the bottom of the list of strategic priorities for western Europe.[27]

Despite the deep resentments to which this gave rise within the country, the Turkish government remained committed to pursuing membership in the EU. In fact, as the Bosnian conflict unfolded, Turkey was engaged in negotiating a customs union agreement with the EU (which came into effect on January 1, 1996). It was in light of those considerations that the Turkish government had to try to ensure that its Bosnian policy did not feed the "Islamist" fears of its Western European partners, nor that it be viewed as being too closely aligned with that of the United States when serious differences of views existed within the Western camp.

Turkish Policy: Rocks and Hard Places

IN STEERING A COURSE through these diverse and often countervailing pressures and influences, the Turkish government displayed considerable prudence in the development of its Bosnian policy. Throughout most of 1992, the Turkish government steadfastly resisted the rising tide of domestic public opinion and the entreaties of the Bosnian authorities for Turkey to provide military assistance to the Bosnian Muslims on a bilateral basis. In June 1992, Turkey hosted a meeting of the foreign ministers of the OIC which promised to support outside military intervention in Bosnia if the UN sanctions failed to deter the Serbs. The Turkish government's response to this escalation of the OIC's rhetoric was, however, relatively muted. It continued to hope that the sanctions would work and that the efforts of the UN and of the EC to end the fighting would succeed.[28] But even as this hope began to fade, Turkey continued to eschew military involvement in favour of a concerted diplomatic campaign to strengthen the resolve of its Western allies against Serbia.[29]

Turkey's military engagement in efforts to halt the Bosnian conflict was relatively slow in coming. It was not until December 1992 that the Turkish parliament authorized the government to offer Turkish troops for the UN peacekeeping force in Bosnia. It took until May 1993 before a Turkish squadron of F-16 aircraft was deployed to the Italian base at Vicenza to support NATO operations for enforcing the no-fly zone over Bosnia. And it was not until 1994 that the UN eventually accepted a Turkish contingent for UNPROFOR. This contingent of 1500 troops was deliberately deployed in Central Bosnia to monitor the disengagement of Muslim and Croat forces and so avoid any risk of it becoming involved in clashes between Serbs and Bosnians. But despite the precautions thus taken by the Turkish government and the UN, the presence of the Turkish contingent gave rise to controversy. Both Serbia and Greece objected to its participation in UNPROFOR and "tried to insinuate that such a move was a decisive step for reestablishing Turkey as a dominant power in the Balkans and thus revitalizing the Ottoman empire there."[30]

Throughout 1993 and much of 1994, Turkey remained actively engaged in diplomatic activity to bring an end to the Bosnian conflict. Whether in its own right or as a leading member of the OIC Contact Group, Turkey maintained continuous relations with the international contact group (USA, UK, FRG, France and Russia) in the preparation of the various conferences that attempted to end the war. In so doing, by and large Turkey "carefully avoided any single-handed activities in support of the Bosnians' case and always aligned its policy with the overall framework created by the moves of its major Western allies and the UN Security Council."[31] The only notable, and largely symbolic, departure from this approach is to be found in Turkish Prime Minister Tansu Ciller's visit to Bosnia in February 1994. In the company of Prime Minister Benazir Bhutto of Pakistan, she went to Sarajevo to express solidarity and sympathy for the long suffering Bosnian Muslims, but was at pains to make clear that her visit should be viewed in a humanitarian rather than a political context. (Whatever credit this visit may have earned her with other Muslim countries and with the Islamist opposition in Turkey was more than nullified by her visit to Israel later that year, the first visit to Israel by the leader of a Muslim country since that of Egyptian President Anwar Sadat in 1977.)[32]

It was not until the autumn of 1994 that the Turkish government found itself confronted with a set of circumstances which led it to make some hard policy choices. These circumstances included: the repeated failures of the efforts of the UN, the EU and the international Contact Group to bring an end to the Bosnian conflict; the resumption of offensive military operations by the Bosnian Serbs; and moves by Russia to take the Milosovic government under its wing. In the face of these realities, "Turkey and the Islamic world grew ever more vociferous in their vocal denunciations of the West's willingness to tolerate a genocide against Muslim peoples in the heart of Europe."[33] The Turkish government in its policy pronouncements began to part company with its European allies, and to align itself more closely with positions held by the OIC and by the United States. In particular, Turkey argued for either lifting the UN arms embargo against Bosnia or taking decisive military action against the Serbs, or both, as a means of re-establishing the military balance. Turkey also became a secret conduit, in breach of the UN arms embargo, for the shipment of arms to the Bosnian Muslims with the consent of the United States. And in pursuit of its military balance policy, following the Dayton accords, Turkey became the United States' main partner in a programme to equip and train the Bosnian army, with the United States providing the equipment and Turkey doing the training.[34]

Conclusion

TURKEY'S PRUDENT and carefully calibrated policy towards the Bosnian conflict can by and large be judged to have been successful. It allowed Turkey to play a leading, but moderating, role within the OIC, without provoking any serious discord in relations with other member states of the organization. Nor did it compromise Turkey's efforts to enhance its relations with the newly independent republics of Central Asia. And in the later phases of the conflict, it certainly served to reinforce Turkey's all-important relationship with the United States.

As a strong advocate of NATO military action to protect the Bosnian Muslims, Turkey could only feel belated justification of its policy when NATO intervened militarily against the Serbs in 1995.[35] More broadly, given its enduring political and security interests in the preservation of the alliance, Turkey could derive considerable satisfaction from the fact that the Bosnian conflict had given NATO a new role and a new lease on life at a time when questions abounded concerning its continued usefulness or relevance in the post-Cold War world. (Turkey gave renewed evidence of its own commitment to the alliance by contributing 1,500 army and air force personnel to the NATO Implementation Force in Bosnia.)

Turkey's policy in the later stages of the Bosnian conflict did not endear it to some of the leading member states of the EU. Did this seriously compromise Turkey's prospects of ever becoming a member of the EU? At one level, the answer would appear to be no. At a summit meeting held in 1999, the EU formally added Turkey to the list of candidates for membership, while recognizing that Turkey would have to overcome numerous economic and political obstacles (including its human rights record) before it could be deemed ready for actual membership.[36] At another level, the answer is far less clear. Did Turkey's involvement in the Bosnian conflict as a Muslim country reinforce the perception that: "Further integration between Turkey and the EU threatens the social and political self-identification of each to an unsustainable degree"?[37] Or did it improve Turkey's chances for membership on the grounds that: "The EU will want to keep Turkey as a security insulator between itself and the Middle East, and to resist at all costs Turkey's becoming a short-circuit between the security dynamics of the Middle East and those of the Balkans"?[38] On these questions, the jury is still out.

Notes

1   This summary of Western concerns and interests is drawn from Lawrence Freedman, "Why the West Failed," *Foreign Policy*, 97 (Winter 1994–95), 53–54.

2   This is the central contention, for example, of Jasminka Udovicki and James Ridgeway, eds., *Burn this House: The Making and Unmaking of Yugoslavia*, second edition (Durham, NC: Duke University Press, 2000). See also Flora Lewis, "Reassembling Yugoslavia," in *Foreign Policy*, 98 (Spring 1995), 135–136.

3   Fred Halliday, *Islam and the Myth of Confrontation* (New York: I.B. Tauris, 1995), pp. 166–167. While both Serb and Croat extremists denounced Izetbegovic's "Islamic Declaration" as a fundamentalist political tract, some scholars claim that it was really little more than a "scholarly document for philosophical discourse." See Carole Rogel, *The Breakup of Yugoslavia and the War in Bosnia* (Westport, CT: Greenwood Press, 1998), p. 86.

4   Ibid., p. 87.

5   Jonathan Landay, "Bosnia – After the Troops Leave," *The Washington Quarterly*, 19/3 (Summer 1996), 70.

6   Quoted in *Turkey Between East and West*, eds. Vojtech Mastny and R. Craig Nation (Boulder, CO: Westview Press, 1996) p. 121.

7   Edgar O'Ballance, *Civil War in Bosnia, 1992–94* (New York: St. Martin's Press, 1995) p. 56.

8   Ali A. Mazrui, "Global Apartheid? Race and Religion in the New World Order" in *The Gulf War and the New World Order*, eds. T.Y. Ismael and J.S. Ismael (Gainesville: University Press of Florida, 1994), pp. 532–533.

9   Ann Elizabeth Mayer, "The Human Rights Jihad" in *The Islamism Debate*, ed. Martin Kramer (Tel Aviv: Tel Aviv University, 1997), pp. 131–132.

10 Final Communique of the twenty-first Conference of Foreign Ministers of the Organization of the Islamic Conference, Karachi, April 25–29, 1993, http://www.oic-UN.ORG/previous/21fc.htm, pp. 11–12.

11 Edgar O'Ballance, *Civil War in Bosnia*, p. 107.

12 Vojtech Mastny and R. Craig Nation, *Turkey Between East and West*, p. 121.

13 Ibid., p. 122.

14 Edgar O'Ballance, *Civil War in Bosnia*, p. 191.

15 The figures used here are drawn from: The International Institute for Strategic Studies, *The Military Balance 1995-96* (Oxford: Oxford University Press, 1995).

16 See for example Kalam Shahed, "Peacekeeping: Bangladesh's Experience in Bosnia" in *Peacekeeping at a Crossroads*, eds. Neil MacFarlane and Hans-Georg Ehrhart (Clementsport, NS: The Canadian Peacekeeping Press, 1997), pp. 168–173.

17 Edgar O'Ballance, *Civil War in Bosnia*, pp. 93–96. See also Ann Elizabeth Mayer, "The Human Rights Jihad," p. 132.

18 *Yugoslavia and After*, eds. David Dyker and Ivan Vejvoda (London: Longman, 1996), p. 174.

19 Vojtech Mastny and R. Craig Nation, *Turkey Between East and West*, p. 152.

20 Ibid., p. 74. See also Graham Fuller and Ian Lesser, *Turkey's New Geopolitics: From the Balkans to Western China* (Boulder, CO: Westview Press, 1993), pp. 152–153.

21 Ekmeleddin Ihsanoglu, "Turkey in the Organization of the Islamic Conference" in *Turkish Foreign Policy: Recent Developments*, ed. Kamal Karpat (Madison: University of Wisconsin, 1996), pp. 75–81.

22 Graham Fuller and Ian Lesser, *Turkey's New Geopolitics*, p. 154.

23 Jeremy Salt, "Turkey's Military 'Democracy'" in *Current History*, 98/625 (February 1999), 76.

24 Turkey's deepening relationship with Israel eventually led to its facing severe censure at an OIC meeting held in late 1997. See ibid., p. 78.

25 *The Middle East and Europe: The Power Deficit,* ed. B.A. Robertson (London: Routledge, 1998), p. 164.

26 Ibid., p. 166.

27 Vojtech Mastny and R. Craig Nation, *Turkey Between East and West,* p. 74. For an interesting and sobering discussion of the issues at stake in Turkey's bid for membership in the EU, see Barry Buzan and Thomas Diez, "The European Union and Turkey" in *Survival,* 41/1 (Spring 1999), 41–57.

28 Graham Fuller and Ian Lesser, *Turkey's New Geopolitics,* p. 152.

29 Ibid., p. 154.

30 Heinz Kramer, *A Changing Turkey: The Challenge to Europe and the United States* (Washington, DC: The Brookings Institution Press, 2000), p. 150.

31 Ibid., p. 151.

32 See Philip Robins, "Turkish Foreign Policy Under Erbakan" in *Survival,* 39/2 (Summer 1997), 84.

33 Vojtech Mastny and R. Craig Nation, *Turkey Between East and East,* p. 123.

34 Heinz Kramer, *A Changing Turkey,* pp. 151–152.

35 Ibid., p. 151.

36 See "The European Union decides it might one day talk Turkey" in *The Economist,* 18 December 1999, p. 42.

37 Barry Buzan and Thomas Diez, "The European Union and Turkey," p. 46.

38 Ibid., p. 52.

Photographs in this volume are the work of German photojournalist
Christian Jungeblodt from his collection *Exodus*.

Notes

Notes

Notes